Barcode in Back

S0-BQY-963

The Politics of Heritage Tourism in China

This volume unravels the politics surrounding behind China's hegemonic project of heritage tourism development in Lijiang. It provides a compelling study of the dialectical relationships between global and domestic capital, the state, tourists and locals as they collude, collaborate and contest one another to ready Lijiang for tourist consumption.

Using rich material from insightful interviews and quantitative data, the authors show how complex tourism development can be even as it strives to do good for the community. Su and Teo investigate the practices of contestation and negotiation of identity within Lijiang; analyze the negotiations that transform material and vernacular landscapes; and suggests strategies that will enable sustained tourism interest in this location. Linking Gramsci's theory on hegemony to the cultural politics of space, this book has two major strengths: it establishes a theoretical framework to conceptualize power relations in tourism space and provides critical insights into the rapidly shifting socio-political landscape of contemporary China. Comparisons with other Chinese heritage sites are also provided.

By addressing the power struggles inevitable in the process of tourism development, The Politics of Heritage Tourism in China provides an innovative understanding of China's dynamic politics in a period of transition. As such, it will address the needs of students and academic scholars working in the fields of China studies, tourism, cultural studies, urban studies, sociology, geography, political science and heritage studies.

Xiaobo Su is Assistant Professor at the Department of Geography, University of Oregon.

Peggy Teo is an independent scholar working on tourism issues in Asia. She is also co-editor of *Interconnected Worlds: Tourism in Southeast Asia* (Pergamon, 2001) and *Asia on Tour: Exploring the Rise of Asian Tourism* (Routledge, 2009)

Routledge Contemporary China Series

The Politics of Heritage Tourism in China

A view from Lijiang

Xiaobo Su and Peggy Teo

Routledge
Taylor & Francis Group

LONDON AND NEW YORK

First published 2009
by Routledge
2 Park Square, Milton Park, Abingdon, Oxon OX14 4RN

Simultaneously published in the USA and Canada
by Routledge
270 Madison Ave, New York, NY 10016

*Routledge is an imprint of the Taylor & Francis Group,
an Informa business*

© 2010 Xiaobo Su and Peggy Teo

Typeset in Times New Roman by Keyword Group Ltd
Printed and bound in Great Britain by MPG Books Group

British Library Cataloguing in Publication Data
A catalogue record for this book is available
from the British Library

Library of Congress Cataloging-in-Publication Data
Su, Xiaobo.
The politics of heritage tourism in China : a view from Lijiang / Xiaobo Su
and Peggy Teo.
p. cm.
1. Heritage tourism–China–Lijiang Naxizu Zizhixian. 2. Tourism–
Government policy–China–Lijiang Naxizu Zizhixian. 3. Culture and tourism–
China–Lijiang Naxizu Zizhixian. 4. Human geography–China–Lijiang
Naxizu Zizhixian. 5. Landscape changes–China–Lijiang Naxizu Zizhixian.
6. Lijiang Naxizu Zizhixian (China)–Antiquities. I. Teo, Peggy. II. Title.
G155.C55S8 2009
915.1'35–dc22
2009003524

ISBN10: 0-415-47808-1 (hbk)
ISBN10: 0-203-87368-8 (ebk)

ISBN13: 978-0-415-47808-3 (hbk)
ISBN13: 978-0-203-87368-7 (ebk)

Contents

Preface

Despite growing academic interest in China's tourism development after its economic reform in 1978, very little has been written about how tourism is linked to broader social and economic transformations and how it has been used for purposes of development. Rather than write about tourism as a way to escape for pleasure and relaxation, we examine tourism as a contested terrain whereby dominance and resistance interact, hegemony is attained, and forces at different scales mediate one another in their interplay. As an extension of important research started on Chinese tourism by both Chinese authors and Western academics, we hope this book can also be an important contribution to elucidating the phenomenon's growth and change in this vast country.

We take this opportunity to express our gratitude to many who have help us bring this research to fruition. First of all, we thank our respondents. They constitute Lijiang and we appreciate their willingness to share their opinions and ideas with us. Friends who helped us during our fieldwork in Lijiang and elsewhere are also acknowledged: Yang Gengfu, Wang Shiying, Bao Jigang, Heather Peters, Peter Su, and Zhu Hong. We also appreciate the help and kindness of Henry Yeung, Shirlena Huang, Lily Kong, Brenda Yeoh, Tim Bunnell, T.C. Chang, Joan Henderson, James Sidaway, Geoffrey Wall, and Tim Winter who provided valuable comments and encouragement at different stages of this project. We likewise thank our University of Oregon colleagues for their strong support: Alec Murphy, Lise Nelson, Pat MacDowell, Andrew Markus, Daniel Buck, Peter Walker, Shaul Cohen, Daniel Gavin, Susan Hardwick, Patrick Bartlein, and Amy Lobben. We thank Wang Gungwu and Yang Dali for permission to work for a short term at the East Asian Institute, National University of Singapore. We are also grateful to Stephanie Rogers, Sonja van Leeuwen and Leanne Hinves for supporting this volume. Finally, Xiaobo expresses his gratitude to his family in China who selflessly supported his pursuit of an academic career and to Chunyuan Huang for her unfailing support.

Xiaobo Su and Peggy Teo

Figures

Tables

Abbreviations

CCP	Chinese Communist Party
CITS	China International Travel Service
CNTA	China National Tourism Administration
CWHMC	Committee for World Heritage Management and Conservation of Lijiang Ancient Town (now Authority for World Heritage Management and Conservation of Lijiang Ancient Town)
GDP	Gross domestic product
GHF	Global Heritage Fund
GNCCS	Global Naxi Culture Conservation Society
LTB	Lijiang Tourism Bureau
NGO	Non-governmental organization
TNC	Transnational corporation
UNESCO	United Nations Educational, Scientific and Cultural Organization
WTO	World Tourism Organization

1 Rethinking the politics of heritage tourism

Space, place and landscape – including landscapes of leisure and tourism – are not fixed but are in a constant state of transition as a result of continuous, dialectical struggles of power and resistance among and between the diversity of landscape providers, users and mediators.

(Aitchison 1999:29)

Cultural relics and historical sites were listed as the main attractions for China in 1994 and became the country's national tourism theme for that year (He 1999). Advocates of history consider this timely, since it represents the beginning of a reversal of the appalling inattention to the nation's rich historical and cultural heritages following the Cultural Revolution. The interest was mainly fueled by the desire to capture a larger part of the world's international tourist market as well as to cater to the growing domestic market. The year is important, marking for the first time the central government's official acknowledgment of the contribution that tourism can make to raising the wealth of the country and giving jobs and economic and social mobility to its people. With this decision comes a heavy responsibility to recognize the possible impacts heritage tourism can have on local communities and on the heritage resources of the country. Within tourism literature, commodification and displacement as impacts have been widely researched (e.g. see Gotham (2007) on New Orleans; Picard (1996) on Bali; Philp and Mercer (1999) on Burma). In China, however, they are only emergent topics. This book attempts to explicate the politics behind China's project of heritage tourism development. The study is based on an analysis of Lijiang Ancient Town, a mature destination that has often been cited as a successful model of tourism policy-making.[1] More specifically, we intend to unravel the dialectical relationships between global and domestic capital, tourists and locals as they collude, collaborate and contest one another in transforming the town for tourist consumption. In discussing these tensions, we will show how complex tourism development can be even as it strives to do good for the majority of the people affected.

Mass heritage tourism began in Lijiang in the 1990s with strong support from the central government. In 1998, then Premier, Zhu Rongji, initiated the "great western development" (*xibu da kaifa*) strategy whose primary aim was to improve economic development in the western region so as to reduce the disparity between itself and the wealthier coastal areas of China.[2] By doing so, the central government believed that national unity would be enhanced and China would acquire greater socio-political stability for the long term (Goodman 2004; Tian 2004; Wang and Hu 1999). Among many proposals to develop China's western region, tourism was singled out as a vital component. Placed under the China National Tourist Administration (CNTA), the main selling points of western China were identified to achieve economic change. They included the area's natural landscape, its rich ethnic cultures, and many important historical sites such as the Silk Road in Xinjiang, the Mogao Caves in Gansu, the mausoleum of the First Qin Emperor in Shaanxi, and ethnic Miao villages in Guizhou (*People's Daily* 2 February 2001). Since then, these resources have been methodically developed by CNTA (Donaldson 2007; Lv 2004; Oakes 1998).

In Lijiang, to make the ancient town into an "international cultural tourism city" (*Lijiang Daily* 9 April 2006), the city has to "internationalize" (*guojihua*) and "modernize" (*xiandaihua*) its landscapes. For tourism to be sustainable, Lijiang must also maintain the authenticity of its unique cultural heritage. Consequently, a balance between the forces of internationalization/modernization and localization/place identity must be achieved. Because of the tensions created by this spatial nexus, invariably, the politics of heritage tourism would involve many groups who are actively inscribing their own agendas with reference to the development and conservation of Lijiang.

In the rest of this chapter, we discuss the critical discourses surrounding tourism politics before setting the background to Lijiang. We then highlight the research arguments and objectives, the methodology behind the collection of information for the analysis of Lijiang, and, finally, the structure of the book is outlined.

Rethinking tourism politics

In this book, we have a specific interest in the cultural politics of space and place. In the *Dictionary of Human Geography*, Jackson (2000a:141) defines cultural politics as "the complex process through which meanings are constructed and negotiated and [...] relations of dominance and subordination are defined and contested." In this definition, meanings are associated with representation and interpretation of places and power relations culminate in social-spatial inclusion/exclusion. Essentially, "how power is exercised, by whom, in what manner of political [and socio-spatial] arrangement and to what end" (Coles and Church 2007a:8) will help us to unknot the complex entanglements inherent in the project of heritage tourism development in a location. More important, according to Peck (2006), the conflicts on meanings and in power relations should not merely be understood from class relations studies, as it has in the past (see Harvey (1978) and Wells (1996)), but should incorporate tensions emanating from cultural factors. Culture is intrinsically "politicized" such that identity, gender, ethnicity, and aesthetics are deeply embedded in conflicts of material interests leading to specific socio-spatial outcomes. He recommends that a synthesis of culture and economy lay at the foundation for rethinking cultural politics.

At the heart of cultural politics in geography is the challenge to deconstruct binary categories such as capital vs labor, economy vs culture, "Self" vs "Other", majority vs minority, and so on (Agnew and Duncan 1989; Rose 1994). One binary in particular – economy vs culture – has affected research in significant ways. To Marx, economic relations and productive forces legitimate class dominance and become universal. It is "as if certain 'laws' of their relations to other activities [act like] *fundamental truths*" (Williams 1972:92, emphasis added, cited from Cosgrove 1983:7). The bias toward the economy as base and culture as superstructure has its critics. Cosgrove (1983:6) points out that Marx's theory denies the cultural realm of beliefs, ideas, and values as integral parts of production, such that "their very important ideological role as weapons of structural maintenance within social and economic formations" is totally ignored.

Materialism only spotlights the dominant in any analysis of politics. In tourism studies, the influential work of Britton (1980; 1982) comes to mind as a good example of this way of thinking. He argued that changes in tourism destinations in the underdeveloped world are outcomes of the process of capital accumulation by transnational corporations wielding strong economic power in a globally interconnected world. Thus, he incorporated the theory of dependency into tourism studies to highlight the imbalance of power relations between global tourism corporations and developing countries, arguing that the international tourism industry is a product of metropolitan capitalist enterprise imposing on "peripheral destinations a development mode which reinforces dependency on, and vulnerability to, developed countries" (Britton 1982:355). In this approach, local cultures, or concretely, the specificities of local community life, social structure, and other cultural factors have been obscured, lumped under the umbrella of dependency, leading to global capitalism colonizing localities into a homogeneous world.

Modernist thinking of politics of the kind described above helps to produce and reproduce the existing hegemonic power of the capitalist West (Nash 2004; Soja and Hooper 1993). This dichotomous binary, which was in intellectual favor from the 1950s to the 1980s, places an unnecessarily high importance to the workings of global capital (Gregory 2000). It has, however, been recently refuted by *new* cultural politics advanced by researchers such as Agnew and Duncan (1989), Cosgrove and Daniels (1988), Dear and Flusty (1998), and McCann (2002) and Rose (1994) who favor a more radical postmodernist sensibility. They argue that those who are peripheralized, marginalized, and subordinated in the modernist social construction of difference *are* capable of action themselves. This argument, under the "cultural turn," focuses on how social structures limit rather than determine social reaction and peoples' experiences (Chouinard 1996), asserting that marginal groups have capacity to re-negotiate power relations by contestation over, or cooperation with, social structures (Aitchison *et al.* 2000; Cosgrove 1992). This new cultural geography embraces the complexities of spatiality rather than advocates spatial essentialism (Dear 2000; Soja 1989; 2000). The new cultural politics of multiplicity and fluidity that fosters "radical openness [and] flexibility" (Soja and Hooper 1993:198) will add to a more stimulating analysis of politics because it assumes agency for all actors involved, and not only the powerful, and certainly not just within the realm of economics.

The "new" cultural politics is, however, not without problems. For example, Thompson (1990) and Sayer (2000) argue that advocates such as Soja and Hooper may have overestimated the agency of the marginalized in reconfiguring social structure. In many cases, we find that multiplicity and difference are still frequently conditioned by *economic* relations and gradually get channeled into the orbit of mainstream society (Harvey 1989a; Jackson 1991; Sayer 2000). As Thompson (1990:330–331) argues, in modern societies, multiplicity and difference are commonly embedded in "social relations which are structured in systematically asymmetrical ways." For example, Langman's (2003:245) analysis of the relation between culture and economy in case studies of carnivals in the USA and Brazil concluded that "[c]onsumption, as sites of otherwise denied pleasure, freedom, agency and *joissance* [actually] serves to sustain late capitalist society." Hence an in-between position is necessary whereby agency advocated by Soja and Hooper is tempered by a good grasp of the material character of cultural production (Williams 1977:33).

Moreover, Soja and Hooper say nothing about the spatial outcomes of the "new" cultural politics even though they introduced the concept of "thirdspace."[3] Hence, conceptualizing politics as almost exclusively in the realm of representations and meanings evades the real economic relations inherent in any distribution and exercise of power. The obsession with cultures, including symbolic, discursive, and representational forms and processes, has impeded a thorough understanding of "the actual, everyday materiality of the places in which people actually dwell" (Latham and McCormack 2004:702). If openness, multiplicity, and diversity are celebrated so deeply and "nothing of lasting or universal application can be said about [the world]," Sayer (2000:30) asks, What meaningful contribution can there be from new cultural politics?

In the main, we would agree with Soja (1989) that spaces are inscribed with complex and sometimes confusing politics and ideologies that go beyond economic relations. Unlike Soja, however, we draw on a cultural materialist approach favoring the interweaving of culture and economy in understanding politics and social change. Cultural materialism, according to Raymond Williams (1980:243) is "a theory of culture as a (social and material) productive process and of specific practices, of 'arts,' as social uses of material means of production." Culture, defined as "a whole way of life," rather than a superstructure labeled by orthodox Marxists, is a constitutive social process which should be understood and interpreted in relation to its underlying system of production (Williams 1958; 1977). Grasping "the indissoluble connections between material production, political and cultural institutions and activity, and consciousness" (Williams 1977:80) will help transcend the economy/culture conundrum or the material/ symbolic dichotomy by highlighting that "all human practices are at once 'material' and 'symbolic' insofar as they signify action within and upon a practical material field" (Peck 2006:112).

In line with this revelation, we reiterate three points concerning the remateri-alization of cultural geography (Jackson 2000b; Lees 2002; Lorimer 2005). First, cultural politics must acknowledge the (re)negotiation of identity and meaning among groups of people as they struggle for power (Jackson 2000a). No matter how hard the dominant try to control and discipline the weak, their position will always be vitiated, as shown by Williams' (1977:125) notable argument that "no mode and therefore no dominant social order, and therefore no dominant culture ever in reality includes or exhausts all human practice, human energy, and human intention." Second, we argue that dominance and resistance are not conceptually abstract; they have spatial outcomes that reflect, reinforce, and reconfigure the power relations of different people/groups. Through these concrete outcomes, people can develop a knowledge of their own place and space as they invest value into the material and social landscapes they encounter, making these spaces meaningful and valued (Jackson 1991; 2000b). Finally, it would be astute to recognize that political economy continues to be *crucial* in cultural politics. As noted by Jackson (1991:225):

> One cannot divorce the 'cultural' aspects of reinvestment or preservation from the apparently 'political' and 'economic' dimensions that produce these chances, but neither can the political economy of urban and regional change be understood without a more fully developed understanding of its cultural politics.

The "power of capital" (Harvey 1993:24) ought not to be devalued.

Besides incorporating the cultural *with* the economic in understanding social change, other important issues relevant to our rethinking is the study of politics beyond the centers of the "West" and of the "state." First, the decentring of the West: Geographers have in postcolonial studies shifted the conceptualization of politics in the "West" to include the "non-West" (see, for example, Bunnell 2004; Sidaway 2002; 2007; Tucker and Hall 2004).[4] In the past, politics has been equated with a political economy in which Western hegemony was consid-ered the culprit of exploitation (Meethan 2004). To facilitate Western tourists' consumption, many destinations in non-Western regions have been constructed as the exotic "Other." However, the binary category of "Other" and "Self" is itself problematic. As Teo and Leong (2006:113) argued, "Othering is contested and subverted by the host and other guests affected by their own genius loci." In this sense, we similarly argue for a multiplicity of worldviews whereby local knowledge about a place and human agency in that place are as important as transnational economic muscle in a contest of the existing social structure. Hence, there is need for a postcolonial analysis that includes non-Western views. In both the production and consumption of tourism, different outcomes can be gener-ated in different localities according to its own spatio-temporal relations in the broader global structure. The variety and changeability of local geo-historical contexts means that the world is not a monolithic entity labeled with the "West." The non-West is "a source of self-theorization and truth claims – the non-West [*is a*] producer, as well as mediator, of knowledge which is extra-local, even global in scope" (Bunnell 2004:20, emphasis added). Nevertheless, the high-lighting of the non-West cannot undermine its (post-) colonial history and its wide connections with the West. As Bunnell (2004:20) has noted, the alternative modernity in the non-Western context, especially in East and Southeast Asia, acts as a way of self-realization and emerges from "(post-)colonial geo-histories of interconnection, not only in the 'economic' domain, but also in terms of the circulation of politico-cultural ideals and practices." Our aim is to conceive tourism politics deep in the "non-West" [or specifically, China] in order to "(re)constitute the world in more discursive terms and thus reclaim epistemological space from the West" (Teo and Leong 2006:112).

This issue is of particular importance to understanding the case of Lijiang as a World Heritage Site. Once a highly popular destination for Western backpackers and group tourists, it is now popular among domestic tourists, mainly the ethnic Han majority. How the state balances the needs of Western tourists, that of domestic Han tourists, and the demands of the local Naxi minority is a lesson on the juxtaposition of westernization, nationalism, and localization as China strives to embrace modernization and globalization. It highlights issues of "agency, representation and especially, the representation of culture(s) under asymmetrical political [economic] and social conditions" (King 2003:383) in the new political economy of post-1978 reform.

Apart from claiming epistemological space through a postcolonial analysis of representation and discourse, this book keeps up with recent calls to pay attention to the experiences of individuals who are denizens of heritage sites undergoing transformation. We will examine how cultural politics manifests in people's quotidian life (see, for example, Jazeel 2006; King 2003; Round 2008; Walks 2008) in which "ordinary" spaces also convey issues concerning control, contestation, and resistance. We draw on the work of the "ordinary," as proclaimed by Amin and Thrift (2002) and Tonkiss (2005).[5] In this discourse, empathy toward ordinary individuals and vernacular landscapes in everyday life is emphasized. Or, as Yeoh (2001:457) notes, there is a need to engage with "material practices, actual spaces and real politics." For example, Lim (2004) contends that Singapore's homosexual community overtly expresses alternative sexuality in everyday public spaces such as beaches and bars to resist dominant heterosexual norms, which are clearly accentuated in the city-state. As Tonkiss (2005:59) puts it,

> The everyday spaces of the street, the subway or the square are sites for a micro-politics of urban life in which individuals exercise their spatial rights while negotiating the spatial claims of others. This is a politics of space as much lived in the body as it is written in law.

That the "ordinary" enters into the arena of politics shows up the importance of many "cultural" dimensions in defining and dividing power relations. So rather than economic relations and the state determining social reaction and individuals' ordinary experiences (Chouinard 1996), they merely place constraints on ordinary people who *have* agency to re-negotiate power relations by contesting or cooperating with the dominant powers (see Aitchison *et al.* 2000; Chouinard 1996; Cosgrove 1992).

The appreciation of "non-West" and "ordinary" should not, however, detract from the analytical attention that needs to be paid to space (Sayer 2000). For instance, Massey (1993:156) argues that space is very open to politics: "space is by its very nature full of power and symbolism, a complex web of relations of domination and subordination, of solidarity and co-operation." In any space, actors generate meaningful (re)actions in terms of their culture and value. They are able to justify whether they follow or resist the order built into the space. Space is therefore more than the outcome of social relations; it can be recognized as an input to shape the power structure, "an active constitutive component of hegemonic power" (Keith and Pile 1993:37). This conception of space begets the notion that politics is dynamic and new equilibriums occur at different times in any one place. This equilibrium is the outcome of negotiations between different groups in that context. On the one hand, the powerful can attain the consent of the governed and maintain their dominance through controlling and disciplining space. On the other hand, the governed can try to resist the imposed order through claiming their own space or to express their discordance if they are discontented with the existing power structure. Both sides have to negotiate with each other and make compromises. Space is thus a container expressing such negotiations and the spatial forms that evolve embody this dynamic equilibrium.

The discussion above about the intersections of culture and economy, the state and the ordinary, and the emphasis given to the non-West has been about negotiation in politics. At this point, we want to clarify two important concepts critical to the idea of negotiation – "dominance" and "resistance." Dominance refers to a condition in which influence or control is exercised over certain objects/people. It can be achieved or asserted through either (1) imposition or coercion by the powerful, or (2) agreement or consent from the weak. Dominance can happen through coercion, collaboration or collusion, not only via economic relations but also in the production of cultural meanings and identity/the superstructural realm of ideology, culture, and politics (Gramsci 1971; Williams 1977). A variable combination of coercion and consent is, according to Gramsci (1971; see also Jessop 1982), hegemony, which is one of the most important concepts in this book. We will elaborate this concept in Chapter 2, but for the time being we clarify that hegemony is designed to capture the complex and dynamic nature of authority and power in our analysis of cultural politics.

Resistance means the act of refusal or opposition to the dominant idea, order, or control. It is not necessarily tantamount to a political movement geared at subverting political authorities in a society (de Certeau 1984; Whitson 2007). Resistance happens "as a reaction against unfairness and injustice, as a desire to survive intolerable conditions, but it may also involve a sense of remembering and of dreaming of something better" (Pile 1997:30). In his seminal work *Weapons of the Weak*, Scott (1985) points out that *everyday* forms of dominance and resistance dwell in not only economic relations of capital accumulation, but also in socio-cultural aspects such as meanings and identity. Described as a "prosaic but constant struggle" (Scott 1985:29), resistance in this research includes self-help, reconciliation, and even withdrawal and does not always imply conflict and confrontation. As Sharp *et al.* (2000:23) put it, "certain resistances are themselves a reproduction or extension of dominating power, rather than a challenge to it." We also want to emphasize the mutual constitution of dominance and resistance, as shown by Routledge's (1997:361) argument that "practices of resistance cannot be separated from practices of domination: they are always entangled in some configuration."

Tourism is an important showground for expression of such cultural politics. Richter (1989:2), one of the leading scholars in tourism politics, argued that tourism is "a highly political phenomenon." Henderson (2003:113–114) shares a similar viewpoint, arguing that the political nature of tourism is "an expression of political philosophy and instrument of policy within and outside of government." Hall (1994) stressed that tourism plays an important role in changing the power structures in host communities. Squire (1994:5) highlighted the relation between tourism and the wider context, asserting that tourism is "a part of [the] larger process of cultural (and economic) transformation." Together, these scholars enunciate the diversity and complexity in tourism politics.

For the most part, past research in tourism politics has focused mainly on two aspects: (1) policy issues and tourism planning and (2) the political economy of tourism (Cheong and Miller 2000). For instance, Richter (1989) linked political science with tourism by exploring the nationwide political dimensions of tourism in her early studies on tourism politics. According to her, policy-led studies on tourism politics concentrate on international relations, public administration, and public policy making. Many recent studies using Richter's ideas have been done on destinations in Australia (Jenkins 1993), Britain (Richards 1995), the Commonwealth Caribbean (Wilkinson 1997), and Greece (Andriotis 2001). These studies also highlight the second aspect of tourism politics in established literature: the political economy of tourism, which draws heavily from dependency theory. As Bianchi (2002:270) summarized, the main argument in this research strand is that "tourism contributed directly toward an extension of metropolitan dominance over weaker destination peripheries and ultimately leads to a loss of self-reliance."

There is nothing wrong with policy- and political economy-led research on tourism politics. However, its resonance with modernist perspectives of politics hinders development within tourism theory (Franklin and Crang 2001). Policy-led studies on tourism politics in geography and other disciplines place the state and capital at the center of tourism politics. As Picard (1996:103) argued, these studies highlight "an objective of social control that will allow the tourist product to be more finely tuned to the demands of the international market." In many cases, "international" market and "Western" market are synonyms. The potential trouble resulting from these studies on tourism politics is that the "ordinary" and the "non-West" have been overwhelmed by the Western capitalism of tourism (Britton 1982; Nash 1977). Consequently, little space is left for resistance. To redress this problem, we purposely include the locals as a counterbalance.

As we pointed out earlier, politics has to transcend "the state" and incorporate many other actors at the global and local levels for a proper analysis of dominance and resistance. Thus, tourism politics is not only associated with the flow of capital and tourists at the global level and national government and policy at the national level but also with socio-spatial transformation involving the ordinary community at the local level. It is widely recognized that tourism development can reconfigure the social structures in different localities by linking transnational cultures (emanating from a global level) with these places, their economies, and their local cultures (Cole 2007; Coles and Church 2007b; Richards 2007). Hence, tourism is not just a logical extension of industrial capitalism into the realm of leisure. Instead, it offers opportunities for local people to modulate transnational cultures and global capital in their everyday lives, according to their own world views and values (Franklin and Crang 2001). The need to explore the mundane of tourism impacts can never be overemphasized.

To sort through agency in tourism politics, both production and consumption aspects of the phenomenon needs to be examined. What is involved in heritage tourism production and how is it consumed? Do they renew existing power structures? Do they offer opportunities to challenge the existing structures? (see Edensor 1998; 2000). In producing as well as consuming tourism, destinations frequently "become sites of contestation where the social structures and relations of power, domination and resistance are interwoven" (Sharp *et al.* 2000:26). The politics of tourism have engendered concerns over who has power to benefit from tourism development and influence the transformation of a destination area, how this is accomplished, and the reasons why specific trajectories are followed. Heavily influenced by dependency theory and core-periphery models, in the literature about the economic impacts of tourism for instance, scholars emphasize that changes in the destinations are as much a result of struggles over underdevelopment as of the process of capital accumulation driven by external capital (Britton 1982). Britton (1982) argued that destinations in the South Pacific became enmeshed in the global tourism system over which they had very little capacity to challenge the international corporations wielding strong capital power. A consequence of this discourse is a language of tourism focusing on the imagination of ethnic groups, cultures, and landscapes that can be presented as commodified objects for sale in the global capitalist economy (Dann 1996). The concepts of "tourist gaze" (Urry 2002) and the "McDisneyization" of tourism (Ritzer and Liska 1997) articulate the power of the global capitalist economy in molding destinations into "a commercial and institutionalized system constructed to satisfy demand for these experiences" of novelty and authenticity, especially those in less-developed countries (Britton 1991:454). Thus, spatial outcomes such as tourist enclaves (Edensor 1998; Herrera *et al.* 2007) and elite landscapes (Peleggi 2005) are observed in different localities in response to this power, which facilitates capital accumulation and social control. Drawing on the Frankfurt School, Britton (1991:454) argued that tourism as a sort of cultural industry represents "a set of institutions and practices designed to facilitate the adjustment of individuals to existing social rules and organizations." Indeed, how tourism is produced is not just an act of capital accumulation but can also be an effective instrument of political and social control. Likewise, how tourism is consumed is shaped by global capital but what is considered "authentic" continues to ferment debate.

Hence, the primary aim of this book is to provide a *holistic* picture of tourism politics by acknowledging the power of global/national capitalist economy in tourism development *and* the agency of individuals and localities to contest this power. Recently, an increasing number of tourism researchers have concentrated on the importance of local factors in mediating global forces (e.g. Chang *et al.* 1996; Cheong and Miller 2000; Gotham 2005a; Jeong and Santos 2004; Joseph and Kavoori 2001; Meethan 2001; Richards 2007; Winter 2007). The main contention is that in tourism development, local people are not merely recipients of global forces but mediate these forces by comprehending, containing, and controlling tourists within their world (Cheong and Miller 2000). For instance, after analyzing tourism in rural Guizhou, China, Oakes (1993:47) argued that "the local does not exist as an oppositional reality to the global, but rather consti-tutes a dynamic cultural negotiation with the changing structures of political economy, a negotiation in which dominant structures are mediated by individual agency." Thus, whether tourism leads to the assertion of a stronger identity via acts of social inclusion/exclusion (Sibley 1995), what is certain is that tourism can potentially open up a contested space for the (re)construction and negotia-tion of local meanings as local communities are brought into the ambit of global tourism influence. Some have in fact argued that "local culture" in destinations can potentially become a mixed outcome of transnational cultures and internal conditions (Cohen 2000; 2004). Others have argued that this mediation between the global and the local can strengthen "a continuity of cultural forms of the past" (Erb 2000:733) and synthesize transnational cultures into different places by (re)inventions and innovations.

In tourism space, there should be room to assert the negotiation between the local and the global, economy and culture, the powerful and the weak, and production and consumption. All the negotiations are central to tourism poli-tics wherein structures and agency interact with each other and influence one another. Social, political, and economic structures set within a geo-historical context can themselves effect change and, while they do not determine, they can constrain or facilitate people's capacities to influence the transformation of destinations. Human agency is crucial and helps individuals to challenge or accept, rather than unconditionally succumb to, the established social and spatial structure. It is our aim to add to discussions on the dialectics by using Gramsci's (1971) theory of hegemony to show how the powerful and the less powerful articulate power to achieve a compromised equilibrium in a case study of Lijiang Ancient Town.

In sum, the rethinking in tourism politics has motivated us to adopt a more critical *geographical* engagement with the politics of heritage tourism in Lijiang.

Influenced by the above-mentioned intellectual debates, we intend to take into account the *geo-historical* contexts of tourism development in the city as well as the *extra-local* connections of its tourism spaces. Hence, we will elucidate the power relations encompassed within Lijiang's heritage tourism, bearing in mind the local, national, and global scales of interaction. The next section elaborates why Lijiang is a very appropriate place for undertaking this engagement.

Lijiang Ancient Town: ripe for an analysis of tourism politics

Lijiang Ancient Town is located in northwest Yunnan, a province in southwest China (Figure 1.1). It lies in the center of the Lijiang Basin and connects the Yunnan-Guizhou Plateau to the Tibetan Plateau. Lijiang Ancient Town is located 2400 m above sea level (Guo and He 1999).

Lijiang Ancient Town has been the home of the Naxi minority group for over 800 years. Because of its unique urban form and authentic lived culture, Lijiang was placed on the World Heritage List by the United Nations Educational, Scientific and Cultural Organization (UNESCO) (1999:7) in 1997:

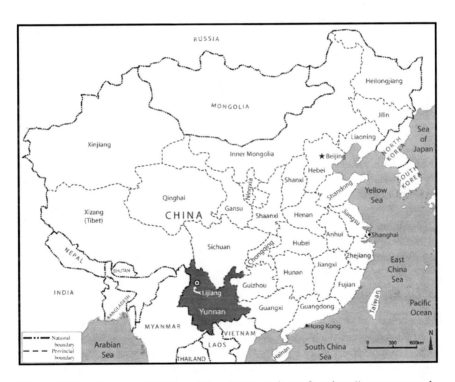

Figure 1.1 Location map of Lijiang, China. Source: redrawn from http://users.ece.gatech. edu/~ydtan/images/china/china_map.GIF: accessed 12 December 2006.

Lijiang, which adapted itself harmoniously to the uneven topography of this key commercial and strategic site, has retained a historic townscape of high quality and authenticity. Its architecture is noteworthy for the blending of elements from several cultures that have come together over many centuries. Lijiang also possesses an ancient water-supply system of great complexity and ingenuity that still functions effectively today.

The town has managed to retain its coherence and sense of history that makes it different from many other Chinese cities where local culture and landscapes have been affected by modernization, wars, catastrophes, or other factors. As a historic city, Lijiang Ancient Town has an abundance of historic buildings and bridges, a canal system that is several hundreds years old and cobblestoned streets that have lasted through the ages. As a cultural city, it is home to the Naxi community who still boasts an abundance of traditional cultural practices in their everyday life. Naxi culture, together with the unique urban fabric, is what Lijiang Ancient Town has come to represent.

After acquiring World Heritage Site inscription, the number of visitors exploded. In 2007 alone, it attracted 5.31 million visitors, most of whom were domestic Chinese tourists (Lijiang Bureau of Statistics 2008). The influx of tourists has brought about dramatic change to the place and to the daily lives of the Naxi. Conservation and protection of the Naxi heritage have been good for the local community but there are many who feel left behind and excluded from the tourist dollar. Hence, it is no wonder that Leask (2006:13) argues, "it is difficult to balance tourism activity with the conservation role, often creating a tension or conflict between the usually large number of stakeholders involved." There is undoubtedly difficulty in reaching a consensus on heritage tourism among the stakeholders as they hold different or even conflicting agendas.

The ancient town has a clear spatial boundary. The line that separates the old town from the new city is clearly demarcated by the local planning authority (Figure 1.2). This boundary has created representations of space as the authorities try to mark out the heritage importance of places by means of development plans and new regulations. Although the new city typifies the monotonous urban landscapes of many coastal cities in China, the old town demonstrates a distinctive cityscape in terms of its historical continuity and cultural disposition. In reality, the new city is a magnet for locals seeking more modern settings. This has made the old town even more of a tourist enclave.

Research rationale and objectives

The restless politics of tourism development in cross-Atlantic countries have been the subject of wide documentation and competing arguments in geography and other disciplines since the 1980s (see, for example, Alsayyad 2001; Boniface and Fowler 1993; Urry 2002). Tourism politics in China, however, has been largely neglected in the English literature. Specific to Lijiang, there are works on anthropology, geography, musicology, and tourism development (du Cros 2006; McKhann 2001; Rees 2000; Wang 2007; Yamamura 2004; Yang 2002; Zong 2005), but few

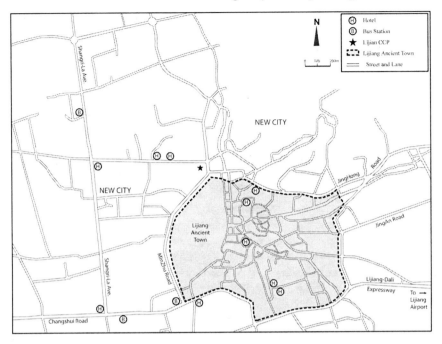

Figure 1.2 Lijiang Ancient Town in the city of Lijiang. Source: Redraw from http://www.soouo.com/emap/1644.htm: accessed 19 May 2006.

that address the politics of tourism development (except for Oakes (1998) and Ateljevic and Doorne (2003) who broach the subject for Guizhou and Dali, respectively). For a country like China, which is undergoing rapid and radical change from a centrally planned system to a market economy and which is also seen as a rising world power (Brandt and Rawski 2008) and an important component of the global tourism industry, this is a serious shortfall. China certainly does not demonstrate less pronounced tourism politics than other countries. More specifically, the transformation and formation of tourism landscapes in China has no parallel elsewhere because the politicization of tourism has led to severe touristification and commodification in numerous heritage sites as demonstrated by Lijiang Ancient Town.

The objectives of this book are three-fold. The primary objective is to examine the practices of contestation and negotiation of identity within Lijiang. Tourism is not only a set of *economic* activities but also "questions of taste, fashion and *identity*" have to enter the inquiry of tourism studies (Rojek and Urry 1997:2, emphasis added). The phenomenon of tourism politics offers a good window into "complex *human and social* engagements, relations and negotiations" (Crouch 1999:1, emphasis added) in the process of tourism development. However, tourism politics has frequently been studied with a one-sided perspective. As Chapter 2 will show, much of the literature in tourism geographies and other tourism studies address one aspect of tourism politics – dominance *or* resistance, production *or* consumption – but not both. By examining the dynamics of dominance *and* resistance and the interplay of production *and* consumption, this book endeavors to incorporate the much-needed dialectical perspective.

The second objective is to analyze the transformation of material and vernacular landscapes of the town so as to articulate the practices and outcomes of dominance and resistance.[6] As different stakeholders, including the state, private investors, tourists, and locals, tussle *and* collaborate/cooperate to control or reclaim space, how precisely are these places socially and spatially transformed? An analysis on tourism politics should not stop at highlighting what has come to be the normative discourses about tourism practices: i.e. debates about authenticity (MacCannell 1976), encounter (Crouch *et al.* 2001), gaze (Urry 2002), and power in the abstract (Cheong and Miller 2000). There is a need to link these practices to the actual geographies of a location to appreciate how tourism politics can actually transform heritage landscapes.

The final objective is to suggest strategies that will enable sustained tourism interest in this location. It is usual that scholars critique what tourism development brings to destinations in peripheral regions all over the world. In doing so, we often lose sight of locals' expectations for a better life. In fact, tourism can be an acceptable mechanism to turn their comparative advantage into productive spaces to help them fulfill their expectations even if this advantage is based on predisposed notions of "primitiveness," "exoticness," and "backwardness." It is inadequate for scholars to be primarily occupied with studying the "faults" of tourism and forget empathy toward the people and place(s) in question. In this regard, the third objective is to propose policy implications for sustained tourism interest in Lijiang to benefit local ordinary people to the utmost.

Fieldwork and data collection

The materials we analyze in this book were collected over several years. A pilot study was conducted in June 2004, followed by three rounds of fieldwork from September to December in 2004, from June to July in 2005, and from June to July 2007, respectively. In the first round, the questionnaire survey, in-depth interviews, participant observation, and site survey were conducted to collect first-hand data. Although not initiated by ourselves, we also observed several focus group discussions on Lijiang's heritage tourism and urban conservation. This became a secondary source of information. In the second and third rounds, we mainly conducted in-depth interviews with tourists and the locals.

Questionnaire survey

A questionnaire survey was designed to give a broad overview of what the tourists and local residents generally thought about Lijiang's heritage tourism. The self-administered questionnaire survey was conducted with visitors between October and November 2004. Before this survey, a pilot test was conducted with 20 domestic and 20 international tourists to uncover problems concerning the clarity of the questions. The survey took place over weekdays, weekends, and public holidays (including the National Day, the highest season in Lijiang's tourism). The time frame covered both peak and off-peak seasons in Lijiang's tourism market. Tourists were randomly targeted in Sifang Square and at the bars and restaurants. It was only at these places that tourists were relatively settled and willing to participate in the survey. The questionnaires were available in three versions – Chinese, English, and Japanese – given according to the respondents' preference. All the returned surveys were checked to see if respondents completed them. Incomplete surveys were followed up accordingly, or discarded if the respondents were no longer available. This ensured a high rate of survey completion. The response rate for the domestic tourist survey was 91.8 percent (303 questionnaires were usable); the rate for the international tourist survey was 90 percent (180 usable). Each respondent was given a small souvenir as a token of appreciation.

The survey adopted a non-probability quota sampling. Prioritizing accessibility, we randomly approached tourists for the survey, regardless of whether they were part of a group or individual visitors, young or old, male or female. This strategy gives a convenience sample. Although possibly all tourists did not have equal probability of selection for this survey (Neuman 2003), every effort was made to ensure that the sample was stratified according to the profile of Lijiang's visitors' profile (Table 1.1).

Table 1.1 shows the demographic profile of tourist respondents in the survey. As far as possible, the quota sample reflected the major demographic characteristics of Lijiang's visitors. Table 1.2 shows the origins of Lijiang's visitors.

The survey among international tourists did not match original statistics very well (Table 1.2). Three reasons account for this discrepancy. First, the Anglo-Saxon tourists were easier to identify physically as international visitors compared to Asian visitors (Japanese, Koreans, Singaporeans, and Malaysians). Second, this survey intentionally excluded those international visitors who cannot understand English, Chinese, or Japanese. Finally, the number of Japanese tourists, although the top international market to Lijiang, has decreased rapidly after 2003 because of sagging Sino–Japanese relations.

The main topics covered in the questionnaire for tourists appeared as three sections. First, the survey focused on what tourists expected to consume and experience in Lijiang Ancient Town. Second, the survey investigated tourists' practice of consumption in the town by asking them for their main activities and for their willingness to come into contact with the town's residents. The final concern was about their knowledge of heritage preservation and tourism development in the town. The items surveyed included their evaluation of different heritage landscapes and the role of the local government in developing heritage tourism.

To ascertain local perceptions on heritage tourism and the state, a mail-back questionnaire survey was carried out at the only school. It borders the ancient town and the new city, with students attending from both sides (see Figure 4.1). The pupils of the school, who ranged in age from 7 to 12 years, were requested to take the questionnaires to their family members or to adult friends to fill in. Altogether, 300 questionnaires were distributed in November 2004 and 260 were returned half

Table 1.1 Demographic profile of survey sample (%)

Demographics	Domestic tourists		International tourists	
	Sample	Lijiang (2003)	Sample	Lijiang (2003)
Gender				
Male	49.2	NA	56.1	NA
Female	50.8	NA	43.9	NA
Age (years)				
19 and below	2.6	5.2	1.1	4.1
20–29	49.2	32.7	36.7	30.1
30–39	32.7	30.1	20.6	31.5
40–49	11.2	18.5	19.4	20.6
50–59	3.6	6.7	11.1	12.3
60 and above	0.7	6.8	11.1	1.4
Educational attainment				
No formal education	0.7	0.7	0	NA
Primary and lower secondary	0.7	1.6	2.2	NA
Upper secondary/pre-college	21.8	23.6	16.7	NA
Diploma and degree	76.9	74.1	81.1	NA
Occupation				
Company employee	40.9	32.4	15.6	13.7
Businessman	8.3	9.3	13.9	10.4
National serviceman	20.8	31.1	3.9	5.2
Professional	12.5	8.2	31.7	41.2
Housewife	0	0	2.2	1.1
Students	5.6	7.0	18.9	6.6
Retired/unemployed	0.7	5.1	7.8	11.8
Others	11.2	6.9	6.1	10.0

Source: Lijiang Tourism Bureau (2005); authors' data.

a month later. Of these, 200 were usable. The sample generally reflected Lijiang's population, except for age, such as those in the 30–39 years old group being over-represented as the pupils naturally sought their parents to complete the survey (Table 1.3).

For local respondents, the questionnaire addressed three types of questions. First, it asked for the negative and positive impacts that tourism brought to their daily life. The aim was to find out whether they gave their consent to the *development* of heritage tourism in Lijiang. The questions subsequently concentrated on how the locals evaluated different heritage landscapes and the *status quo* of Naxi culture. They were also asked to assess the local government's role in heritage preservation and tourism development.

In-depth interviews

The in-depth interviews produced qualitative data from different respondents who had been engaged in Lijiang's heritage tourism and urban conservation for

Table 1.2 Place of origin of visitors

	Sample		*Lijiang (2003)*
	No.	*Percent*	*Percent*
Domestic tourists			
North China[a]	32	10.6	9.4
Northeast	3	1.0	1.4
East	78	25.7	24.9
South-middle	86	28.4	26.7
Southwest	84	27.7	27.3
Northwest	16	5.3	4.1
Hong Kong/Macau	4	1.3	6.2
International tourists			
Europe[b]	76	42.2	32.9
USA/Canada	44	24.2	15.6
Asia[c]	44	24.4	43.6
Australia	13	7.2	6.1
Other continents[d]	3	1.7	1.8

Source: Lijiang Tourism Bureau (2005); authors' data.

[a]The district division is based on the report from the Ministry of Civil Affairs, China, http://www.xzqh.org/QUHUA/index.htm (accessed 5 May 2006).
[b]European countries covered by the survey include Netherlands, Switzerland, UK, Belgium, Sweden, Germany, Denmark, Austria, France, Portugal, Norway and Spain.
[c]Asian countries include Japan, Israel, Singapore and Malaysia.
[d]Other countries include Algeria and Ecuador.

Table 1.3 Profile of local respondents

	Sample		*Lijiang in 2000*	
	No.	*Percent*		*Percent*
Gender				
Male	108	54.0		51.3
Female	92	46.0		48.7
Age (years)				
19 and below	16	8.0	14 and below	26.2
20–29	11	5.5	15-64	67.9
30–39	138	69.0	65 and above	5.9
40–49	26	13.0		
50 and above	9	4.5		
Ethnicity				
Han	78	39.0		42.3
Non-Han	122	61.0		57.7

Source: Lijiang Bureau of Statistics (2006); authors' data.

Table 1.4 Composition of tourist interviewees

	Gender[a]	Age[b]	Origin	Nights of stay	Occupation[c]
International tourists					
IT1	M	60	Canada	2	R
IT2	F	30	UK	2	NS
IT3	M	30	Argentina	2	CE
IT4	M	30	Macau SAR	4	P
IT5	M	40	Canada	2	B
IT6	F	42	Canada	2	CE
IT7	M	30	Malaysia	10	B
IT8	F	50	France	2	P
IT9	M	35	Australia	4	CE
IT10	F	30	Israel	3	P
IT11	M	55	Italy	7	R
Domestic tourists[d]					
DT1	M	35	Beijing	3	CE
DT2	F	33	Beijing	3	CE
DT3	F	30	Hunan	5	P
DT4	M	35	Beijing	3	CE
DT5	M	40	Guangdong	3	P
DT6	F	26	Yunnan	3	S
DT7	M	35	Guangdong	15	CE
DT8	F	20	Beijing	3	S
DT9	F	35	Sichuan	5	B

Source: authors' data.

[a] M = male; F = female.
[b] Age (years) was given or estimated.
[c] B = businessperson; CE = company employee; NS = national service; P = professional; R = retired; S = student.
[d] All domestic tourists are Han people.

many years. These interviews were arranged through informal contacts or our *guanxi* (literally, personal social relations). This arrangement made it possible to obtain their voices without external intervention. Two interviews were conducted by email. Altogether, 91 interviews were garnered and the composition of all interviewees is listed in Tables 1.4–1.8.

An interview generally lasted between 45 minutes and an hour. Some key respondents were interviewed twice. All interviews were done in either Mandarin or English. For the two local respondents who could not speak Mandarin, we used an interpreter. The majority of the interviews were tape-recorded, with permission. On only rare occasions did respondents not approve recording. For these, we noted down the key words they used and recapped their ideas immediately after the interviews.

For the locals, the interviews focused chiefly on:

- a comparison of the town under different periods
- the impacts of tourism on their lives and on the town

- their interaction with tourists
- and the socio-spatial transformation of Lijiang's heritage landscapes.

We began with a set of warm-up questions inquiring about their knowledge of and relation to Lijiang before advancing to open-ended questions indicated from either the information they introduced or issues they were familiar with. The purpose of this format was to allow respondents to "talk about the subject in terms of their own frames of reference" (May 1993:112), and especially ordinary people to express any potentially hidden transcripts (Skeggs 2002:369). As we

Table 1.5 Composition of local interviewees[a]

	Gender[b]	Age[c]	Occupation	Residence[d]
L1	M	30	Employee in Naxi music troupe	A
L2	M	70	Manager in a Naxi music troupe	A
L3	M	35	Guesthouse manager	A
L4	M	70	Manager in a Naxi music troupe	N
L5	M	25	Taxi driver and tour guide	N
L6	F	45	Guesthouse manager	A
L7	M	20	Employee in a Naxi music troupe	A
L8	M	40	Manager in a tourism firm	N
L9	M	25	Bar owner and silverware shop manager	A
L10	M	60	Employee in a Naxi music troupe	N
L11	F	60	Guesthouse owner	A
L12	M	60	Guesthouse owner	A
L13	F	20	Employee in a tourism firm	A
L14	M	36	Manager in a travel agency	N
L15	M	30	Senior tour guide	N
L16	M	61	Employee in a Naxi music troupe	N
L17	M	30	Amateur musician	A
L18	M	50	Representative of an NGO	A
L19	F	30	Doing National Service	N
L20	M	60	Retired	N
L21	F	60	Head of a dance team	N
L22	M	60	Head of a dance team	N
L23	M	55	Guesthouse owner	A
L24	M	60	Retired	N
L25	F	45	Head of a primary school	N
L26	F	55	Head of a Naxi cultural school	N
L27	M	65	Retired	A
L28	F	50	Retired	A
L29	M	67	Retired	A

Source: authors' data.

[a]All local interviewees are Naxi.
[b]M = male; F = female.
[c]Age (years) was given or estimated.
[d]A = Lijiang Ancient Town; N = Lijiang New City.

Table 1.6 Composition of migrant merchants or workers in tourism

	Gender[a]	Age[b]	Ethnicity	Length (years)[c]	Origin	Occupation
OM1	F	28	Han	2	Jiangsu	Guesthouse manager
OM2	F	35	Bai	5	Yunnan	Silverware shop owner
OM3	M	40	Unknown	5	Taiwan	Owner of a gift shop and a bar
OM4	M	23	Han	2	Yunnan	Tour guide
OM5	M	35	Han	4	Sichuan	News vendor
OM6	M	30	Han	5	Yunnan	Silverware shop manager
OM7	M	50	Han	4	Guangdong	Executive manager of a tourism firm
OM8	M	26	Yi	4	Yunnan	Bar employee
OM9	M	60	Han	3	Hubei	Artist
OM10	F	40	Han	2	Hebei	Guesthouse manager
OM11	F	35	Han	3	Hunan	Owner of a bookshop with café
OM12	M	40	Naxi	3	Yunnan	Employee in a tourism firm
OM13	M	40	Han	10	Sichuan	Gift shop owner

Source: authors' data.

[a]M = male; F = female.
[b]Age was given or estimated.
[c]Length refers to how long interviewees have had a business in Lijiang.

Table 1.7 Composition of government officials interviewed

	Gender[a]	Age[b]	Ethnicity	Governmental body
G1	M	55	Naxi	Dongba Cultural Museum
G2	F	40	Han	CWHMC[c]
G3	M	60	Naxi	Mu Palace
G4	M	45	Naxi	Lijiang Tourism Bureau
G5	M	45	Naxi	Nationality and Religion Bureau, Ancient Town District
G6	M	45	Naxi	The Bureau of Culture, Ancient Town District
G7	M	35	Naxi	Lijiang Tourism Bureau

Source: authors' data.

[a]M = male; F = female.
[b]Age (years) was given or estimated.
[c]Committee for World Heritage Management and Conservation of Lijiang Ancient Town.

Table 1.8 Composition of other interviewees

	Sex[a]	Age[b]	Occupation
OI1	M	50	Senior research fellow at the Dongba Cultural Institute and a town resident
OI2	M	60	Architecture professor in Kunming Polytechnic University, Han
OI3	M	60	Senior research fellow in Yunnan Social Research Institute, Naxi
OI4	F	50	Senior consultant with the Culture Unit in UNESCO, Bangkok
OI5	F	20	US researcher on Naxi culture

Source: authors' data.

[a]M = male; F = female.
[b]Age (years) was given or estimated.

hoped, the unstructured interviews not only yielded specific information but also opened up new avenues for research. For instance, some local respondents reminded us that they had ambivalent feelings about tourism development and their attitudes to tourism were shaped by China's economic and social transition and by globalization. These were incorporated into our analysis of tourism politics in Lijiang.

For government officials, however, we prepared a series of questions which we showed them before carrying out the interviews. Designed in accordance to the governmental bodies they belonged to, the main focus was their official view of the role the local government plays in Lijiang's heritage tourism and urban conservation. These officials were also asked to list the important policies their departments formulated or carried out for heritage tourism and to explain the rationale. It is generally very difficult to interview officials in China as they are wary of talking to a stranger, and our interviews were no exception. To avoid any possible rejection and misunderstanding, we approached them directly in their own offices where they had a sense of authority. Additionally, the questions were framed with a sense of respect and to encourage them to talk, such as "What do you think of the newspaper reports on Lijiang?" and "Can you explain the types of investments Lijiang Ancient Town attracts?"

For tourists, merchants, and others, semi-structured interviews were conducted. The main foci were commodification, the role of government, tourism impacts, and heritage preservation. Semi-structured interviews enabled us to "have more latitude to *probe* beyond the answers and thus enter into a dialogue with the interviewees" (May 1993:111, original emphasis).

Two ethical issues emerged during the interviews. First, the questions asked during the interviews were not supposed to trouble the respondents. If they felt intimidated by the questions, we immediately changed the topic. On several occasions, the respondents expressed their unwillingness to answer our questions or to elaborate their answers. The second issue was privacy. At the beginning of any interview, we assured the respondents that their identity would be kept strictly confidential and that their anonymity would be guaranteed by using pseudonyms if a direct quotation was extracted from their interview data. Respondents were requested to check the transcripts of their interview data in order to convince them that all data were accurately recorded.

Participant observation

Participant observation yielded data about the everyday workings of tourism politics in Lijiang. Through engaging in tourism activities and observing locals' daily life and the physical aspects of the town, we sought to understand and explain the actions of people who occupied the town and prompted the socio-spatial transformation of Lijiang's heritage landscapes. Participant observation allowed us to move beyond "a merely cerebral relationship and develop more intuitive or gut-level feelings about what it is like to be 'a native' in this particular time and place" (Fife 2005:72).

We conducted various forms of participant observation in our fieldwork. We joined the dance teams in the town center to watch the interactions between dance performers and tourists, despite occasionally becoming the object of tourists' gaze. Additionally, we participated in all tourism activities in the town to gain a better understanding of them. We attended local concerts, both commercial and spontaneous, to develop our knowledge of Naxi music and to uncover how Naxi music survives in different settings. More often than not, we stayed in the town center or the streets where tourists clustered so as to observe how they "performed" in these settings and how tourism consumption activities such as shopping were done. We also roamed the streets where tourists seldom visited and locals still maintained their community ties. In these streets, we observed how Naxi everyday life went on in the presence of tourism.

Site survey: mapping tourism businesses

Site survey is a method of spatial mapping and analysis in combination with observation and measurement (Dovey *et al.* 2001). According to Dovey *et al.* (2001:321), spatial analysis "consists of a series of layered mappings of the study area including pedestrian access networks, public/private ownership, functional mix and streetlife volume." Writing about the contested backpacking landscape in Bangkok's Khao San Road, Teo and Leong (2006) employed this method to map visible details of the road. According to Teo and Leong (2006:115), the method was to verify secondary data and delineate "the constituent components of the physical space" for analyzing "the negotiation of spaces by the different groups." Much used in tourism geographies, the method has proved its value for studying urban historic districts (Ashworth and Tunbridge 1990; Pearce 1998).

In this research, site survey as a method focused on the functions and owner-ship of the houses (on the ground floor) along the main streets in Lijiang Ancient Town. It generated data about the spatial distribution of businesses and depicted the commodification and spatial transformation of Lijiang's heritage landscapes.

The data can be used for analyzing the outcome of the negotiations among different groups and detecting the relevant social and economic mechanisms underlying the spatial distribution of tourism businesses.

The survey was done in November 2004. All houses in the town were occupied as shops or residences, or remained vacant. In the light of the customers and the business contents that shops held, all shops surveyed were classified into three categories: namely, tourist-oriented shops, resident-oriented shops, and general shops that aimed at tourists and residents without obvious preference (Table 1.9). The identification of a shop relied on "the Business License in Scenic Zones in Yunnan Province" issued by the Committee of World Heritage Management and Conservation of Lijiang Ancient Town (CWHMC), the statutory body in charge of heritage preservation and management of the town. Supervised by CWHMC, the business contents of a shop are officially documented on the license and no changes are allowed without approval. Identifying who are targeted by the shop depended on the shopkeeper's confirmation or on-the-spot observation. The survey also covered the ownership of a house, referring to whether local or migrant merchants were running the business. In addition, the average house rent

Table 1.9 Categories of businesses in Lijiang Ancient Town

Shop type	*Business content*
Tourist-oriented shops	
Bars	Food and beverage
Book/CDs	Sale of brochures, guide books, maps, and CDs
Ethnic costume	Naxi, Bai or Tibet style costume
Guesthouse	Accommodation with less than 20 rooms and only a few facilities[a]
Hotel	Accommodation with over 20 rooms and some facilities
Local specialties	Yunnan tea, medicinal materials
Naxi Music Hall	Music and dance performance
Clothing	Fashion wear and T-shirts with Dongba words or ornaments/trinklets
Souvenir	Silvercraft, woodcarvings with Dongba inscriptions; paintings and chimes
Tourism Services	Travel agents and sale of camera periphery
General shops	
Clinic	Hospital, clinic
Grocery	Supermarket
Public services	Bank, telecommunications, post office
Restaurant	Food and beverage
Resident-oriented shops	Barber, tailor, video rental, repair shops

Source: authors' data.

[a]CNTA sets 20 rooms as a criterion to differentiate guesthouse from hotel (GB/T 14308-1997) (China National Tourism Administration 1997).

on different streets was investigated to draw a link between the common routes traversed by tourists and the distribution of tourism businesses in Lijiang.

Three points need elaboration about the site survey. First, hawkers or casual stalls were not included. These stalls did not obtain business licenses and changed their locations frequently since CWHMC forbade them in the town. It was hard to locate them on the map. Generally, their number was less than 20 in the town. Second, we have to admit that the survey contains small errors because of the inaccuracy of the town map we used and the inadequate information about the shops. Finally, the survey only focused on the main streets that tourists frequently visited and ignored the streets where few tourists patronized and those where locals resided without tourists' intrusion. The area surveyed covered over 65 percent of the core area of the town. These three points indicate that the survey does not have complete validity, as it does not cover the entire town. That notwithstanding, the survey is useful for understanding socio-spatial changes in the core of the ancient town.

Secondary data

In this research, we also relied on secondary data. We collected several urban planning reports and government regulation documents on how to implement heritage management and accelerate tourism development. The planning reports provided us with an opportunity to analyze how the authority and planners constructed Lijiang's heritage and resolved the pressing tensions between development and conservation. The examination of such reports sought to identify changes or continuations as a result of overt legislative commitments regarding heritage production.

A considerable amount of information about the history of Lijiang Ancient Town was accessed through almanacs and annals about Lijiang. The materials included a government-made visual CD on Lijiang Ancient Town, many brochures for tourism products, postcards, and guide books. The local newspaper, *Lijiang Daily*, was also an important source of secondary information. We looked at information from 1994 to 2008 to find reports about heritage, Naxi culture, and tourism development relevant to Lijiang Ancient Town. *Lijiang Daily* is actually the mouthpiece of Lijiang's Chinese Communist Party (CCP) committee. The reports from *Lijiang Daily* were selected for analysis because they constitute important, continuous, and official narratives about heritage tourism from the local authority that became propaganda for the local Naxi community. These reports ranging from 1994 to 2008 covered the stages of take-off to high development of Lijiang's tourism sector.

We also accessed necessary statistics from different governmental bodies in Lijiang to sketch out Lijiang's tourism. The statistical data provided a chance to trace the trajectory of tourism development in Lijiang and substantiate the importance of the tourism sector to Lijiang society. The data covered tourist arrivals and receipts in Lijiang from 1996 to 2007. Nevertheless, these data are not viewed as all-encompassing, as their reliability and validity are not highly assured.

We gathered tourists' personal accounts, such as comments in some shops' notepads and notes in travel forums on the Internet. Newspaper reports published outside of Lijiang were also included in the analysis. Two points require elaborating. First, people now rely on mass media like the Internet and newspapers to construct their knowledge about Lijiang and/or for expressing their experiences. For people who do not have an opportunity to visit Lijiang, the messages in the mass media are potentially influential in shaping their anticipations about what Lijiang will be like. For those who have visited Lijiang, the mass media provide them with an arena to share their experiences with others or to reconstitute the knowledge they have gleaned from their tour. They are the "authors," seeking to consciously write about Lijiang. Second, the mass media outside of Lijiang represent the voice of the national or global forces. They disseminate the mainstream values and beliefs of China or even the world and perpetuate certain expectations of Lijiang's heritage tourism. The analysis of current media text helped explore the breadth and diversity of the cultural meanings of Lijiang Ancient Town. The main agents of mass media for this study included *People's Daily* (*renming ribao*), *China Daily*, *Xinhua News Agency*, *Yunnan Daily*, Tianya Club (the most popular Internet forum in China), Lonely Planet and its forum, and tourists' blogs.[7]

The structure of the book

Chapter 1 outlines the theoretical influences of this book and provides a sketch of Lijiang and how the empirical data were gathered. Chapters 2 and 3 offer the theoretical framework for our analysis, including the important geo-historical underpinnings that influenced the development of Lijiang Ancient Town. In Chapter 2, Gramsci's theory of hegemony and recent work on representational practices and capital accumulation in tourism studies are drawn upon to elaborate how the cultural politics of heritage tourism can be conceptualized in terms of a compromised equilibrium between the powerful and the less powerful as the processes of production and consumption of tourism landscapes take place. Here, we argue that the representation of heritage and the socio-spatial transformation of heritage sites are outcomes of an ongoing dialogue between producers and consumers of heritage tourism that have been affected not only by economics but also by politics and culture.

Chapter 3 elucidates the commodification and politicization of tourism in post-Mao China. Rather than reducing China's transition to a story of an economic miracle, we will be concerned with the dynamic state–society relations that inflect the contested space of tourism. To conceptualize China's dramatic transition, which was initiated in 1978, we identify four themes in this chapter: (1) the shift from a planned economy to a socialist market economy; (2) the revival of Chinese nationalism; (3) inter-urban competition and urban coalition; and (4) the rise of consumerism and social stratification. These themes help us to explore changes in the political economy of the country, the significance of nationalism, and the growth of consumerism in China, which have been responsible for the politicization and commodification of China's heritage. The history of Lijiang

Ancient Town is a history of domestication and acculturation of the peripheral minority groups by the Han majority in the center. Valuable heritage landscapes that originate from smaller minority groups are able to woo nostalgia-seeking urban Han tourists, bringing about rapid modernization in Lijiang. Nevertheless, exact tourism landscapes that emerge involve a dialectic process in which various role players encode/decode heritage as they negotiate for an acceptable position in the pursuit of power and capital.

Chapters 4 and 5 examine the production and consumption of heritage tourism in Lijiang. Informed by a global–national–local nexus, we start by analyzing the dominant discourses about Lijiang's tourism development and the practices by which different groups of people propel Lijiang into the global economy via tourism (Chapter 4). In particular, we explore their underlying agendas that help produce the landscapes. Chapter 5 focuses on tourists and how they consume heritage and exert their influence on the representation of heritage landscapes. It also unveils the tensions and compromises between tourists and tourism developers, and between domestic and international tourists.

Chapters 6 and 7 move beyond production and consumption to investigate the actual socio-spatial transformation of Lijiang. The main concern is to discuss the negotiations of dominance and resistance, and their outcomes. Chapter 6 shows commodification of the material, vernacular, and symbolic landscapes of Lijiang as the town gets turned into a space of tourism consumption.

Chapter 7 looks at how the local indigenous Naxi endeavor to (re)build their own place-bound identity to mediate the influences of global and national forces. An analysis of locals' readings of heritage tourism reveals that they do not completely embrace or deny tourism development; rather, they maintain an ambivalent feeling toward heritage tourism. Informed by the neo-Gramscian approach to cultural politics, we argue that the locals do make use of heritage tourism as a means to strengthen their role in heritage transformation and to enhance their own socio-economic status. Local agency in heritage tourism is exemplified in three ways: (re)claiming space for a sense of place, Naxi language education and identity building, and local involvement in heritage tourism. Finally, in the last chapter, we also provide some recommendations to sustain tourism in Lijiang Ancient Town without detriment to the locals.

2 The cultural politics of tourism

Exploring the complexity of hegemony

At the outset, we want to clarify the definition of heritage tourism. According to Zeppel and Hall (1992:47), heritage tourism is based on "nostalgia for the past." It is centered on "what we have inherited, which can mean anything from historic buildings, to art works, to beautiful scenery" (Yale 1991:21). Linking heritage and nostalgia, Kibby (2000:140) argues that heritage tourism represents "a way of recuperating the past for contemporary tourists, and is part of a wider nostalgia for traditional social values, and an appreciation of the way things were, or at least are perceived to have been." In many cases, these transitional social values and cultures are disappearing and heritage tourism provides a reason to rejuvenate them: sometimes for economic gain, other times simply for strengthening political/cultural fortitude. Thus, Alsayyad (2001:14) concludes, "all heritage is socially manufactured, and [...] all transitions have the potential to be consumed."

In the context of urban heritage, a great deal has been written about how urban authorities package their tangible cultural heritage such as historic buildings, monuments and artifacts, and intangible heritage such as living tradition, memory, and folklore into heritage products in order to heighten a city's competitiveness in the global era of travel and tourism (Ashworth and Tunbridge 1990; Graham *et al.* 2000; Kearns and Philo 1993; Yeoh 2005). The strategies used include urban regeneration, waterfront rejuvenation, and urban redevelopment (Chang and Huang 2005; Harvey 1989a; Smith, N. 2002; Teo 2003). Collectively known as the "heritage industry" (Hewison 1987), cities have managed to turn their economies around from the declining manufacturing sector to the profitable service sector. In the absence of traditional resources to compete for large capital investments and jobs, heritage tourism is a cultural strategy that has a great deal of potential (Zukin 1998).

Changes in tourist taste have also helped the industry. For instance, leisure under Fordism was a natural extension of assembly line production, being "morally sound and consistent with 'rational corporate expectations'" (Harvey 1989a:126). When corporations and families stopped influencing leisure in post-modern society (Lash and Urry 1994), individuals took responsibility for their own consumption. Thrift and Glennie (1993:44) argue that consumers of today pay a great deal more attention to "the fostering of individuality [and to] projects of self-actualisation." Heritage tourism is often a convenient vehicle to achieve these goals because it renders itself to the accumulation of cultural capital. Cultural capital here refers to knowledge, skill, education, and other advantages that can enhance an individual's status in society (Bourdieu 1984; 2001; Munt 1994). Heritage encompasses an ensemble of inherited features that constitute an extraordinarily rich exhibit of the uniqueness of any society. The historical continuity and past glory embodied in heritage landscapes provide a chance for tourists to imagine the history in their own terms, according to their own values and life experiences. The imagination about history in their minds generates "a deeper meaning and a sense of worth beyond material possessions" (Yeoman *et al.* 2007:1128), allowing them to socially distinguish themselves from other consumers by the wealth of their knowledge (Munt 1994; Richards 1996). For many heritage tourists, they do not simply seek new experiences, they pursue "a statement of taste" (Shaw and Williams 2004:24).

This global popularity of heritage tourism has also permeated into China. As we documented in Chapter 1, China's mass heritage tourism can be traced back to 1994 when a nationwide inventory was made of the country's cultural relics and historical sites. Since then, heritage has become a vital tool for accelerating economic development in many localities. On the surface, the goals are commendable as their aim is principally to raise wealth for the people and boost local economic development. Thus, city governments all over the country make special efforts to package their heritage resources to win titles such as World Heritage Status or National Historic City. "[R]ather than a wish to protect the site in question [they are ...] driven by a desire for economic gain" (*China Daily* 25 July 2006:4).

Besides economic development and capital accumulation, the popularity of heritage tourism has raised other new issues. As articulated by Jackson (1991:225), we wonder "whose past is being preserved, how is it being represented, and whose interests are served by such unavoidable selective readings?" Kearns and Philo (1993) maintain that the production of heritage resides on a selective appropriation of the past to create what Boyer (1994:11) calls "a utopia of rationalised space." The production of "utopian heritage" is ruled through the sophisticated capitalism of the tourism/leisure industry, which strengthens socio-spatial control of the heritage site and has a tendency to domesticate history as it sees fit (Ashworth and Tunbridge 1990; Harvey 1989a; Zukin 1995). As Gotham (2005b:1114) observes in the case of New Orleans's Vieux Carre, tourist consumption contributes to the formation of a gentrified space by bringing in "more upscale and affluent population[s]." Tourist/leisure enclaves ensue, as exemplified by Bugis Street in Singapore (Chang 1997), Xintiandi in Shanghai (He and Wu 2005), SoHo in New York (Zukin 1995), and Docklands in London (Butler 2007), to name a few.

Although the stamp of bureaucracy and capital is clearly marked on the production and consumption of heritage at these sites, they are also replete with signs of struggle and resistance from individuals and groups who may not be totally agreeable with the state of affairs. The production and consumption of heritage are not simple processes. Tourism sites are borne out of complex exchanges, competitions, and collaborations between local groups, as well as national and international forces in relation to capital, labor, and culture. In other words, the (re)presentation of heritage landscapes conveys "a multiplicity of quite different and even competing 'ideologies'" in terms of their stances and values (Tunbridge and Ashworth 1996:49). Heritage (re)presentation and socio-spatial transformation of many sites are filled with tensions about the authoring of heritage that will inevitably reveal how dominance and resistance between the powerful state and capital and the less-powerful individuals within society become expressed.

In the remainder of this chapter, we situate heritage in a global–national–local nexus to understand identity building and capital accumulation in relation to different scales. The production and consumption of heritage transcend the boundary of certain locales and have wide socio-economic relations at other scales because of intense globalization. Thus, heritage sites become "scaled places" (Marston 2000:221) which are "the embodiment of social relations of empowerment and disempowerment and the arena through and in which they operate" (Swyngedouw 1997a:169).

Subsequently, we examine different heritage sites to elaborate two interrelated aspects of tourism politics: (1) acts of dominance and resistance in the production and consumption of heritage, and (2) the commodified heritage landscapes as the socio-spatial outcomes consequent on the first point. Finally, we detail Gramsci's theory of hegemony and explain how a neo-Gramscian approach that incorporates resistance, negotiation, representation, and the interplay of production and consumption is useful as a theoretical framework to structure the empirical analysis of this book.

Heritage in a global–national–local nexus

Globalization is probably the most misused concept in social sciences. The term has been described as "time-space compression" (Harvey 1989a) or time-space shrinkage with "new fluidities of astonishing speed and scale" (Urry 2000:33). Globalization is a powerful force that speeds up the velocity and intensity of interconnections between capital, people, ideas, and information all over the world. Teo and Lim (2003) observed the following about globalization: (1) the forces of globalization are powerful so that they can threaten to homogenize the world and result in "a borderless global economy" and society (Teo and Lim 2003:288, see also Ohmae 1990); (2) a counterargument is that globalization does *not* necessarily overwhelm local particularities and cultures, but is frequently mediated by local factors and in turn generates place-bound uniqueness in different locations; and (3) so as not to reify the global/local dichotomy, space is acknowledged to be in a "perpetual [state of being] redefined, contested, and restructured" as a consequence of globalization (Swyngedouw 1997b:141). This book understands globalization to be a socio-spatial process and "a *dialectical* process of homogenization and differentiation" (Yeung 1998:292, original emphasis). As Agnew and Corbridge (1995:219) argue, globalization "opens as many doors as it shuts" insofar as it invents certain inextricable conditions for (de)centralization and (dis)empowerment. The results are derived from the convergence between the general forces on the global scale and the national and locality-specific factors.

Whereas globalization remains an important research item, recently, more attention has been given to "locality." Many scholars argue that the local is inevitably intertwined with global forces (Brenner 1999; Gotham 2005a; Swyngedouw 1997b).[1] Robins (1991:35) specifically asserts that locality should be viewed as fluid and relational spaces, "constituted only in and through its relations to the global." From a neo-liberalism standpoint, Brenner (1999:433) argues that cities need to supply relatively immobile infrastructures to "the world-scale circulation of capital" to make possible the accelerated physical movement of commodities and labor through space. To territorialize capital and skilled labor to facilitate this circulation, cities have to come up with "immobile, place-specific assets and externalities that either cannot be found elsewhere or cannot be abandoned without considerable devalorisation costs" (Brenner 1999:442). In the "struggle for place," a localization of heritage and tradition is central to the continuity of identity and community in the global economy. Uniqueness of "place-specific assets" serves only to enhance local competitiveness. This book argues for a global–local nexus to explore the cross-scalar power geometry in which "the 'local' and the 'global' are mutually constitutive, theorized not in terms of unilinear commodity chains but via complex circuits, networks and flows" (Jackson 2000b:10).

Although far more can be said about the cultural politics of heritage in a global–local nexus, it is appropriate at this point to bring in the role of the nation state in influencing the representation and provision of heritage. The desire for nation building and economic development has to be singled out since most countries have a colonial history and their economies are "less developed." The nation states in developed countries such as the USA and the UK also harness heritage landmarks to serve special political purposes such as national identity building (Pitchford 1995; Pretes 2003). As Hall (2005:24) points out, the British heritage has become "the material embodiment of the spirit of the nation, a collective representation of the British version of tradition, a concept pivotal to the lexicon of English virtues," for the purpose of constructing a shared national identity and binding each individual into the larger national story.

Boyd (2002) argues that the meanings of heritage can vary in terms of the geographical scale of analysis. At the *global* level, natural and cultural particularities at heritage sites are heavily emphasized in order to attract worldwide attention. At the *national* level, especially in an Asian context, these particularities are played down, giving way to a collective national imagery. The purpose is to promote the *whole* country as a united tourism destination. For example, slogans are nationalized, such as "Uniquely Singapore," "Amazing Thailand," and "Incredible India." Geographical differences re-emerge at the *local* level and help the people to build a sense of place and identity. Hence, reference to the scales provides a lens to examine the multiplicity of heritage representations and the complexity of identity building, all of which are inextricably bound up with the context where they emerge and the scale that this context is situated in. One good case to show the multiple meanings of heritage at different scales is Bali, Indonesia.

Michel Picard's work on heritage and cultural tourism in Bali articulates how the interconnection of forces at different scales is played out. Using Bali's global tourism prestige and its economic significance, the Balinese resolve on controlling their own fate by using heritage as a means to "obtain full recognition of their [own] ethnic identity from the state and to improve their position with Indonesia" (Picard 1997:184). This process, also known as Balinization, is an arduous struggle as the Balinese seek to establish a local identity and reify the representational spaces of localities and of lived experience. The efforts for Balinization, however, are always constrained by the structural forces of globalization and nationalization, i.e. "Indonesianization." On the one hand, Bali cultural heritage has to conform to the rules of global tourism production when tourism developers market and promote Bali as a destination for global visitors (Picard 2003). Thus, Bali is an exotic site to the world, "a meeting-place of the romantic South Seas and the mysterious Orient" (Hitchcock 2001:106). On the other hand, Bali is compelled to contribute to nation building and national integration as the Indonesian government in Jakarta uses Bali heritage and culture to represent Indonesia as if thousands of islands that comprise Indonesia were "a single distinct set of unique cultural features" (Picard 1997:198). In this regard, Bali is a showcase of Indonesian "high culture." The "Indonesianization" of Bali then bolsters a linear image that can be decoded by its audiences, i.e. Balinese, other Indonesians and the global community.

Due to a tourism-driven reconfiguration of socio-spatial structures, Bali, as well as many other heritage sites in the world, become easily "displaced and connected to images of other places in a global circulation" (Coleman and Crang 2002:4). Tourism, therefore, not only brings a universality of mass culture to destinations but also reasserts local place-bound identities in different localities and contributes to the rise of nationalism (Massey and Jess 1995).

The case of Bali provides many insights for the study of Lijiang's tourism politics as these two sites share many similarities, but their differences also yield new lines of inquiry to the established literature. Unlike Bali, where global visitors constitute the main tourism market, Lijiang is visited largely by domestic tourists. To date, tourism literature in English has rarely focused on domestic heritage tourists in Asian countries, with a few exceptions such as Edensor (1998), Gladstone (2005), Nyíri (2006), and Winter (2005). Domestic tourists not only bring nationalist discourses into heritage sites but also are gradually taking over the Asian tourism market (especially in China and India). Analytic attention is therefore needed to inquire how these national forces can shape different destinations, and to examine identity building in relation to different scales by placing heritage in a global–national–local nexus. The danger that tourism can bring an "end [to] geography" (Yeung 1998:292) via homogenization is real. Hence, we will analyze the concrete acts of dominance and resistance as they determine the fate of heritage within a global–national–local nexus.

Cultural politics in tourism

The dynamics between dominance and resistance in heritage tourism has remained the focus in a number of publications (Burns and Novelli 2006; Harrison *et al.* 2005; Smith and Robinson 2006). This dynamics is not just a guest–host issue, but also involves tourism enterprise, government, and even international organizations in the process of producing and consuming heritage. For example, urban conservation in many cities does not reinforce locals' sense of place to heritage sites, but is implemented on the basis of "economic viability and [hence] favor[s] commercial (leisure) activities" (Teo and Huang 1995:589). However, new local interest groups and alliances are emerging within our increasingly globalized societies and these groups have very different alternatives and agendas on heritage from those in power. They have been principally responsible for converting heritage sites into contested spaces.

Within China, the issue of the politics of heritage tourism has received some academic attention. A particular concern draws upon the relation between place making and identity building in peripheral places where minority groups of people reside, such as Yunnan's Zhongdian (Kolås 2004) and Dali (Ateljevic and Doorne 2003), Guizhou (Swain 1990), Sichuan (Nyíri 2006), and Hainan (Wall and Xie 2005; Xie 2003). These authors have argued that tourists, both domestic and international, have been interested in minority heritage and culture in China and the ethnic groups are either passively or actively resisting the representations of their ethnic culture and heritage for the sake of tourism revenue alone. Some scholars from mainland China are also concerned with tourism politics (Liu 2005; Wang and Liu 2005). Their main attention is on the relations between heritage preservation and tourism development, policy implications to promote heritage tourism, and heritage management. These studies have provided information for understanding the politics of heritage tourism in China's southwest region and elsewhere.

Tim Oakes's research stands out in the scholarship on China's tourism politics. In his discussions and analyses of tourism in modern China, Oakes (1998) interprets China's modernity as a tense and paradoxical process. In the case of Miao villages in southeast Guizhou province, for example, Oakes (1998) argues that tourism-driven cultural revival has helped to preserve local identity and tradition. External capital originating from the majority Han, and supported by the state, has overtaken indigenous sectors and incorporated Miao people into the broader labor and commodity markets of the tourism sector. Selling local folk tradition and heritage to tourists helps the Miao to earn an income on the one hand and molds these villagers into the state project of socialist modernity on the other (Oakes 1998). Oakes (1995; 1998) conceptualized the dominance of Beijing as a form of internal colonialism, whereby the Han majority can exert influence and control over the Miao minority groups and the control is being perpetuated through the mechanism of tourism development.

The villagers in Guizhou, however, are not passive receivers of the dominance imposed by the state and capital. Oakes argues that they struggle to maintain their identity and construct local culture by "directly manipulating tourism's falsifications" (Oakes 1998:12). In the case of the Azure Dragon Village, tourism has seen the local Tunpu people become "transform[ed ...] into enterprising subjects of heritage promotion and self-regulation" (Oakes 2006:33). Noteworthy, however, is the fact that it is the rural elites who orchestrated the representation of the culture. It is also they who receive the most profit from tourism. From Oakes' (1998) work, we surmise that the ordinary villagers have a very meager influence on the production of tourism. These cases in Guizhou have revealed that heritage sites in China are full of contestation. In the name of tourism, the state and capital can shape local ethnic and heritage landscapes for political and economic interests. In response, the ordinary masses will also mediate these powerful forces.

Another strand of research in the cultural politics of tourism concerns the role of tourists, which has come under the microscope. In the past, many scholars, including Oakes, shed little light on how tourists formulate and resist the dominant version of tourism development. For instance, Adams (2003) asserts that Ke'te' Kesu', a world heritage site in Indonesia, is the product of a long-term interplay between local groups, national government, and international organizations. These studies assume that tourists merely stand by in the politics of heritage tourism and have insignificant influence on the (re)production of heritage. Such an assumption that overemphasizes the production of heritage not only stifles a full understanding of the meanings of heritage but also "misses the processes of interaction between the producer and consumer" (Selby 2004:188).

We argue that tourists actively participate in tourism politics to transform destinations in terms of their agendas. Instead of being passive objects of tourism structure, tourists "explore and experience sites of consumption, and their practices contribute to the ways in which places are constituted" (Shaw and Williams 2004:23). In heritage sites, tourists do not simply consume the sight, but actively construct and reproduce "shifting, unstable and contested" (Urry 1994:238) meanings through their alternative readings and resistance. Hence, the juxtaposition of (1) enclavic spaces which are carefully staged and regulated and (2) heterogeneous spaces with loose surveillance and improvisation (Edensor 1998) indicate that tourists are capable of influencing how landscapes evolve because their preferences also need to be taken into account. These spatial outcomes also emerge in many heritage sites, such as Penang (Teo 2003) and Bali (Minca 2000). On the transformation of tourist space around the Taj, Edensor (1998:198) admittedly predicts that "the extension of an enclavic, highly commodified form of tourist space will be matched by the shrinkage, marginalization or even disappearance of heterogeneous tourist space." Despite the power of the state and corporate capital and Edensor's pessimistic prediction, the current existence of heterogeneous spaces surely reflects resistance from the marginal groups (including small and medium tourism enterprises and independent tourists). This juxtaposition of enclavic and heterogeneous space spatially exemplifies the equilibrium of tourism politics.

Tourists are far from a homogeneous group and different groups of tourists may have different types of consumption. For instance, Muzaini (2006:158) points out that the backpackers in Southeast Asian destinations seek to "distance themselves not only from other conventional mass tourists but also from each other." The tensions between tourists need to be accounted for. With the rise of Asian tourism (Winter *et al*. 2008), well-known destinations in Asia may increasingly encounter conflicts between their conventional Western customers and a burgeoning group of Asian tourists. Teo and Leong (2006) offer an insightful study of these conflicts through a postcolonial analysis of backpacking in Khao San Road, Bangkok. The authors observed that Asian backpackers constructed their own spaces of consumption to evade and contest the domination of space exercised by their Western counterparts and the tourism brokers who try to cater to Western backpackers (Teo and Leong 2006). Thus, popular Asian tourist sites epitomize tensions and negotiations over the representation of place among different groups of tourists and between producers and consumers.

We have detailed that dominance and resistance are two interrelated components of tourism politics and that they involve many groups such as heterogeneous groups of tourists and of locals, tourism enterprise both large and small, and the government. Tourism politics not only draws on dominance and resistance but also yields spatial outcomes and transforms local society. By synthesizing production and consumption, the commodification of heritage landscapes offers a point of departure to understand socio-spatial transformations as a consequence of the tourism politics. Commodification provides an apt demonstration of the intersection between economic relations and cultural politics.

Generally, commodification refers to "the process by which things and activities come to be evaluated primarily in terms of their exchange value in a context of trade" (Goulding 1998:837). Regarding the process of commodifying heritage, Strange (1996:435) enunciates, "in the search for profit, image enhancement and the exploitation of the past, a sanitised and easily consumable historical experience emerges, while heritage and history become the major assets for continued growth and development." Although the commodification of heritage landscapes has become popular, the relationship between commodification and the socio-spatial transformation of heritage landscapes deserves closer consideration. Among many viewpoints about the relation, three are notable.

The first viewpoint emphasizes that commodification gives local culture a new strength to survive in an increasing globalized world. Commodification can bring about some socio-cultural benefits, such as protecting historic buildings, keeping folk traditions alive, and affirming local identity (Markus and Cameron 2001). In the process of constructing culture and redefining ethnic space in rural Guizhou, the commodification of local everyday life and culture, according to Oakes (1993), links ethnic identities to a broad network of capital accumulation and cultural production. Therefore, commodification potentially empowers the locals to "effectively maintain a sense of autonomy" by integrating them into the tourism system and reviving local tradition (Oakes 1993:58–59).

The counterargument is that commodification denigrates the meanings of built environments and cultural assets (Philp and Mercer 1999). Hall (1994) argues that the mass-scale production of souvenirs, driven by commercialization and trivialization, leads to low quality and sameness, and possibly degrades cultural meanings in the artwork. In his seminal study of the Alarde, a public ritual in Fuenterrabia, Spain, Greenwood (1977) described the negative impacts of commodification. As the ritual was reoriented to suit tourists, the locals were unwilling to participate in it any more. Greenwood (1977:135–137) argues that a 350-year-old ritual "died" as it became a performance for tourist dollars and its meaning was "gone." To him, commodification is simply to value culture by the pound. In other words, culture is nothing but to be "packaged, priced, and sold like building lots, rights-of-way, fast food, and room service, as the tourism industry inexorably extends its grasp" (Greenwood 1977:136). Greenwood's arguments had strong influence on the later research on cultural commodification. Commodification has two relevant implications: "the reduction of the complexity and richness of the urban heritage to a few simple recognizable and marketable characteristics" (Ashworth and Tunbridge 1990:54) and the selective appropriation of local history in terms of visitors' experience (Boyd 2002; Dwyer 2004).

The third viewpoint is developed by Cohen (1988) who argued that commodification does not totally destroy the meaning of a cultural product but rather infuses new meanings into local culture. In particular, he (1988:383) asserts that:

> Tourist-oriented products frequently acquire new meanings for the locals, as they become a diacritical mark of their ethnic or cultural identity, a vehicle of self-representation before an external public. However, old meanings do not thereby necessarily disappear, but may remain salient, on a different level, for an internal public, despite commoditisation.

This account is compatible with his argument that authenticity is socially constructed and the social connotation of authenticity is open to negotiation (Cohen 1988:374).

These debates yield many insights regarding the commodification of heritage landscapes and also raise issues which have not been fully addressed in the existing literature. First, heritage tourists not only consume material landscapes like buildings and cityscapes in heritage sites but also vernacular landscapes such as rituals, dance and daily life, and even symbolic landscapes such as the Statue of Liberty in New York, the Freedom Trial in Boston, or the Liberty Bell in Philadelphia as insignias of freedom and liberty. The commodification of different types of heritage landscapes generates different outcomes and "takes diverse forms over time and space" (Williams 2004:64). Second, commodification not only dwells in economic transactions between tourists and locals but also has associations with socio-cultural relations in destinations since it influences as well as is influenced by culture. Last but not least, commodification has implications for symbolic values which we will elaborate later (Britton 1991; Crang 2004). For now, suffice it to say that these insights challenge the binary thinking of commodification as good or bad. In fact, commodified heritage landscapes are outcomes of negotiation where stakeholders jostle for control.

The different outcomes of commodification in heritage sites are pertinent to the interaction between production and consumption within a certain context. According to Jackson (1999:104):

> As commodification extends its reach into an ever-widening range of domains, the commodity form has become increasingly universal. But the significance that is attached to specific commodities differs markedly from one place to another according to their contexts of production and consumption.

Drawing on these arguments, this book explores how commodification transforms, socially and spatially, the heritage landscapes of Lijiang Ancient Town.

In the above discussion on cultural politics of tourism space, we highlight the importance of a dialectical thinking of power relations in tourism. As we have noted in the first chapter, politics is immanent in space. Power is relational and its existence "depends on a multiplicity of points of resistance: these play the role of adversary, target, support or handle in power relations" (Foucault 1990:95). Hence, our study probes into the power of capital and bureaucracy in China's heritage tourism; but, in addition, using a neo-Gramscian approach, we also assess *grassroots reactions* being either compliant or resistant to the production and consumption of heritage. The next section will elaborate this approach and establish a conceptual framework to structure the following empirical discussions.

A neo-Gramscian analysis of cultural politics

Gramsci's conception of politics obviously differs from the orthodox school of Marxism. He not only explores class struggles and the mode of production but also interrogates the cultural and social dimensions of power relations through his attention to lifestyles, education, ways of thinking, consciousness, and the cultural formation of the masses. In *Selections from the Prison Notebooks*, Gramsci (1971:144) writes that politics exists because "there really do exist rulers and ruled, leaders and led." According to Bocock (1986:16), Gramsci's politics contains two notions: "classes are constituted by the dominant mode of production and ... groups other than classes may become potential agents of change, that is, able to aim at constituting their economic and political world." Following Gramsci, we argue that the division of "ruler" (the powerful) and "ruled" (the less powerful) draws on both economic foundations and socio-cultural factors like ethnicity and gender. The bridge that links the ruled and the ruler, according to Gramsci, is "hegemony."

Gramsci's theory of hegemony has been widely examined in the literature (Anderson 1976; Bates 1975; Bocock 1986; Cox 1993; Jackson 1989; Jessop 1982; 1990). In this research, hegemony will be considered in relation to cultural politics. Unlike Russian Marxists like Plekhanov and Lenin, who stressed that hegemony is a strategy for the destruction of capitalism and hegemonic leadership is "a situation of uncontested political supremacy" (Jackson 1989:52), Gramsci maintains that hegemony is a *concept* about the balance of power, and synthesizes consent and force into this balance. Gramsci (1971:12) elaborates this notion using two aspects:

(1) The 'spontaneous' consent given by the great masses of the population to the general direction imposed on social life by the dominant fundamental group; this consent is 'historically' caused by the prestige (and consequent confidence), which the dominant group enjoys because of its position and function in the world of production.
(2) The apparatus of state coercive power which 'legally' enforces discipline on those groups who do not 'consent' either actively or passively.

Gramsci considers that politics stems not solely from class conflicts but also from group tensions. In Gramsci's (1971:161) opinion, "hegemony is ethical-political" but he also insists that "it must also be economic, [it] must necessarily be based on the decisive function exercised by the leading group in the decisive nucleus of economic activity." Jackson (1989:53, emphasis added) interprets hegemony as "the power of a dominant class to *persuade* subordinate classes to accept its moral, political, and cultural values as the 'natural' order." Both Gramsci's notion of hegemony and Jackson's interpretation resonate with our own critical thinking of tourism politics that was earlier discussed in Chapter 1.

Writing about how to attain hegemony, Gramsci propounds two corresponding processes: (1) winning consent of the allies and (2) coercively pruning or weakening opposing forces. In other words, through "a variable combination of coercion and consent," the powerful can maintain its hegemonic power (Jessop 1982:146). To win consent of the masses, "account [has to] be taken of the interests and tendencies of the groups over which hegemony is to be exercised, and that a certain *compromise equilibrium* should be formed" (Gramsci 1971:161, emphasis added). Nevertheless, the compromise that the powerful makes for equilibrium *cannot* threaten its own dominance. In times of need, the powerful can wield coercive force to prune or weaken any overt resistance such as protests and terrorism. In this sense, hegemony is not a fixed state, but a historical concept residing in the dynamic process of dominance and resistance among different groups. Linking hegemony to cultural studies, Raymond Williams (1977:113) argues that

> The reality of any hegemony, in the extended political and cultural sense, is that, while by definition it is always dominant, it is never either total or exclusive. At any time, forms of alternative or directly oppositional politics and culture exist as significant elements in society. ... That is to say, alternative political and cultural emphases, and the many forms of opposition and struggles, are important not only in themselves but as indicative features of what the hegemonic process has in practice had to work to control.

Because of its openness and multiplicity, hegemony is not an ossified relation to define dominance and subordination, but a dialectic and transformative process in which all social groups have to negotiate for a favorable position for capital accumulation, identity building or other purposes through compromise, consent, and coercion (Williams 1977). Therefore, any space becomes a contact zone where people interact with each other to reach a temporal compromise.

Gramsci claims that the means by which one group or class wins hegemony over another not only relies on *controlling* relations of production alone or employing power machinery such as the army, police, and law. Rather, it also relies on the fact that the ruled may be willing to pay consent to the rulers so that dominant beliefs and values can penetrate into people's consciousness and become naturalized in their daily life to obey and follow. As Williams (1977:110) beautifully expresses,

> Hegemony is then not only the articulate upper level of 'ideology,' nor are its forms of control only those ordinarily seen as 'manipulation' or 'indoctrination'. It is a whole body of practices and expectations, over the whole of living: our senses and assignments of energy, our shaping perceptions of ourselves and our world. It is a lived system of meanings and values.

To secure their consent, the rulers have to not only justify and maintain its dominance but also to leave some space to accommodate the opposing values so that hegemony is at the end of the day, "a *negotiated version* of ruling class culture and ideology" (Bennett 1986:xv, original emphasis). In this sense, the sphere of politics becomes the "expressive form of the common general interests of a society" (Mouffe 1979:10) and the result is the dynamic process of contestation and negotiation among various groups.

Gramsci goes further to elaborate three dimensions of hegemony – intellectual, moral, and political – a triangle synthesizing different forces in achieving and maintaining hegemonic power in a given state. This triangle illustrates Gramsci's efforts to reconfigure the Marxist concept of "superstructure" and break away from orthodox Marxism that has been argued as "being only a theory about economically determined classes and their actions" (Bocock 1986:35). Gramsci elaborates that politics can fuse economic relations and superstructure as an entity where "power was exercised and hegemony established" (Bocock 1986:35). In Gramsci's notion, the superstructure is not a passive reflection of socioeconomic relations. It contains two important components: civil society and political society. Civil society is the ensemble of private "organisms" – schools, churches, etc. – which "contribute in molecular fashion to the formation of social and political consciousness" (Bates 1975:353). Political society is synonymous with the "state" (Gramsci 1971:12). As Gramsci (1971:12) notes, "[t]he two levels correspond on the one hand to the function of 'hegemony' which the dominant group exercises throughout society and on the other hand to that of 'direct domination' or command exercised through the state and 'juridical' government." This account implies that civil society pertains to consent while political society to coercion. Simply put, hegemony is equal to consent plus coercive forces.

The importance of civil society cannot be underestimated.[2] It is an important arena for intellectuals to impart and interpret mainstream ideologies to the masses and for individuals to endure or dispute these ideologies. On the one hand, intellectuals perform as propagators of contending cultures. The term, "intellectuals," in this context, is not strictly confined to cultural or social elites, but broadly refers to those related to producing and distributing ideas and knowledge (Strinati 1995:171) or those associated with what has been called the culture industry (Adamson 1980). The intellectuals' role is to "succeed in creating hegemony to the extent that they extend the world view of the rulers to the ruled, and thereby secure the 'free' consent of the masses to the law and order of the land" (Bates 1975:353). On the other hand, human consciousness enables individuals to determine whether they comply with "the external environment," i.e. the mainstream ideologies. Gramsci boldly announces that "all men are philosophers" (Gramsci 1971:323), suggesting that individual's philosophies emanate from three basic aspects: (1) language, which carries a totality of preoccupied notions and concepts in a society; (2) common sense, including tradition and customs; and (3) popular religion and folklore, such as superstitions, beliefs, and ways of seeing the world and of acting. Because of their alternative philosophical dispositions, the subaltern surely cannot accept the rulers' orders and ideologies. In sum, consent from civil society, therefore, is contingent on two interrelated aspects: (1) whether the intellectuals construct the hegemonic discourses of the rulers successfully and (2) whether the mass accept them in terms of their morality.

Gramsci has revealed that the effective way to achieve consent is *persuasion*. Persuasion can construct a hegemonic alliance by forming "a national-popular collective will" and "intellectual and moral reform" (Gramsci 1971:132–133, see also Ghosh 2001:21; Hoffman 1984). One salient form of persuasion is education, which is an instrument activated by intellectuals in civil society, and through church, school, the mass media, and other organizations. Furthermore, Gramsci affirms that the consent from civil society, and through persuasion (i.e. intellectual and moral leadership), is more effective in attaining and maintaining hegemonic leadership than coercive forces, as it requires fewer resources to do so and, more importantly, fatigues the subordinate groups into compliance with the ruling moral order and reduces the possibility of overt resistance.

The critical theory of hegemony developed by Gramsci is of importance to examine cultural politics in contemporary society. It dialectically conceptualizes the dominance–resistance relation and recognizes that many groups are able to anchor their agendas to a state of hegemony. *Moral* hegemony empowers individuals with agency to determine whether they accept or contest the dominant discourses, although this sort of agency is definitely conditioned by *economic* power. Strinati (1995:166) specifies that

> Gramsci's theory suggests that subordinated groups accept the ideas, values and leadership of the dominant group not because they are physically or mentally induced to do so, nor because they are ideologically indoctrinated, but because they have reason of their own.

Intellectual hegemony highlights the importance of education and propaganda in achieving consent from the masses through imposing a collective will on them. Without a doubt, mass culture itself is a form of education in late capitalism. *Political* hegemony is imbued with force and coercion to guarantee the implementation of the beliefs and ideologies of the rulers and to "constitute 'a people' who are subject to it (the ruler)" (Bocock 1986:36). An integration of economic, political, intellectual, and moral factors in Gramsci's theory of hegemony provides a valuable mechanism to examine how a compromised equilibrium between dominance and resistance is reached and a hegemonic leadership is attained.

However, Gramsci's theory of hegemony arguably necessitates theoretical advancement as it has several fundamental problems with reference to the studies of cultural politics. First, Gramsci says that hegemony is based on economic relations but does not sufficiently clarify the relationships between economic relations and political, intellectual, and moral dimensions of hegemony. The Marxist-related economic reductionism in Gramscian thought runs the risk of simplifying the relation between people and their philosophies, i.e. culture, common sense, and language. In the sphere of cultural politics, the concept of "culture" becomes increasingly important and has numerous bearings on economic activities, as shown by the upsurge of the "cultural turn" (Gibson and Kong 2005). The paradigm of this "cultural turn" focuses on how the social structures *limit* rather than determine social reaction and people's experience (Chouinard 1996), and how marginal groups renegotiate power relations by contestation over, or cooperation with, social structures (Aitchison *et al.* 2000; Cosgrove 1992). In essence, the paradigm heightens, in Squire's (1994:5) words, the "political edge and concern with cultural politics and power relations." Hence, it is necessary to correlate Gramsci's notion of hegemony with a broader conception of cultural politics to unpack how individuals harness their culture to accept or resist the hegemonic power.

Second, Gramsci privileges the dominant group in the narrative of hegemony. From his perspective, the resistance made by the less powerful to hegemony does not make sense although he mentions that a compromised equilibrium between the rulers and the ruled is an imperative to maintain hegemony. The theory itself is, according to Strinati (1995:173), "a dominant ideology thesis."

Finally, heavily influenced by Marxism, Gramsci prioritizes the process of production and underestimates the importance of consumption, as evinced in his arguments on Fordism. We argue that consumption is not a compliant reaction to production or a simple form of social reproduction. Instead, it becomes a crucial terrain in which many forces continue to strengthen hegemony significantly more by the consent of the masses than by the machinery of reigning force.

Keeping the research objectives in mind, the following section addresses the above-mentioned problems and establishes a neo-Gramscian approach by incorporating representation, the interplay of production and consumption, and resistance and negotiation into Gramsci's existing theory of hegemony.

Hegemony in tourism space

In his seminal book *The Production of Space*, Henri Lefebvre (1991) questioned whether the exercise of hegemony leaves space untouched and whether space is merely the passive locus of social relations. His own answer was an absolute "no!" Drawing on Gramsci's theory, Lefebvre emphasizes that hegemony implies more than an influence or a use of repressive violence and coercion, but rather a power exercise over society as a whole through human mediation, including culture and knowledge. He further demonstrates the active role of space, "as knowledge and action, in the existing mode of production [and consumption]," arguing that hegemony makes use of space "on the basis of an underlying logic and with the help of knowledge and technical expertise, of a 'system'" (Lefebvre 1991:11). Although Lefebvre does not specify the means of persuasion, consent, and coercion for attaining and maintaining hegemony, he aptly elaborates the ways by which the ruling class seeks to maintain its hegemony through building rationalized and disciplined space to instruct people's spatial practices and to dominate their consciousness and mentality. The ultimate goal is to establish hegemonic power in space and eradicate any mismatch between "the objective structure and the subjective beliefs" (Cresswell 1996:20).[3] Lefebvre's work provides insights for us to understand how hegemony is maintained and contested in the spaces of tourism.

As we seek to demonstrate in subsequent chapters, the development of heritage tourism in China is a state project for various purposes, among which is to deploy the representation of heritage landscapes to transmit certain values and ideologies to the audience, i.e. tourists and locals. Within the scope of cultural politics, representation is a key concept to reveal how cultural hegemony is attained and maintained (Lefebvre 1991). Representation is "a set of practices by which meanings are constituted and communicated" (Duncan 2000:703). In this sense, it is *meanings* that account for representational practices whereby members of social groups develop an attachment to certain cultural forms. Through the representation of "self" and "other," the powerful are able to construct hegemonic discourse(s) and reinforce their values and orders (Cresswell 1996). Meanwhile, the weak can also use representation to contest hegemonic discourse(s) in the context of their own philosophies. As a means of attaining hegemony, representations serve different agendas of particular groups in expressing symbolic meanings (Jackson 1989).

Representational practices not only constitute and convey meanings, but also "contribute to the production of knowledge – which is closely related to social practices enabling some to have more power to speak than others" (Morgan and Pritchard 1998:34). For instance, the representation of heritage, imbued with a selective nature of what should be presented to tourists and other consumers, "contribute[s] to the creation of public memory that shapes understanding of the place and of the processes that created it" (Waitt and McGuirk 1996:12). Therefore, the hegemonic role of representation, relying on its very tangible and visible materiality, is to make that "which is socially constructed appear to be the natural order of things" (Winchester *et al.* 2003:66). Therefore, representation can "serve the dual purpose of reinforcing and defining group identity while simultaneously order[ing] complex difference into a simpler, homogeneous entity which ... [can be] easily appropriated" (Duncan 1993:44). To understand how sites are represented, it is necessary to analyze "how they were 'colonized' socially and temporally as sites of desire, power and weakness" (Duncan 1993:43). The effective means of colonization, according to Duncan, is the discourse of the "other." The imagination of the "other" frequently imposes predisposed values to representational practices which have some bearings on reality, as shown by Said's seminal work of Orientalism. According to Said (1978), Western Europeans historically developed a hierarchical worldview to help them imagine the "other," i.e. an Oriental world, and to justify what should be appropriated to represent the "other" in the Western society. Said argued (1978:21–22)

> The Orient was almost a European invention, and had been since antiquity a place of romance, exotic beings, haunting memories and landscapes, remarkable experiences .... That Orientalism makes sense at all depends more on the West than on the Orient, and this sense is directly indebted to various Western techniques of representation that make the Orient visible, clear, 'there' in discourse about it.

The purpose of imagination and justification is to stabilize and naturalize their Western-centric worldview. The Orientalist perspective does not merely stand out in imaginative geographies, but also concretizes in material landscapes.

One notable thesis that discusses the representation of the "other" in cultural geography was done by Anderson (1988). She unpacks the cultural hegemony in the representation of the "other" (i.e. Chinese) in the race-definition process in Chinatown, Vancouver. According to her, the changing landscape of Chinatown not only reflects the dominance of whiteness over Chinese people but also helps to intensify the existing power structure through the spatial manifestations of Chinatown. This geographical articulation of hegemonic discourse illustrated in Anderson's work resonates with the argument made by Cosgrove and Jackson (1987:99): "[T]he geography of cultural forms is much more than a passive spatial reflection of the historical forces that molded them; their spatial structure is an active part of their historical constitution." Similarly, Duncan (2000:703; emphasis added) pinpoints that "representations not only reflect reality, but they help to *constitute* reality."

The problem with Anderson's work and many others on representation lies in underestimating the resistance of the "othering" objects to hegemony. In Anderson's eyes, many practices done by the Chinese, like developing a place-bound pride to Chinatown and making donations to build a Chinese Cultural Centre in Chinatown, were inferior to "the century-old moral order of 'us' and 'them'" and contributed to "the perpetuation and toleration of European appellations of identity and place" (Anderson 1988:145). This argument is problematic. Although the resistance occurred within a particular condition, i.e. cultural revival in tourism development, and did not subvert the existing power structures, these practices definitely represented Chinese peoples' efforts to denaturalize the landscape of Chinatown and challenge the dominant racial ideology. The notion of "othering" in tourism is also examined by many scholars (Edensor 1998; Tucker 2003; Tucker and Hall 2004). In line with Desforges (1998), Teo and Leong (2006:119) inform that "othering is the way Western tourists build their knowledge of the world and help themselves gain cultural capital among their own people."

In many cases, it is never easy to naturalize the dominant ideological system for hegemony. Take Penang in Malaysia as an example. Writing about the cultural conflicts in Penang, Teo (2003) demonstrated that the government-led strategy of imagineering Penang to facilitate heritage tourism raised discontent among several local stakeholders, including the environmental and conservation NGOs (non-governmental organizations), and among individual residents. As a hegemonic discourse, this strategy threatened to "marginalize the community from the space they occupy" (Teo 2003:560). The discontent signifies resistance in Penang. In the case of Kuala Lumpur's Petronas Twin Towers, Bunnell (1999:18) described the grand project of symbolic discontent among the public, arguing that unhappiness arising from the project contributed to "an on-going reworking of the would-be hegemonic vision" of "world class" Malaysia. Winchester *et al.* (2003) identify resistance as two-dimensional, involving the powerful and the marginal in a contest against each other. Resistance in this book refers to how the marginal or the less powerful offer an "alternative reading" to mediate the powerful (Kong and Yeoh 1997:214), and even to reclaim space away. Resistance is a representational practice to mediate and mitigate dominance.

An array of tactics can stimulate resistance. For instance, any discontent and its concrete actions can undercut the everyday exercise of domination. As Winchester *et al.* (2003:125) note:

> Resistance may be symbolic and overt. It may be symbolically contestatory through the creation of extraordinary landscapes, but also through appropriating everyday landscapes. It may take the form of open defiance, direct action, legal action, negotiation or collaboration and change form within.

Smith (2002) reveals that there are two types of resistance in contemporary China – ordinary resistance and dissident resistance. The former is about cultural politics, referring to the less-powerful individuals or groups attempting to "author or create identities for themselves that are beyond the reach of the state and other dominant groups" (Smith 2002:1641); the latter relates to radically social and political movements to achieve certain goals. We focus mainly on the former, a tactic to develop "a hidden transcript" representing "a critique of power spoken behind the back of the dominant" (Scott 1990:xii).

Through resistance, the less powerful not only formulate their alternative readings but also seek to "appropriate (and transform) space, to make new spaces" (Pile 1997:16). They are willing (and able) to exemplify their resistance in a disciplinary space and reify the hidden transcript to see the light of the day. The embodiment of dominance and resistance reflects hegemony in space. On the one side, in order to attain hegemony, the powerful have to impose their orders and ideologies on both the public space and the private sphere of the less powerful and, consequently, intensify disparity so that many other groups become "a silent majority" (de Certeau 1984:xvii). On the other side, different "philosophies" offer some "weapons" to the weak or the marginal to resist the prevailing orders or hegemonic discourse by constructing their own space (Scott 1985). This space aims to "create their own sphere of autonomous action and self-determination within the constraints placed on them by the 'strong'" (Kong and Yeoh 1997:216–217).

The less powerful can influence or even change the existing power structure, actively rather than passively, only if they exercise their resistance in the political and economic spheres. As Duncan and Sharp (1993:478) highlight:

> The empowering function of marginal sites of resistance and subversion cannot be realized, however, if confined within the realm of dialogue alone, without access to the political and economic resources necessary for rectifying the imbalance in the flow of representational power; if these can be attained, the margins have the potential to become nodes in a more decentered, less binary, and less hierarchical spatial organization of society and configuration of representational power.

Consumption is an effective means of the less powerful to rectify the imbalance, as they can wield their buying power to attain necessary economic resources. According to de Certeau (1984:xvii), "the tactics of consumption, the ingenious ways in which the weak make use of the strong, thus lend a political dimension to everyday practices." Gramsci, who noticed this kind of everyday practices, went on to talk about resistance in popular culture. Writing about consuming detective novels, for instance, Gramsci (1985:377) argued that people read them to "revolt against the mechanical quality and standardization of modern existence, [as] a way [to ...] escap[e] from the pettiness of daily life." Ultimately, "the rhetoric of consumer choice is ... progressive in as far as it can be transformed into the actuality of persons with the resources to become empowered, arbitrating the moralities of institutions that provide goods and services" (Miller 1995:41). This arbitration on production signifies that consumption transcends the conventional function of social reproduction and serves as an empowering instrument of resistance for the less powerful in cultural politics.

The tensions between both groups are then "softened" through negotiation. The process of negotiation ties with "a collaborative pursuit of joint gains" for the purpose of forging an agreement or compromised equilibrium between the dominant and the weak (Gibson *et al.* 2006:276). The socio-spatial outcomes of tangible or intangible negotiation can be envisioned through the (re)presentation of landscapes, as landscapes conceptually reflect the "symbolic constitution of material production [and consumption]" (Cosgrove 1984:59).

The concepts of representation, dominance, and resistance are incorporated into a neo-Gramscian approach for exploring the politics of heritage tourism in China. The approach considers how different groups of people dominate and resist each other to reach a *compromised equilibrium* within the process of production and consumption of tourism landscapes. The representation of heritage and the socio-spatial transformation of heritage sites are the result of ongoing dialogue of dominance and resistance among producers and consumers of heritage tourism. This dialogue is based jointly on these groups' economic foundations and philosophical underpinnings. The approach enhances Gramsci's theory of hegemony by addressing the three limitations identified in the previous section. It also establishes the strong link between this theory and cultural politics. It is necessary to reiterate that a Gramscian notion of politics is structured by the efforts of the powerful to "win hegemony and by the forms of opposition to this endeavor" (Bennett 1986:xv). Building upon this approach, we establish a conceptual framework (Figure 2.1).

The significance of this conceptual framework will now be discussed. First, the framework highlights the importance of economic foundations and cultural dispositions in tourism politics. As Cosgrove (1984:56, emphasis added) argues:

> the economy conceived as the production of material goods, and culture conceived as the production of symbols and meaning, coexist and continuously reproduce social relations through the action of living human beings. Economy and culture, structural necessities and human actions, interpenetrate and relate dialectically, *each structuring the 'other' as it is structured by the 'other'*

Cultural politics entails the interconnectedness of (1) economy and culture and (2) production and consumption, both of which have been incorporated into the framework. In this regard, we argue that the politics of heritage tourism is not

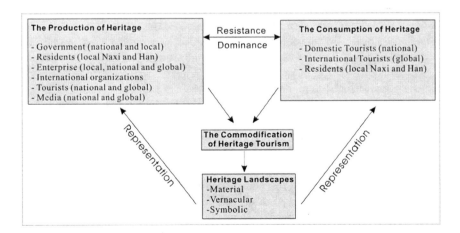

Figure 2.1 Conceptual framework.

simply manipulated by the economic and political power derived from capital and bureaucracy to produce heritage for consumers. It does involve endless nego- tiations among many groups who capitalize on their cultural values and economic foundations to construct or destabilize the hegemony of heritage tourism within certain contexts. More often than not, the state and enterprise can mobilize their economic and political power to suppress others to construct heritage repre- sentation and socio-spatial transformation in heritage sites in favor of their own interests.

Second, this framework anchors the interplay of production and consumption with tourism politics. The production and consumption of heritage tourism are intertwined, with each affecting the other in dialectical ways. Extending Stuart Hall's (1980) conception of "encoding/decoding," Johnson (1986) proposes circuits of culture to analyze the interplay of production and consumption. According to Johnson, the meanings of cultural products are always circu- lated and transformed through production, texts (cultural forms), consumption (readings), and lived cultures within certain geo-historical contexts. Johnson's framework, as detailed, can be helpful in understanding the power relations behind the production and consumption of heritage landscapes:

(1) Tourism/leisure developers start to package heritage resources for tourism within the obligations of local heritage value and global tourism environment.
(2) The text (or the meanings of landscape), including linguistic interpretation and visual expression of heritage, converts the economic relations embed- ded in heritage production into a diversity of cultural forms for tourist consumption.
(3) Through the consumption of landscape, tourists formulate their readings and knowledge of heritage landscape in terms of the universal morality and their particular cultural values.
(4) Tourists' consumption of service and goods together with their readings could be incorporated into the receivers' and locals' lived culture, and particularly influence the social relations in heritage sites.
(5) The changes and transformations in lived culture and heritage landscapes feed back into the production of heritage for tourism/leisure.

The above-illustrated circuit of heritage tourism can avoid privileging produc- tion or consumption in tourism politics. It also places heritage representation and the socio-spatial transformation of destinations in a dense network of inter- actions between (1) producers and consumers and (2) structure and agency (Cook and Crang 1996; Selby 2004). Furthermore, the circuits acknowledge "the active potential of 'ordinary' people to transform and subvert meanings in the course of cultural production and consumption" (Ateljevic 2000:376).

Third, this framework not only articulates the acts of tourism politics, i.e. domi- nance and resistance, but also pinpoints the resultant socio-spatial outcomes. The outcomes, as shown in Figure 2.1, refer to the commodified heritage landscapes.

In the case of Lijiang, three forms of heritage landscapes have to be identified: namely, material, vernacular, and symbolic:

(1) Material landscape refers to historic buildings and urban fabric that is distinctive of Lijiang Ancient Town. These material assets possess strong historic significance and have been ratified by UNESCO and the state in China.
(2) Vernacular landscapes are expressions of Naxi everyday life. As "a product of spontaneous cultural forces" (Hough 1984:10–11), this sort of landscape is bound up with rootedness and memory and helps locals to engender a sense of ownership. Through their music, dance, costume, and religion, Naxi people can increase involvement and strengthen a sense of place and build solidarity against external influences.
(3) As a social assertion of power, symbolic landscapes reflect a cognitive mapping of identities (Cosgrove 1984). As Scott (2001:12) points out, symbolic landscapes serve as means of entertainment, communication, self-enrichment, and social positionality and their production has become "the frontier of capitalist economic expansion." In the case of Lijiang Ancient Town, the coexistence of Naxi minority and Han people is symbolic of political tolerance in an increasingly inclusive and open China. Some Naxi cultural icons, commodified to highlight the uniqueness of Lijiang's heritage, constitute another sort of symbolic landscape.

These landscapes are embroiled in Lijiang's internal particularities and external geo-historical conditions. As a consequence, they are invested with contested meanings in relation to different groups. We will ease out the tensions in the (re) presentation and commodification of these three important landscapes.

Finally, this framework transcends the normative guest–host relations and positions many groups under the banner of tourism politics. As a heritage site that is attracting millions of tourists, Lijiang Ancient Town draws many interest groups who want to partake in and influence its heritage tourism. The framework exposes several forces in different geographical scales to the power relations in the production and consumption of heritage in Lijiang. At least six main forces are involved in tourism politics in Lijiang, each with different objectives:

(1) Of all the statutory boards, the CWHMC and the Lijiang Tourism Bureau (LTB) should be underscored; they each play a crucial role in enacting and implementing the various heritage conservation and tourism development plans.[4]
(2) Tourism corporations provide services and commodities for tourists. As they make profit from tourism businesses, they have to keep up with the changing taste in Lijiang's tourism market and comply with laws and government regulations.
(3) Naxi and Han residents live and work in the ancient town or in the adjoining new city, who may work, buy things, or have family members and friends living in the ancient town. For the Naxi in particular, it would be important

to understand how they build their identity as it is rooted in Lijiang and also how they view themselves vis-à-vis others. It is notable that this book over-looks other minority groups who also live in Lijiang. (They are the Bai and Yi. A shortage of space does not permit a full-fledged discussion.) The focus will remain on the Naxi, as the minority group referred to in this book, while the majority refers to the Han.

(4) International organizations are concerned with the balance between conser-vation and development. They provide some financial and technological support to maintain the town, but feel unhappy with the threat of tourism as it is perceived to be contaminating Lijiang's heritage value. In addition, their advice probably influences the state's decision on Lijiang's development.

(5) Tourists who come from the rest of China and foreign countries. In the earlier stages of tourism development in Lijiang, international tourists were the main market. As of today, domestic tourists dominate the market and are exerting more influence on Lijiang than international visitors.

(6) Mass media agencies include television, Internet websites, travel magazines, and newspapers. They come from local Lijiang, the rest of China, and the international community. *Lijiang Daily* is the mouthpiece of the Chinese Communist Party Committee in Lijiang and its news reports reflect the will of the local authority.

The intersection between these groups leads to a multi-layered and cross-scalar geography of dominance and resistance.

The politics of heritage tourism is embedded in the production and consumption of heritage. Many groups of people are entwined in resistance and dominance to maintain and/or destabilize a hegemonic state of heritage tourism. Partly because of the ranges of the groups and their various agendas and interests, partly as a consequence of the powers held by the producers and the alternative philosophies attained by the consumers, and partly due to the changing geo-historical contexts descended on Lijiang, the geography of dominance and resistance tends to be relentless and dynamic. The (re)presentation of three forms of heritage landscapes in Lijiang is the result of their readings and practices of politics in the process of heritage production and consumption. In sum, this framework can address the questions proposed by du Gay *et al.* (1997:3) – "how it [heritage] is represented, what social identities are associated with it, how it is [and what is] produced and consumed, and what mechanisms regulate its distribution and use."

Conclusions

This chapter has examined the politics of heritage tourism. Heritage tourism is not politically neutral. The cultural politics of heritage tourism necessitates a comprehensive consideration. A critical concept to inquire about power relations in heritage tourism is *hegemony*. By mobilizing economic and political power, dominant groups formulate a shifting set of ideas and discourses by means of which they "strive to secure the consent of subordinate groups to their (hegemonic) leadership" (Strinati 1995:170–171) in tourism development and heritage preservation.

Heritage tourism, as discussed, has various bearings on politics, place, people, and time (period). Exploring the politics of heritage tourism opens a window to observe and inquire how people "appropriate space, to make new spaces" to renew or resist the existing power relations (Pile 1997:16). As Squire (1994:5) aptly articulates, "tourism is about meaning and values which are both taken for granted and socially constructed. Landscapes become tourist places through meanings ascribed to them by visitors and promotional agencies." More recently, Aitchison *et al.* (2000:4) argue that tourism landscapes are regimes of significa-tion in which "the production, representation and consumption of landscape are mediated by sites and process of leisure and tourism." An acknowledgment of the cultural politics in heritage tourism potentially develops the methodological avenues in tourism geography. The next chapter will reveal the geo-historical contexts that influenced the development and formation of Lijiang Ancient Town and, furthermore, elucidate the commodification and politicization of tourism in post-Mao China.

3 Locating Lijiang

Connections and process

This chapter provides a retrospective overview of the geo-historical context of Lijiang's heritage tourism. It elaborates China's tourism developments during the transitional period from planned economy to market economy with a final focus on the *historical* site of Lijiang as a popular destination.[1] The primary aim is to uncover how diverse geo-historical forces, interests, and sentiments are responsible for framing the current tourism politics in Lijiang. There are two important signposts to note.

First, revolutionary utopianism, which characterized Mao Zedong's regime (1949–78) and the pragmatism of Deng Xiaoping's era from 1978 onward color the historical trajectory of changes in China's tourism industry (Ci 1994; Dirlik and Zhang 1997; Knight 2007). Although change followed "a path not so distant from those of Europe and North America" (Walker and Buck 2007:65), "continuation of Party rule, the continuation of large-scale state enterprises as a unit of social organization, the continuation of strong, unquestionable political control of the media and the continuation of many rhetorics and practices of socialism" (Latham 2006:7) affect how Lijiang develops as a tourist destination.

The second signpost to guide our understanding of Lijiang's tourism politics is the historic importance of the old town as the link in the tea trade between Yunnan and Tibet. The long-standing connections with Tibet have created, since historical times, geo-political tensions between the many minority groups in Yunnan and the Han majority. Trepidation about the ethnically different peripheral regions in China is well documented (see, for example, Brown 1996; Harrell 2001; Turner 2005). Oakes' (1998) work on Guizhou, for instance, talks about a "colonial" history of Han control over non-Han ethnic minority groups. This chapter unveils the implications of such historical links on Lijiang's integral identity for consumption by domestic tourists.

China's tourism in a transitional period

Since 1978, China has been untergoing unprecedented change, with the central government in Beijing endeavoring to replace the centrally planned model of Mao's reign with a market economy system. This change has resulted in stronger global ties with capitalist and other economies (Keith 2005; Rawski 1999).

According to Rawski (1999:139), there has been a "gradual replacement of state control with market allocation," culminating in democratization, decollectivization of sectors, privatization of state-owned enterprises, and land and property reform (Bian 2002; Brandt and Rawski 2008; Naughton 1995). In the next sub-sections, we detail four dramatic shifts to provide a better understanding of their implications for tourism: (1) the transformation from planned economy to socialist market economy; (2) the revival of Chinese nationalism; (3) urban competition and inter-urban coalition; and (4) the rise of consumerism and its effects on social stratification.

The state: from planned economy to socialist market economy

The entrenchment of the socialist market economy in China was a gradual and incremental process. In late 1978, Deng Xiaoping came into power after the Third Plenum of the Eleventh Communist Party Congress. With the support of his allies in the Party and the army, he immediately embarked on his experiment of developing China's market economy by a policy of "Reform and Open" (*gaige kaifang*). Very few people (probably including Deng himself) expected China to achieve an average annual growth of 9.6 percent in real gross domestic product (GDP) as it did between 1978 and 2006 (Yao 2007). For the Party leaders, the initial purpose of the reform was simply to modernize China to "catch up" with the developed countries in the world. To rid existing ideological impediments to his experiment, Deng introduced a philosophy of economic pragmatism to replace the legacies of the planned economy and to remove the dogmatic ways in which people strictly followed the instructions of the great leader Mao Zedong (Gittings 2005). The essence of Deng's policy was the "four modernizations" in the fields of agriculture, industry, science and technology, and the military. Eventually, in Deng's mind, China would build a Chinese model of socialism where the populace benefited from moderate affluence (*xiaokang*), i.e. material well-being and a modern way of life for everyone (Liu 2004).

Deng's market-driven yet pragmatic system was very different from Mao's planned economy. Mao's planned economy stressed the state's authority in organizing the country's economy, whereas Deng's system prioritized market mechanisms in distributing and optimizing capital, resources, and manpower. According to Kornai (1992), planned economies rely heavily on the state's comprehensive plans and a system of collective ownership. In order to implement a planned economy, the state has to be powerful and bureaucratically centralized so that civil society has no ability to contest or constrain its decision making. Not surprisingly, under Mao's decree, China used a top-down approach to control and instruct the economic activities of both corporations and individuals by means of coercive administration. A utopian image of affluent communism was promulgated through the Party's propaganda machinery to persuade the mass population to accept that a planned economy was the only way to better the lives of all. Under Mao's leadership, the Chinese Communist Party (CCP) obviated market mechanisms from China and adopted an isolationist self-reliance to handle foreign relations. Accordingly, Chinese citizens were rigidly confined to the people's communes (*renming gongshe*) in rural places or to different government-owned work units (*danwei*) in cities (Lin *et al.* 2005). For the most part, there was no overt dissonance from them.[2]

In contrast to Mao, Deng endeavored to build "socialism with Chinese characteristics"[3] and emphasized that socialism does not mean shared poverty (Gittings 2005). In Deng's down-to-earth perspective, the idea of economic pragmatism required a downplaying of the ideological conflict between socialism and capitalism in making economic policies, as shown by his famous quote: "It doesn't matter if a cat is black or white, so long as it catches mice." The key principle, according to Ko (2001:3), is to create "a synthesis of economic liberalization and political authoritarianism." More and more, there is a decentralization of power to enable people to manage their own production and consumption but Party influence remains strong, albeit in a behind-the-scenes way.

The road toward a socialist market economy has not been smooth. The call for democratic reform from some quarters was overt and triggered considerable social tension that culminated in the riots at Tiananmen Square in mid-1989. By 1992, Deng Xiaoping had come to totally embrace the concept of a market economy for China's development. He stated simply but firmly during his tour of south China:

> *Development is the absolute principle.* We must be clear about this question. If we fail to analyze it properly and to understand it correctly, we shall become overcautious, not daring to emancipate our minds and act freely. Consequently, we shall lose opportunities. Like a boat sailing against the current, we must forge ahead or be swept downstream.
>
> (Deng 1994:377; emphasis added)[4]

Deng's willingness to experiment has paid off: not only has there been continuous economic growth for China but also it is now a member of the World Trade Organization and hosted the Olympic Games in 2008. Another very good example to show its embrace of global capitalism can be found in tourism.

Before 1978, tourism and travel was politically motivated. It was collectively provided by the state and not available to ordinary citizens. All social activities, including travel, were overwhelmingly associated with production. Any pursuit of consumption that transcended the need to maintain life was regarded as inappropriate because it contradicted socialist values and beliefs prevalent at that time. Tourism was a collective provision during 1949–66 that served mainly the domestic elite: namely Chinese compatriots or foreign delegations from socialist countries.[5] Some destinations such as Beidaihe resort in Hebei province, for instance, were accessible only to political leaders and party cadres for relaxation or to national model workers as an award for their exemplary behavior (Xu 1999). Additionally, international guests from socialist countries frequently visited several designated destinations such as Suzhou, Guilin, and Shanghai. Serving these guests was essentially "a top-down political task" without any commercial

Table 3.1 International tourist arrivals to China, 1965–78

Year	International tourist arrivals
1965	12,877
1968	303
1970	Less than 800
1971	1,599
1975	Less than 25,000
1976	Nearly 50,000
1978	229,600

Source: He 1999.

incentive (Xu 1999:57). Tourism, thereby, became one of the diplomatic tactics deployed by the newly established republic to strengthen friendships with other socialist countries (Zhang, G. 2003). During the Cultural Revolution (1966–76), tourism stagnated, as illustrated by the numbers in Table 3.1, and its sole function was a purely political reception for limited foreign guests. A revival of the tourism sector occurred only after 1978 when the central government accorded tourism an economic function to earn foreign currency much desired at that time.

Generally, China's inbound tourism industry underwent rapid growth after 1978.[6] The big change occurred at the first national tourism conference held in September 1979 when the central government made calls for repositioning tourism as an economic activity instead of a political tool. By 1986, tourism had become formally incorporated into China's national plans for social and economic development. The State Council described the tourism industry as the 'kingpin' in China's service sector in 1992. Subsequently, where possible, provincial governments made it a pivotal industry in their local economic development plans.

To date, this industry has kept a steady pace of development despite the unrest caused by the Tiananmen trauma, the East Asian financial crisis, the terrorist attack on the USA on 11 September 2001, the outbreak of SARS (severe acute respiratory syndrome) in 2003, global economic recession in 2007, and fierce international competition. China has built its reputation as a globally well-known destination with diverse attractions and a mature tourism infrastructure. *Lonely Planet* (Harper *et al.* 2005:3) describes China as a unique destination:

A journey through this colossus of a country is a mind-boggling encounter with the most populous and perhaps most culturally idiosyncratic nation on earth. Whatever China does to you – entertains, stimulates, beguiles or bemuses – you will witness a country undergoing a spectacular transformation. … China remains huge and wild enough to satisfy your explorer instinct, and, crisscrossed with an extensive transport network, you won't be left high and dry.

Not surprisingly, Francesco Frangialli, Secretary General of the United Nations World Tourism Organization (WTO), predicts that China will become the world's top tourist destination before 2020 (*China Daily* 8 February 2008). Furthermore, China not only acts as a high-quality international destination but also undertakes an active role in shaping the global tourism market through its domestic and outbound tourism.

The backbone of Chinese tourism is in fact domestic in origin. Mass domestic tourism in China burgeoned in the mid-1980s (Xu 1999). Rising affluence generated a strong demand. In 1999, the State Council announced a new public holiday scheme that allowed for three week-long vacations (called "golden week holidays") around May Day, National Day, and the lunar Chinese New Year, respectively.[7] The scheme, which meant to boost domestic demand and stimulate retail consumption, with the idea of accelerating economic restructuring in many vacation spots (*People's Daily* 5 February 2006), was a tremendous success. China's domestic tourism is now in the millions and "involve[s] the masses of people, not just the elite" (Gottdiener 2000:13).

In 2000, the central government made an official stand to prioritize domestic tourism. Accordingly, it urged local governments and tourism developers to provide special products and services suitable for domestic visitors. An example of such special products is "red tourism" or visits to former revolutionary bases of the CCP and landmark sites of important political events. These trips are part of patriotic education for the Chinese masses. According to He Guangwei, the then China National Tourism Administration (CNTA) director, "the promotion of 'red tourism' is a need to eulogize the brilliant cause of the Party, inspire and carry forward China's national spirit" (*People's Daily* 22 July 2004). As a result, CNTA, together with CCP's Department of Propaganda, recommended 30 tourism routes and 100 classic red tourism sites, including Jinggangshan and Ruijin in Jiangxi Province and Xibaipo in Heibei Province. In 2004 alone, tourism revenues in 20 major red tourism sites amounted to over 20 billion Chinese yuan (*People's Daily* 25 March 2005). By commoditizing CCP's own heritage, red tourism helps to strengthen CCP-orchestrated nationalism among domestic tourists and enables ex-revolutionary bases to catch up with the pace at which the market economy is growing.

The rapid development of domestic tourism in China can be attributed to factors such as increasing disposable income and leisure time, the improvement of residents' physical and mental quality, the growing need for communication, and the social advancement of China (Liu 2002). According to He (1999), China's domestic tourism industry provides diverse products to satisfy different people with various purchasing abilities. Figure 3.1 shows international and domestic tourist numbers in China from 1985 to 2005.

In line with the boom in the domestic tourism market, China's outbound tourism is also growing steadily. More and more, Chinese people are able to leave mainland China to visit Hong Kong, Macau, and foreign countries either for work or personal reasons, resulting in "an unparalleled explosion in Chinese travel" and a "crash course" in the global tourism industry (*The New York Times*

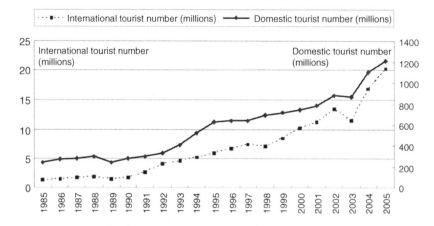

Figure 3.1 International and domestic tourist numbers, China, 1985–2005. Source: Compiled from CNTA 2006; He 1999; Zhang *et al*. 1999.

17 May 2006). According to *People's Daily* (15 February 2008), CNTA has designated more than 130 countries and regions as approved destinations and, in 2007, China's outbound tourism amounted to 41 million people, in comparison with 34 million in 2006. On 17 June 2008, the first-ever (after a long hiatus) Chinese group tour to the USA was described by the National Tour Association as "a momentous groundbreaking occasion for the United States and the economic growth of travel and tourism" (*Reuters News* 17 June 2008).

Tourism is hence highly subject to desired policy goals within mainland China (Lew *et al*. 2003; Sofield and Li 1998; Wen and Tisdell 2001; Zhang *et al*. 1999). From a political extravagance to an instrument to earn foreign currency, tourism has been treated quite differently in the distinctive eras of China's political development. Compared to the roles of tourism set in 1986, the state now endows the sector with more economic wherewithal to curb fundamental social problems and echo the principle of market-driven pragmatism. From 1978 onward, the central government, local agencies, and the market have acted as regulators and participants in tourism development and in capital accumulation. In addition, the balance between centralization and decentralization in the tourism sector has become more dynamic as the local authorities have increased their bargaining power vis-à-vis the central government. The more the Chinese people travel, the less tourism is associated with political status; instead, it is now an integral part of Chinese lifestyle.

The revival of Chinese nationalism

The first wave of modern Chinese nationalism emerged in the early twentieth century when Sun Yat-sen mobilized a nationalist movement to overthrow the Qing Dynasty. This nationalism reached its peak during the May Fourth Movement in 1919 when university students, workers, and business persons overtly demonstrated their anger at the Manchu government's impotence to protect national sovereignty against Western and Japanese penetration. The immediate consequence of this movement was the founding of the CCP by a group of Marxist intellectuals. By focusing on the inadequacies of the Qing Dynasty, Mao Zedong, the CCP leader, became a firm guardian of China's national interest. Riding the back of anti-Japanese sentiments during the Second Sino–Japanese War (1937–45), Mao ultimately triumphed during the Civil War (1946–49). After 1949, however, Mao Zedong and his colleagues weakened nationalism and replaced it with communism (Chen 2005).[8]

Mao aside, it is now widely accepted that a new form of Chinese nationalism has emerged since the mid-1990s (Zhao, S. 2000, Zhao, D. 2002; Zheng 1999). The new nationalism does not awaken the nation as the national independence movement did in the late 1940s and early 1950s. Rather, today's nationalism aims to build a strong sense of belonging among the Chinese people so as to foster a political ideology that would facilitate social control in the country.

The current revival of Chinese nationalism responds to both external and internal factors. Externally, the latest narrative – China Threat – has a huge potential of suppressing and/or denigrating China's rapid development (Zhao 2000). Many Chinese are purportedly upset by hostility from some Western countries, especially the USA, about human rights issues such as in the recent March 2008 riots in Tibet. Even a high content of lead poison in toys or the export of contaminated food constitute China-bashing to some Chinese. Well-educated intellectuals, such as Xiao Gongqing and Liu Kang, have advocated a nationalistic rhetoric such as *China Can Say No*, a well-received book. The protest against the US missile attack on China's embassy in Belgrade in 1999 during the time of the Kosovo War is reflective of further anxiety on the part of the Chinese.[9] The 1 April 2001 spy plane collision over the South China Sea and, more recently, the disruption of the Beijing 2008 Olympic torch relay in Paris have fostered more hard-line nationalist sentiments.[10] This type of nationalism is not directly manipulated by the CCP, but emanates from what has been called the "century of humiliation," starting from the First Opium War (1839–1942) and lingering after the establishment of the Peoples Republic of China (PRC) in 1949 (Gries 2004; Liu 2004). The popularity of Western mass culture in China is also seen as a challenge, stimulating intellectuals to revive Confucianism as a means to protect China's unique identity. To many scholars, Chinese nationalism is characterized by "a politically-motivated (re)essentialization of Chinese culture … in order to resist Western 'cultural hegemonism'"(Schubert 2001:143–144). In other words, the kernel of Chinese nationalism is, historically and currently, to withstand external aggression and maintain an independent nation with unique cultural traditions and a strong national identity.

Internally, the revival of nationalism responds to a belief crisis in socialism. After the collapse of the Mao regime in 1978, a growing number of skeptics of socialism and collectivism questioned the CCP's orthodox ideology and its legitimacy. At the same time, the rapid pace of modernization and reform in the 1980s resulted in numerous social and political problems such as corruption, unemployment, and inequality in incomes. The radical reform of state-owned enterprises resulted in millions of workers being laid off, not to mention serious embezzlement cases following the privatization of state-owned assets. This and the income gap between the rich and the poor resulted in public disobedience and nationwide protests (Liu 2004; Tang 2002).[11] These phenomena have concerned observers, who believe that the CCP faced strong challenges to its authority, standing on what Zhao (2006) called a "fragile legitimacy." This point has been captured by Liu (2004:12), who argued that "the crisis lies precisely in the incompetence of the state in reproducing social cohesion and a broad alliance of the general public in the face of widening social and economic polarization." To unite the Chinese people, an alternative "imagined community" came into formation (Anderson 1983) in the form of a CCP strategy called "pragmatic nationalism" (Chen 2005; Zhao 2006). This strategy entails a persuasive political discourse centered around a sense of belonging to the country in order to help the CCP to legitimize its authority in China.

According to Zhao (2006), pragmatic nationalism is a political maneuver that the Party uses to bolster public faith in the current political system and to bind the country together during a period of rapid transition into a post-socialist country. The CCP harnesses a patriotic rhetoric to rally public support, arguing that "the strong leadership of the CPC [CCP] is the fundamental guarantee for China's socialist modernization, for national unification and social harmony and stability, and for the unity of over 1 billion people as they work together to create a bright future" (*China Daily* 16 November 2007). Conveying explicitly that the CCP is the guardian of the people's interest, this discourse aims to foster nationhood by including everyone in the economic progress of China.

Further clarification is provided by two points. First, it is imperative to understand that Chinese nationalism emerges at a time when the legacy of traditional social values and the doctrine of communism and collectivism are collapsing, but the social and political order of a healthy society has not yet been consolidated. It is in this period of transition and upheaval that Chinese nationalism emerges as part of a project to reconstruct a new social reality under a strengthened political structure. Second, the CCP plays an important role in controlling and manipulating the rhetoric of Chinese nationalism. The Party channeled nationalist sentiment into the love for the CCP and the country; it acted as the defender of China's national interests; it had the ability to lead the Chinese people into modernization that is supported by political stability and economic prosperity. Valorizing Chinese nationalism reinforces the CCP's authority. Wang Gungwu (1996, cited from Ko 2001:18) rightly observes that the essence of China's revived nationalism "combines elements of both preservation and renewal, but ties in the faith in a glorious past more directly with a vision of a great future." Despite some critiques, Chinese nationalism probably serves as "a new source of pragmatic/ ideological strategy for China to cope with internal tensions and the challenge of globalization" (Ko 2001:20).

Some researchers working on cultural nationalism (Guo 2004; Zhang 1999) and ethnic nationalism (Gladney 1994; Harrell 2001; Zhao 2004) elaborate the

Table 3.2 China's tourism themes, 1992–2008

Year	Theme	Year	Theme
1992	Friendly Sightseeing	2001	Sports and Health of China
1993	Landscape Tour	2002	Folk Arts of China
1994	Tour of Cultural Relics and Historical Sites	2003	Culinary Kingdom of China
		2004	Catch the Vernacular Lifestyle
1995	Folk Customs Tour	2005	Beijing 2008 – Welcome to China
1996	Holiday Tour		
1997	Visit China 1997	2006	Rural Tourism
1998	Urban and Rural Tour	2007	Harmonious Urban and Rural Tourism
1999	Ecological Environment Tour		
2000	Century Tour – China's World Heritage	2008	Olympic-themed Tourism

Source: He 1999; http://english.gov.cn/2006-02/08/content_182522.htm.

formation/orientation of Chinese nationalism and its policy implications. Very little literature, however, has actually addressed how the state disseminates the messages of Chinese nationalism to the masses and the responses to these messages. In his seminal book *Imagined Communities*, Anderson (1983:184) argues that the state harnesses certain "institutes" to illuminate its style of thinking about its domain and to forge "a totalizing classificatory grid" to govern the society under its control. We use this for the Chinese state. We argue that the Chinese state uses domestic tourism as a way to educate the masses about history and culture shared in an imagined community.

We show two strategies used in Chinese tourism. First, the state employs a common theme for the consumption and imagination of China. The CNTA is responsible for framing the annual tourism theme for China (Table 3.2). The themes rally the Chinese together in a common consumption of a nationalistic message. For instance, the theme in 2006 directly responded to President Hu Jintao's call to build "a new socialist countryside," whereas the theme of 2007 resonates with President Hu's decree to build a harmonious society. These themes portray a united image to both the Chinese people and to the global community in order to facilitate a common sense of Chinese nationalism. As Chang (2000:35) asserts, "by prescribing themes to places, planners inadvertently freeze their identities and stultify their potential to evolve organically, effacing their myriad histories on the one hand while confining their future to a pre-ordained narrative on the other." To boast about these resources of China is to "praise the idea of the nation" (Lanfant 1995:33). In this regard, tourism in China becomes "an agent in the state's projects of national integration" (Oakes 1998:157).

The second way that tourism can forge national unity and ethnic harmony is by intensifying the cultural and economic interaction between the richer coastal regions and the poorer inland areas of China. In 1999, the central government launched a program to develop the western inland region, which accommodates 75 percent of the country's ethnic population and 60 percent of the rural poor (see Chapter 1). In his visit to Sichuan in 2001, the then vice-premier, Qian Qichen stressed that tourism could contribute to development of the western region. By utilizing their rich natural and cultural resources, tourism can generate jobs and create economic and social mobility (*People's Daily* 9 October 2001). Along with many other senior state leaders, Qian has constantly reiterated the significance of tourism in poverty alleviation and national harmony building. Tourism has been used as a mechanism to improve locals' living conditions in peripheral regions and to unite the non-Han population under the CCP's leadership.

Hence, Yunnan in southwest China (Figure 3.2) serves as a good example for understanding tourism and Chinese nationalism. Yunnan hosts 25 ethnic minority groups, who accounted for 38 percent of its population in 2000 (National Bureau of Statistics of China 2002). Yunnan is one of the poorest provinces in China. In 2004, its GDP ranked nineteenth and its per capita twenty-ninth among 31 provincial level units in mainland China (National Bureau of Statistics of China 2005). The tourism industry only took off after the Yunnan CCP committee

Figure 3.2 Map of Yunnan. Source: redrawn from http://www.xbq818.com/tu2/xbq1/dt-yunan.jpg: accessed 20 April 2006.

and the provincial government sought to impel tourism development in the middle 1980s. To implement the strategy of the great western development, the central government invested heavily in Yunnan's infrastructure to improve its accessibility to facilitate tourism development. Furthermore, with the support of the central government, Yunnan's provincial government hosted the Kunming International Horticultural Exposition in 1999. This event promoted Yunnan as a well-known tourism destination to both international and domestic visitors. Yunnan's major selling point is its numerous minority groups, which have been packaged by Yunnan Tourism Bureau as quintessential tourism products. Dan Zeng, the then vice secretary of the Yunnan CCP committee, stressed that Yunnan's uniqueness fundamentally rested on its 25 minority groups and their cultural attractions, which are important to improve the competitiveness of Yunnan's economy (*Yunnan Daily* 15 June 2004).

The significance of tourism to Yunnan society is considerable. In 2005, the receipts from the tourism sector accounted for 5.9 percent of the whole of Yunnan's GDP and contributed to 2.58 billion Chinese yuan in taxes, which is 9.8 percent of Yunnan's financial revenues (*Yunnan Daily* 7 February 2006). Bai Enpei, the Yunnan CCP leader, explicitly stated that the tourism sector in Yunnan can stimulate provincial economic growth, alleviate poverty, facilitate global awareness of Yunnan, and advance sustainable development (*Yunnan Daily* 29 April 2006). The benefits for the minority groups are substantial. According to *Yunnan Daily* (29 October 2000), tourism can expose the minorities to a global market economy, as large inflows of tourists enter the places they live.

Hence, how much tourism can contribute to Chinese nationalism in China necessitates further exploration and analysis. It is obvious that tourism can be a useful mechanism to promote China as a united country possessing diverse cultures and to mold the peripheral regions and peoples into mainstream society through economic and cultural instruments.

Urban competition and inter-urban coalition

Urban competition is a direct consequence of economic decentralization. In the early 1980s, the central government endeavored to improve the cities by allowing the provincial and city governments to possess some autonomy to accelerate their own local economy. The rationale was that cities are "the engines of growth to propel national economic development" (Ma and Wu 2005:8). Major changes introduced by Deng Xiaoping in the form of the four special economic zones (Shenzhen, Zhuhai, Xiamen, and Shangtou) opened up China and connected it to the global economy from 1979 onward. In 1984, the central government opened 14 coastal cities and built 11 economic development districts. All of these places were granted privileges so as to attract foreign investment and talent, and capture advanced technology. During the late 1990s, the central government implemented a series of reform activities in the fiscal budget and in land leases in order to endow local governments with financial incentives to speed up the urban economies. The reform means that local governments have to be responsible for most of their own profit and loss. The leaders were motivated, as success helped them to advance their own careers. As Xu and Yeh (2005) argue, the decentralization of power and the redistribution of finance eventually goaded local governments to shift from being a passive agent of the central government to an active promoter and manager of urban development. As a result of this shift, there is "greater entrepreneurialism, more intense inter-urban competition and the conscious promotion of place-specific development strategies" (Parkinson and Harding 1995:67).

The race for investment and technology has fueled inter-urban competition since the middle of the 1980s, as shown by the disputes between Shanghai and Beijing for the position of economic capital, and Guangzhou and Shenzhen for leader position in the Pearl River Delta (Wu 2002). Hong Kong also joined this race by competing with Shanghai to be the national economic center (Hong Kong Trade Development Council 2001). Besides jobs and investments, rankings for "best place" to live were also taken into account. As McCann (2004:1910) argues, these rankings had a "treadmill" effect in that "every city feels an external pressure to upgrade continually its policies, facilities, amenities and to stave off competition and maintain its position in the competitive urban hierarchy." Grand flagship developments as well as face-lift projects were undertaken to enhance their urban image. Driven by their own political objectives and strong belief in urban modernization, city leaders in China did not really consider the price of development and the real needs of their urban residents.

Urban competition extends to the tourism sector insofar as the urban authorities desire to attract tourist flows and enhance the prestige of their cities on a national scale. For instance, hundreds of cities are eager to obtain titles such as "National Excellent Tourism City" and "National Historic City." Currently, the shift toward a more proactive business-driven entrepreneurship in the mindset of local authorities is a common trend, not just of mainstream economic development but also of the tourism industry. Many historical cities make significant efforts to reinvent themselves as places of consumption and to develop a cultural economy on the basis of their diverse and vibrant heritage (Wu 2003). One example is Xintiandi in Shanghai. In 2000, with the support of Shanghai government, Hong Kong-based developer Shuion Group invested heavily in the project of Xintiandi and turned the historic Shikumen (stone-arched) residential houses into high-class restaurants and bars that boast a fusion of Western and Chinese flavors. Thousands of residents were relocated and a majority of the houses were torn down. After renovation and beautification, the remaining historical houses soon became a must-see item for middle-class tourists and Shanghainese who come to Xintiandi to enjoy nostalgia. Xintiandi certainly helped elevate Shanghai's place in the global arena and brought generous economic returns to the developer. This win–win situation indicates an emerging entrepreneurial governance in China's urban development. Nevertheless, the expensive consumption in Xintiandi spatially excludes ordinary locals who cannot patronize the shops in the renovated Shikumen, turning it into an elite landscape for a specific clientele.

That local governments strive to tailor historical sites for the title of World Heritage Site reveals its political and economic import. As pointed out earlier, the economic benefits far exceed altruistic wishes to protect the sites. As a World Heritage title can sharply increase a city's cultural capital and competitiveness, many city governments rush to spend public monies to beautify their places. Some cities have even resorted to reconstruct what has been destroyed. For instance, in the city of Changsha, the capital of Hunan Province in central China, the local government mobilized public finances of up to 80 million Chinese yuan to reconstruct a well-known but dilapidated viewing platform in the core area of a nature reserve (*Xinhua News Agency* 31 August 2006). The popularity of these pursuits can be attributed firstly to the fierce urban competition for external investment and international tourists and, secondly, to an increasing number of "nostalgia-struck" Chinese.

Emerging a little later than urban competition, inter-urban coalition is an important way to handle the fierce competition of the global era. As Ma (2001:1555) observes, the growth of inter-urban coalition in China is not simply attributable to the predisposed grand strategies from the central government, but is the consequence of regional states' response to "the decentralization of power, the deregulation of local economic development, and the globalization of capital." In contemporary China, three mega-urban regions – Yangtze Delta led by Shanghai; Pearl River Delta led by Hong Kong and Guangzhou; and Bohai Rim Region led by Beijing and Tianjin – are rapidly taking shape. These "mega urban units are essential nodes linking the local and global economies, and they function as spatial nexuses in the web of flows of goods, capital, technology, and information" (Ma 2001:1553). The city governments in these regions see that spatial proximity can be harnessed to advantage in a collaborative effort to achieve growth.

Apart from these mega-urban regions, there are mega-tourism districts that contain an agglomeration of diverse tourism products. A well-known case is the Great Shangri-la Ecotourism Zone, an amorphous tourism coalition impelled by the provincial governments of Yunnan, Sichuan, and Tibet. This zone covers 82 counties and aims to be a world-class tourism district (*Xinhua News Agency* 29 September 2005). In order to take advantage of complementary attractions, the governments of these provinces forged an inter-regional tourism cooperation plan that would take best advantage of the area's Shangri-la myth. They jointly invested approximately 4.3 billion Chinese yuan to improve the infrastructure of the zone (*Xinhua News Agency* 29 September 2005). Yunnan launched a plan in 2004 to incorporate Dali, Lijiang, Diqing and Nujiang (see Figure 3.2) into the Shangri-la Tourism Zone of northwest Yunnan. Focusing on Lijiang's world heritage value, the rich ethnic cultures of the region and the spectacular natural landscapes with diverse ecological systems, the Yunnan provincial government aims to build this sub-region into an international-class tourism zone (Yunnan Tourism Bureau 2004).

As a new spatial configuration, tourism regionalism facilitates the commodification of place as all tourism elements in the region are mobilized and packaged together to cater for the global tourism market. In the case of China, it is the Chinese state that controls and exploits "the resources of the market or the growth of the productive forces in order to maintain and further its rule" (Lefebvre 1991:112). This rule is frequently mediated by the market forces. By nailing down the connections between the nation state and the world/domestic market, tourism regionalism is incorporated into the state mode of production to achieve the grand project of developing China's western region.

The rise of consumerism and its effects on social stratification

As in Western society, consumerism in contemporary China bespeaks the manner in which the Chinese are constructing their identities in the new era of reform. In the past, people relied on their political status to distinguish themselves from others. Political status was defined by many factors, such as household registration, urban–rural cleavage, CCP membership, or position in the administrative hierarchy. Under an all-inclusive social welfare system and the collective allocation of necessities, poverty was a perpetual condition and people had no chance to differentiate themselves even though their political status may be different. Collective egalitarianism went to extreme so that any form of consumption beyond the necessary was deemed as a remnant of capitalism, and hence to be frowned upon. Eventually, the Mao-styled uniform conveyed an image of the Chinese as *equal* members of a nation rather than essentially *social* beings.

Marketization after 1978, however, marked the demise of absolute collective egalitarianism. It liberalized commercial firms to provide commodities and services and initiated a commercial blitz across China. It set people free to pursue their own economic profit legally. It encouraged people to purchase goods and services for themselves. As a result, cultural and economic variables gradually replaced political status in differentiating Chinese people.

Hence, marketization and consumerism have grown hand in hand. Since the mid-1980s, rising income has enabled Chinese people to have more free time and disposable expenditure on consumption (Chao and Myers 1998; Croll 2006; Ngai 2003). In addition, the consumption of goods and services has extricated the Chinese people from the rigid control of the state and further inspired them to earn money to expand their consumer choices and pursue their own desired lifestyles. Fashion has been instantaneously incorporated into people's everyday life in metropolises like Beijing and Shanghai. Taste has become an emblem of both economic and cultural capital and is used as an indicator of social class. Scholars who have researched this call it "China's consumer revolution" (Chao and Myers 1998; Davis 2000; 2005). This consumer revolution may afford Chinese citizens the freedom of choice and a sense of individualism, but we also agree with Ngai (2003:475), who argues that it acts as "a new mode of governmentality of the Chinese state" as people's desire for commodities and services is subject to economic capital and political powers. Writing about changing institutions and economic transition in the Chinese cities, Wu and Ma (2005:276) argue that this type of consumer revolution does not necessarily undermine state hegemony, and in fact it "helps to legitimize the regime of accumulation and opens all sorts of imaginative venues for capital accumulation, while at the same time forming spaces of resistance." As Zhang (2006) observes, the rise of tourism in Kunming, the capital of Yunnan Province, has caused massive destruction of historical buildings and community life in its inner-city neighborhoods.

Tourism allows Chinese urbanites to seek temporary reprieve from the big cities. Seeking the sublime and "authentic" rural life is a trend common among middle-class consumers. Born during or after the Cultural Revolution, they are spared the strict Communist indoctrination of their parents' generation and have only experienced a world that functions as a market economy. Hence, distinction through personal consumption has facilitated "a corresponding differentiation and specialization of leisure (and tourism) pursuits" (Britton 1991:453).

Another outcome of marketization is class distinction, which has been on the rise since the opening up of China (Bian 2002). In Lijiang, those who can afford, seek nostalgia in heritage that has seemingly withstood the test of time. Peripheral regions like Yunnan, Tibet, and Guizhou have been imagined and portrayed as a frontier which will release the tourist consumer from the stifling confines of "modernity" in China (Wang 1999b). The tentative withdrawal from big cities to peripheral destinations emerges as "an ideal that acts to resist or invert the dominant rational order of the mainstream institutions in modernity"(Wang 1999a:361). In contrast, as many middle-class people dither over their next destination, there are as many who struggle for their next meal. In the eyes of the minority poor in these exact places of Yunnan and Guizhou, tourism is a luxury beyond their means and as such, they are excluded.

This section has discussed China's tourism in a transitional period. It reveals that tourism has not merely been an economic sector, but, more importantly, a system situated within a whole spectrum of transitional processes, including marketization, commodification, nationalism, power decentralization, and rising consumerism. These processes have fostered more politics in numerous destinations across China. We argue that such politics ought to be discussed, grounded on an understanding of the local geo-historical contexts of China and, in the next section, of Lijiang itself.

The formation of Lijiang's heritage

In a basin (*Lijiang Bazi*) 2,400 m above sea level, Lijiang Ancient Town is nestled against the Yulong Snow Mountain (or Jade Dragon Snow Mountain). The surrounding mountains are strewn with rivers, streams, and waterfalls and create an idyllic environment for tourism. It is here in the more accessible basin that the town's residents come into contact with other groups living elsewhere.

A brief on Naxi society

The origin of the Naxi people is fraught with uncertainty. Some scholars such as Fang (1981), a well-known Naxi historian, suggest that the ancestors of the Naxi can be traced back to nomads who roved a strip of land between the Yellow and Yangtze rivers in Qinghai and Gangsu provinces during antiquity. For unknown reasons, a group of nomads started a thousand-mile-long journey to the south and eventually settled down in the area along the upper Yangtze River, where most of the Naxi people are now residing. Archaeological evidence dug up in the 1980s and 1990s, however, questioned this theory. He (2001) proposed that the Naxi are a part of the Yi Group (literally, tribe group) living in Yunnan and Sichuan or that they are the original indigenous residents of Lijiang Basin. Clarifying the origin of the Naxi people has been an exercise of diligence, as the documentation helps local authorities authenticate the antiquity of this group and allows them to weave a better story to sell to the tourists.

Historical records show that Lijiang Basin was incorporated as a part of the ancient Qin Dynasty (221–206 BC). During the Han Dynasty (206 BC to 220 AD), the region in which the Naxi people lived was documented as part of Yi Prefecture (Yi Zhou). Administrators were dispatched to this prefecture, but the authorities seemed to have little impact on Naxi daily life. At the end of Song Dynasty (AD 960–1279), the ancestors of the Naxi settled down to life as an agricultural civilization and it was during this time, at the end of Song Dynasty, that Lijiang Ancient Town was built.

In 1253, Kublai Khan, the grandson of Genghis Khan and the founding emperor of the Yuan Dynasty (1271–1368), commanded his army to attack Yunnan.[12] The leader of the Naxi groups, A'liang A'hu, succumbed to Kublai Khan. In return, the Yuan emperor awarded several official titles to the Naxi leader and allowed him to govern the minority groups in the Lijiang area on his own (Guo and He 1999).[13] This political affair had two important implications. First, the administrative arrangement became the seed for a native chieftain system that gradually became prevalent in the peripheral southwest regions of China where thousands of minority (or non-Han) groups reside (Shin 2006).[14] Under this system, the ruling authorities in the Yuan Dynasty and later the Ming Dynasty (1368–1644) appointed local elites, or tribal leaders, to the highest official order and promised no alteration to the existing economic and political relations in the empire's frontier areas in exchange for peace and obedience. The native chieftains enjoyed a high degree of administrative and spatial autonomy (Herman 1997). To some extent, this system was helpful for economic advancement and social stability in peripheral China. In their book *The History of Naxi Groups*, Guo and He (1999) argue that the political arrangement was a radical change for the Naxi because Lijiang was brought under the jurisdiction of the central government and Naxi chieftains were appointed by the center ever since. The second implication is that A'liang A'hu and his successors could successfully expand their control over other smaller and dispersed Naxi groups and prevent invasion from other minority communities. Learning from the political system popular in the Central Plain, Naxi chieftains established a scheme to facilitate their own effective control over the Lijiang area.

During the era of the Ming Dynasty, an attempt was made to consolidate the control of the empire's peripheral regions. In the autumn of 1381, Emperor Zhu Yuanzhang (*hongwu*) appointed Fu Youde as the General of the Southern Expedition (*zhengnan jiangjun*). General Fu was tasked with the job of conquering the region around Yunnan (Rock 1947). In 1382, the troops arrived at

Lijiang Basin and the chieftain A'jia A'de submitted to the Ming. In the same year, Emperor Zhu set up an autonomous prefecture in Lijiang[15] (Lijiang Fu[16]) to incorporate this area into the map of the Ming Empire (Duan 2000). In 1383, Emperor Zhu gave a Han-styled surname "Mu" to A'jia A'de and his offspring (Gong 1988). In the perspective of the chieftains in the peripheral regions, a Han-styled surname was a huge largesse from the central government and a signifier of recognition from mainstream Han society. In addition, Emperor Zhu granted hereditary status to the Mu clan and legitimized its dominion over the minority groups living in Lijiang (Lijiang Office for Editing Local History 1997). In response, the Mu chieftains and their offspring had to pay loyalty to the central government by keeping this marginal area stable, withstanding Tibet's intrusion on Han society and contributing to the Ming Empire's finances. With the support of Ming emperors, the Mu chieftains expanded their territory further into Tibet and Sichuan and accumulated abundant fortune from the area's mining and salt industries (Guo and He 1999).

Also during the Ming Dynasty, Han culture started to influence Naxi society. This influence took place as the Yunnan provincial government openly supported Han culture in Lijiang and in its other frontier areas. The Mu chieftains and their family members took an active part in learning Han culture. They invited many Han scholars and intellectuals to Lijiang to teach Han culture and etiquette and encouraged their children to take part in the nationwide imperial examinations to win scholarly honor and official recognition granted by the central government (Guo and He 1999; Fang 1981). They even encouraged Han Taoism, Han Confucianism, and Tibetan Buddhism to flourish in Lijiang. The Naxi people absorbed these external religions into their own to form the so-called Dongba religion. But this cultural fusion took place at a very slow pace due to the poor transportation system in this region.

Geo-historical connections of Lijiang Ancient Town

The construction of the town allegedly started from the late Song Dynasty (960–1279). At that time, the local authority, controlled by the elite clan of A'liang A'hu, decided to select the town's current location, which was called Dayechang, to build its new administrative center (Guo and He 1999). Dayechang was originally dotted by several small villages situated along the Yu River (*yuhe*) where the villagers made a living as farmers (Mu 1997). The location was probably chosen for its excellent water supply (Ebbe and Hankey 2000) and the surrounding hills that could protect the people from the chilly winds coming from north of Yulong Snow Mountain.

To create a habitable place, A'liang A'hu's clan dredged a tributary on the west side of the Yu River (Mu 1997). The tributary, called West River (*xihe*), expanded the town's built area and enabled more residents to access water conveniently. The empty space between the Yu River and West River was converted into a daily market. It was named Sifang Square. Several more canals were dug that reached every corner of the town. Additionally, Mu chieftains mobilized hundreds of villagers and merchants living nearby to settle down in the town and provided land for them to build houses along the rivers or the canals (Mu 1997).

Lijiang underwent a dramatic change from an autonomous state to a vassal prefecture affiliated to the central government during the Qing Dynasty (1644–1911). After overthrowing the Ming Empire, the emperors of Qing were determined to bring the indigenous groups in peripheral regions into the Han embrace just in case they caused rebellions and challenged the dominion of the empire. This policy was called *gaituguiliu*, or as Dreyer (1976:11) translated, "to change from native to regular administration." Emperor Yongzheng (c1723–35) initiated this policy. Regarding the rationale, the emperor explained:

> Due to their evil nature, the barbarians living under native chieftain rule are continually subjected to unspeakable cruelties. Thus, I have ordered my provincial officials to recommend plans that will abolish the native chieftainships and bring the barbarian population under [our] administrative control. I take this action only because the unfortunate people living in these frontier areas are my innocent children. I hope to free them of such hardship and make their lives safe and happy.
>
> Emperor Yongzheng, the veritable records of the Yongzheng Reign
> (*Da Qing Shizong xianhuangdi shilu*), cited from Herman (1997:47)

The policy was an effective instrument for the Qing Empire to embark on a long-term plan to abolish the native chieftain system and eradicate the political barriers so that the Empire would bring the frontier areas in Southwest China under its direct jurisdiction. In 1723, the Mu chieftain was demoted to *tu tongpan* (a native sub-prefect), which did not carry any official power (Rees 2000; Rock 1947).[17] In the spring of 1724, Yang Bi, the first official dispatched by the Qing emperor, reached Lijiang and took office as the magistrate of Lijiang to directly govern the minority groups in Lijiang (Guo and He 1999).

This shift brought fundamental and substantial changes to Lijiang's social organization as well as for the town (Jackson 1979; Rock 1947; White 1997). Guo and He (1999:355–56) affirmed that *gaituguiliu* exposed the Naxi to other ethnic groups in the region. Hence, there was cultural reconstruction as well as urban expansion. The Qing dismantled the serfdom-based economy installed by the Mu chieftains and introduced feudalism, which was the prevalent socioeconomic system of people who lived in the Central Plain.[18] They also encouraged local people to use advanced technologies imported from the Central Plain to improve their agricultural production. In addition, the Han officials popularized Han culture and Confucian thoughts as a way to "educate" the minority groups in Lijiang. They set up schools in the town and appointed scholars from the Central Plain as teachers. The first school in Lijiang, Snow Mountain College (*xueshang shuyuan*), was built in 1725 (Guo and He 1999). Subsequently, a Confucian temple was built. From these institutions, Han culture was widely disseminated to Naxi society and could be learned by ordinary Naxi people and not the elite alone. The new educational system led to further transformation of Naxi society, since Han culture had penetrated into everyday life.

Education had other impacts. He (2001:24) asserts that education "impair[ed] the traditional culture of Naxi ethnicity, as shown by the wane of Dongba culture." Dongba culture is itself still in a process of evolution. Dongba religion comes from Naxi primeval society but has synthesized Han and Tibetan Buddhism. During the Qing era, Dongba culture weakened as people associated Han culture with progress. Naxi intellectuals actually belittled Dongba religion and the Naxi shamanistic priests, the dongbas.

Undoubtedly, *gaituguiliu* ushered in a period of change in which Han culture infiltrated Lijiang's local communities and expedited cultural transformation. As manifestations of soft power, cultural communication, religious teachings, and Confucian values cushioned hard power like the hierarchical administration and military operations of the Qing. Through cultural institutions like schools and temples, the local intellectuals so willingly accepted Han culture that they could recite Han classics and use ancient Chinese language to write poetry although they were almost unable to speak Chinese for daily communication (Guo and He 1999; Rees 2000). Many Naxi people felt proud of their children's learning of Han culture and endeavored to support their education. To date, this state of cultural hegemony has remained effective, but domestic tourism has replaced the old forms of "soft power."

Urban expansion, initiated by the empire Han officials, also changed the town. The new urban development largely resembled popular urban planning layouts in the Central Plain and consisted of many buildings housing Confucianism, Taoism, Buddhism, as well as the local Gods. Apart from these religious buildings, schools and yamuns (administrative buildings in ancient China) were also constructed to remind Naxi people of the influence and governance from the Central Plain. The new urban form of the town deepened the integration of Han culture into Naxi society. After *gaituguiliu*, the Han officials selected a field in the east of the town to construct the new official mansion which is a cluster of buildings after Han architectural styles. The mansion was enclosed by a clay wall that eventually collapsed (Mu 1997). During the 1940s, the wall was all but gone and only "a remnant of it exists today around the ruined yamen" (Rock 1947:180). This text clearly indicates that like many ancient cities in the Central Plain, Lijiang had a city wall in its history.[19] In addition, the new government dug a new ditch to the east of Yu River known as the East River (*donghe*). The East River irrigated the fields in the east of the town and supplied water to the new official mansion. Sifang Square continued to be a daily market and also became the node to link the government mansion and Mu Palace, which was still inhabited by the Mu clan. It was during the early *Guangxu* period (1875–1908) that Sifang Square was tiled over by slate slabs (Mu 1997). During this period, the town accommodated 900 households or about 3,000 residents (Yunnan Committee for Five Series of Books on Ethnic Issues 1983).

After overthrowing the Qing Dynasty in 1912, the revolutionary Kuomingtang government set up its official administration in Lijiang. The long-running conflict between the central government in Nanjing and the warlord provincial government in Kunming, however, weakened intervention and control from the capital and left enough space for Naxi people to develop their local economy on their own. Commerce in Lijiang Ancient Town continued to flourish. It reached a peak during the 1937–45 war against the Japanese. During this period, the Japanese army controlled the majority of Chinese land and blocked China's exports. That caused the emergence of Sino–Indian trade as an important channel to supply daily necessities to Kunming and other cities in Yunnan. The trade was carried on horseback and the main commodity was tea. This commercial link between Yunnan and Tibet or India became known as the Tea Horse Road (*chama gudao*). The road was full of danger and hardships and many merchants lost their lives on this route.

Lijiang was a major trading hub where traders from both sides, Yunnan and Tibet/India, would conduct business. Sifang Square was the market and a staging point for caravans on their way to Tibet and India (Ebbe and Hankey 2000). As a result, markets in Lijiang and other cities in north Yunnan were filled with commodities from places like the USA, India, the UK, and Japan. The town became an unparalleled commercial market on its own (Yunnan Committee for Five Series of Books on Ethnic Issues 1983). This was the first wave of internationalization in Lijiang's history. At the peak of commercial development, it is estimated that the town accommodated more than 1,200 shops of differing businesses (Lijiang Prefecture Committee for Editing Local Records 2000). In addition, dozens of local people who gained their wealth from the Tea Horse Road started building grand houses in the town to show off their wealth. Many of these grand houses had a hybridized architectural style of Han, Tibet, and Naxi origins. This wave of internationalization, albeit transient and hasty, ostensibly portrayed a grand picture of Lijiang Ancient Town's commercial glory and global connections in its history. Nowadays, this picture has inevitably been utilized by the local government to justify the flooding of tourism business outlets in the ancient town and to launch ambitious plans to restore its past glory.

Liberation from the reins of the Kuomingtang took place in Lijiang on 1 July 1949 when the CCP took authority officially, an event marking a new era for the Naxi people and for Lijiang Ancient Town (Lijiang Prefecture Committee for Editing Local Records 2000). In the early 1950s, the central government in Beijing started to identify ethnic groups (*Minzu shibie*) and created a number of autonomous units where any ethnic group formed a majority. The local governments in these districts were granted partial autonomy. The Naxi were among those identified and were granted autonomy in 1961 (Guo and He 1999).[20] This is the first time that the central government in Beijing identified the minority groups in Lijiang and "labeled" them Naxi. Like many other minority groups, Naxi people were granted several favorable benefits such as financial subsidies and tax cuts. The purpose was to prompt local development to occur in order to reduce the economic disparity between the autonomous districts and other Han-dominated places.

The socialist ideologies of Mao undermined Naxi culture further after the establishment of the PRC in 1949. All previous social and political structures were dismantled as soon as the Naxi communities fell under the new socialist regime. The local government forbade the practice of the Dongba religion and other "superstitious" activities because they were regarded as contradictory to atheism upheld by the CCP (Guo and He 1999). As a result, religious practices disappeared in Lijiang Basin and completely faded in the town itself. The government discouraged Naxi traditions and replaced Confucian education with the new socialist model. Landlords, capitalists, and their offspring were discriminated against or even afflicted in the many political movements supported by Mao Zedong; their grand houses were overtly confiscated for public administration or other purposes. The function of Sifang Square also changed. Instead of a commercial hub to connect Tibet and Yunnan, it became a small business center serving town residents and villagers in its vicinity.

The town fabric underwent a big change after 1949. In order to house an increasing number of administrative institutions, the government expropriated the farm lands along the East River to construct many concrete buildings during the 1950s. Since the town could not afford any more land for new development, the government had to relocate many administrative bodies to the new city that had begun construction in the mid-1950s. The turbulence of the Cultural Revolution, undoubtedly, "resulted in the destruction of many ancient landmarks and cultural artefacts" in Lijiang (Rees 2000:33). For instance, the Mu Palace was confiscated and its ancient buildings were completely destroyed in the middle of the 1970s. The administrative buildings – yamuns, schools, temples, and pavilions built in the Qing Dynasty – were completely demolished because they were part of the "old society."

At the time of the development of the new city, the boundary between the ancient town and the new city did not exist. As such, a number of unsightly buildings in armored concrete could be found in the town and they even replaced the traditional timberwork houses. Between 1978 and the early 1980s, the town was relatively undisturbed and the Naxi people underwent a peaceful period when Lijiang was almost marginalized as it is far away from the agitated centers of reform occurring in China's coastal regions or at the capital. This static state was interrupted when the provincial government decided to develop tourism in north Yunnan in 1994 and Lijiang Ancient Town was henceforth inscribed in the World Heritage List in 1997.

Peter Goullart, a Russian citizen who spent eight years in Lijiang Ancient Town from 1941 to 1949, describes Lijiang as a "little-known and all but forgotten, ancient Nakhi (Naxi) Kingdom of south-west China" (Goullart 1955:217–218):

> I had always dreamed of finding, and living in the beautiful place, shut off from the world by its great mountains, which years later James Hilton conceived in his novel Lost Horizon. His hero found his 'Shangri La' by accident. I found mine, by design and preseverance, in Likiang [Lijiang].

The Shangri La mythology in Goullart's dream has generated far-reaching resonance with millions of international and domestic tourists since Lijiang was opened
to the global tourism market in the early 1990s. Lijiang Ancient Town has undergone rapid change from a forgotten kingdom to a desirable and popular destination,
a radical change that has brought various problems to Naxi society and also empir-
ically revealed the politics of heritage tourism in the context of transitional China.

Lijiang as a World Heritage Site

The value of Lijiang Ancient Town as a World Heritage Site can be understood
from two aspects: its material landscapes depicting its urban fabric and residential
buildings and its vernacular landscape constituted by costume, religion, language
in the form of pictographic words, and music.

The town has a remarkable water supply system that consists of the Yu River,
West River, and East River which originate from the Black Dragon Lake located
1 km north of the town. Water is channeled through several meandering tributaries,
yielding a complex network of water supply. Historically, town residents either
retained the canals as their private pools or channeled them into "three-eyed" wells
for public usage.[21] Besides sustaining everyday life, this water system also beauti-
fies the cityscape. The alignment of the streets to the canals renders Lijiang a unique
urban fabric, which contrasts sharply with the rigid grid-like layout in many other
old cities in the Central Plain. Furthermore, these canals have cultural connotations.
They represent the close affinity the Naxi have with water and with the natural
environment. This water system has become a selling point for attracting tourists.

Naxi people have developed their own style of buildings by mixing local with
Han and Tibet architectural styles. Currently, no other architecturally incompat-
ible buildings are allowed to be constructed in the core area of the town. After an
earthquake in 1996, concrete buildings in the town that had collapsed were not
replaced in order that the town could comply with World Heritage Site guidelines.
Any reconstruction since 1997 has followed strict codes of regulations to the
historical architectural styles of the past. As all the streets and lanes in the town
are paved with cobblestones, Lijiang Ancient Town effuses an old world charm
that is hard to replicate (Figure 3.3).

As for culture, Naxi people have retained some of their traditions in spite
of Maoist socialism. For instance, the older women still wear Naxi costume,
speak the Naxi language, play Naxi ancient music, and so forth. Naxi women
traditionally wore sheepskin capes. Now the cape has given way to "a lighter,
synthetic-looking version," similar in style to the original attire (Rees 2000:151).
Seven circular ornaments form a distinctive pattern on the capes. They symbolize
female diligence, following after the sureness of the appearance of the sun, moon,
and stars as night turns to day. The revised version of Naxi attire is a popular item
for tourist photography.

Most Naxi people subscribe to a combination of Buddhism, Taoism, and indigenous animist belief, i.e. the Dongba religion. The Dongba religion has thousands
of gods, but no specific temples or priests. Rituals center on maintaining harmony

Figure 3.3 A bird's eye view of Lijiang Ancient Town. The buildings in the town
generally have two or three storeys and are equipped with gable roofs. By
itself, each buildings would be modest, but, together, they are spectacular.
Source: authors' photo.

between humans and nature. Historically, priests of this religion were ordinary
farmers who understood the ancient pictographic scriptures and hence could
preside over the ritual ceremonies. The rituals consist of offerings and dances to
worship ancestors and nature, and/or to expel evil spirits. Currently, there is no
one in the town who can actually perform Dongba rituals but its philosophy still
permeates. In the town, Dongba Gong (the Dongba temple) is the only place to
catch a Dongba ritual, although this is a shortened and staged performance done
for touristic purposes rather than as a form of worship.

As an extraordinary system of hieroglyphics formed 1,000 years ago, the ancient
Naxi language includes pictographic words, special pronunciation, and grammar
(Figure 3.4). The scripts of the Dongba religion, e.g. "The Myth of Creation," is
in this language. It is said to be the only living primitive hieroglyph in the world
(Guo and He 1999; personal interview with Respondent O2). In 2003, UNESCO
formally included the ancient Naxi Dongba literature manuscripts in the memory
of the World International Register. According to UNESCO (2005:1),

> As a result of the impact of other powerful cultures, Dongba culture is
> becoming dispersed and is slowly dying out. ... The problem of how to
> safeguard this rare and irreproducible heritage of mankind has become an
> agenda for the world.

This title, together with the town as a World Heritage Site, distinguishes Lijiang
further from other destinations. In the town, apart from some Dongbas, very few

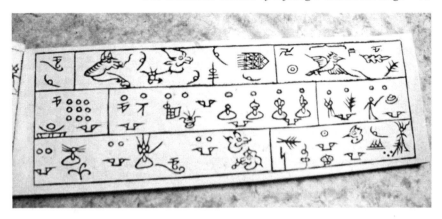

Figure 3.4 Dongba pictography taken from a religious script. Source: authors' photo.

people can understand the hieroglyphics. However, the language is printed on greeting cards and souvenirs such as bracelets and key chains even though merchants and tourists do not understand what the inscriptions say.

Naxi ancient music dates back to the Han Dynasty (AD 25–220). Crystallizing three antiquated musical forms – Taoist rites, Confucian ceremony, and literary lyrics – Naxi ancient music is known for its unique traits. The music maintains 24 tunes and rhythms which are already lost in the Central Plain. Therefore, this music is treated as a "living fossil" of Chinese music (Ebbe and Hankey 2000). In Lijiang Ancient Town, Naxi people now try to preserve the music by playing it frequently at their community centers or in their own houses. The other way in which Naxi music has kept alive is by professional musicians performing Naxi music for tourists.

Conclusions

The 30-year-long (1978–2008) development of tourism in China can be understood as a move to fulfill China's desire to be globally recognized. Built upon four identified themes – i.e. a shift from a planned economy to a socialist market economy, the revival of Chinese nationalism, urban competition and inter-urban coalition, and the rise of consumerism and its effects on social stratification – that encapsulate China's transition, this chapter has revealed the politicization and commodification of China's tourism in a transitional period. As Sofield and Li (1998:387) argue, tourism development in China is "highly politicized," as it serves the national goals of modernization on the one hand and remains loyal to socialism on the other. Consequently, the conflation of both politicization and commodification of tourism charts a unique direction for Lijiang's tourism development.

In this chapter, we have illustrated how the Yunnan provincial government had mobilized its natural landscape, minority groups' culture and heritage in courting tourists' attention. In China, many governments in peripheral regions harness tourism as a form of *development* so as to catch up with their coastal counterparts. The diverse natural landscapes and vibrant minority groups' culture and heritage are the main selling points in attracting both domestic and international tourists. Tourism development has sped up both *modernization* and *internationalization* in western China. It has also led to socio-spatial transformation in these peripheral regions and brought far-reaching impacts to ethnic communities. In this sense, it is necessary to conceptually link tourism to socio-spatial transformation, economic restructuring, and nation building, to understand the context in which Lijiang's tourism politics is observed.

This chapter has also outlined a brief history of Lijiang Ancient Town. It is a history of domestication and Hanization. China's modernization process allows some amount of soft power to integrate the peripheral regions into mainstream Chinese society, in which tourism is a central component. Because Lijiang Ancient Town is so attractive, tourism had drawn the town into a web of relations involving global capitalism, the state, and the locals as landscapes get produced, consumed, and commodified. The next chapter examines the process of Lijiang's immersion in heritage tourism.

4 Producing heritage

Lijiang's immersion in global tourism

Any system of representation, in face, is a specialization of sorts which automatically freezes the flow of experience and in so doing distorts what it strives to represent.

(Harvey 1989a:206)

Representations of space ... are remarkably dependent on images of break, rupture, and disjunction. The distinctiveness of societies, nations, and cultures is based upon a seemingly unproblematic division of space, on the fact that they occupy "naturally" discontinuous spaces.

(Gupta and Ferguson 1992:6)

This chapter focuses on Lijiang's immersion in the global system of tourism and the practices of heritage production and representation. It aims to reveal the negotiations and struggles between processes of globalization reified through transnationalistic forces, nationalism through Beijing-based polices and Han-centered values, and local practices in tourism development and heritage preservation. In so doing, we place Lijiang in a global–national–local nexus to analyze how dominant and subaltern forces converge in Lijiang's tourism development.

We now discuss what we mean by a global–national–local nexus. Unlike many destinations in Western countries that are more globally recognized, Lijiang Ancient Town, as with many other sites in Asia such as Bali in Indonesia and Angkor Wat in Cambodia, has to strive for a favored position in the global tourism market. The process of gaining a foothold in this market requires engagement with many forces at different geographical scales. At the *global* scale, transnational corporations (TNCs), international organizations, and global mass media are known to exert a strong influence on how tourism products evolve. However, heritage tourism is never a purely economic industry involving only flows of capital and people. It is also associated with political symbolism at the *national* level,[1] which is arguably more prominent in Asia because many countries in this region have struggled or are struggling with nation building in the postcolonial era (Edensor 1998; Henderson 2007). Scholars have shown that nationalist discourses are heavily invested in heritage sites, especially those that have a World Heritage Site status, as this helps to facilitate the project of nation building in the country

(Adams 2003; Edensor 1998; Henderson 2003; Munasinghe 2005; Peleggi 1996; 2005). China is no exception.

It would, however, be foolhardy to assume that national is equivalent to *local*. This generalization masks existing asymmetrical relations between the national and the local. Where minority groups reside, the term *local* suggests more complex relations that need to be untangled. Tourism presents many forms of "realities" to the world and can reconstitute socioeconomic relations between the local and the national as it likes. By scaling (global/national/local) Lijiang's heritage production, we address Mitchell's (2001:279) call to find a language "with which to understand just how ... appropriation [is ...] at once local and global" within a national territory. In other words, we will show that the politics of heritage tourism in Lijiang Ancient Town entails a balancing act that seeks to accommodate global, national, and local interests.

To analyze Lijiang's immersion into heritage tourism, we now investigate the actors who play a dominant role. At the top of Lijiang's hierarchy of decision making is the secretary of the CCP branch of Lijiang, directly appointed by the Yunnan CCP committee in Kunming and supervised by the CCP central committee in Beijing. The administrator oversees the authorities in charge of tourism planning and heritage preservation in Lijiang, including the many statutory boards responsible for the drawing up and operation of policies that bring to fruition Beijing's recommendations. Apart from the local authorities such as CWHMC and LTB, other influential actors include the World Bank, UNESCO, Lonely Planet, many TNCs at the global scale, the State Council in Beijing, the Yunnan provincial government in Kunming, and domestic tourism corporations at the national scale.

This chapter begins with an elaboration of the hegemonic discourses on Lijiang's heritage tourism. Tourism producers who construct these discourses not only interpret and shape Lijiang's heritage landscapes but also use heritage landscapes as important instruments to persuade locals to accept their values and arguments. In addition, the practices employed by global forces to bring Lijiang to the world and to bring the world into Lijiang are examined for the impacts that globalization can have on the town. The congruence this has with national forces such as the State Council and the Yunnan provincial administration will also be uncovered. The final part focuses on local practices in developing Lijiang's heritage tourism.

Hegemonic discourses in Lijiang's heritage tourism

To make Lijiang a successful attraction, local authorities have constructed three discourses around the ancient town, which it sells successfully with the help of transnational groups like Lonely Planet and UNESCO: a "perfect" destination that tourists would never want to give a miss; unique Naxi culture which is still very much alive and practiced and hence should be experienced; and Lijiang is a showcase of the success of heritage preservation and a model for the world to emulate. These discourses make Lijiang very appetizing as an attraction site.

The imagination: a "perfect" tourist destination

The local government and tourism developers have carefully packaged Lijiang as a "perfect" tourist destination. As local leaders claim, Lijiang is a "permanent heritage site" that will never suffer from the invasion of modernization. It is an "Oriental Venice" locked in time where its charm lies in its canals and waterways, which will perpetually play a role in the social and economic life of its inhabitants (*Lijiang Daily* 8 May 2004).

Lijiang Ancient Town is a choice site for anyone who wants to escape from the drudgery of city life. An advertisement to promote Lijiang in Shanghai, for instance, emphasizes that it is a big contrast to large cities (*Shanghai Star* 1 August 2002):

> When you get tired of the busy urban life, why not slow down a bit? Lijiang, a poetic place in South China's Yunnan Province, offers a heavenly escape from earthly troubles and anxieties ... Following Daoism [Taoism], the harmony between nature and man is the basic principle throughout constructions [sic]. Its simple elegance, closeness and peacefulness qualify it as a poetic dwelling place .... Unlike the city's skyscrapers, its quiet beauty is close to nature.

Like many others, this advertisement highlights Lijiang's stark contrast to the modern cities of China. Furthermore, Lijiang incarnates the myth of Shangri-la, a creation of Western writers. Bishop (1989), for instance, portrayed southwest China in general, Tibet and northwest Yunnan in particular, as a paradise full of sacred symbols. This initial imagination started in the eighteenth century and culminated in James Hilton's (1933) *Lost Horizon*. Hilton invented the paradise Shangri-la at the foothills of the Himalayas where people are isolated from the external world and enjoy a simple yet satisfying life free from stress and unhappiness. By the time the Shangri-la myth came into Chinese awareness, many urban dwellers were ready and had the means to seek the "lost horizon." A place with beauteous nature as well as rich tradition, Lijiang is viewed by many as a romantic forgotten place frozen in time. "Backwardness" and "nature" are contrasted with "modernization" and "human centeredness" with the intention to turn Lijiang into the "other," reinforcing existing imaginations of what China's peripheral places are like. Lijiang's local government is complicit in grounding this image. He Zixing, the incumbent Lijiang CCP Secretary, proudly stated that "Lijiang Ancient Town is a place for human beings to find a spiritually ideal homeland" (*Lijiang Daily* 2 February 2004). The suggestion behind the word "homeland" is significant, because it alludes to Lijiang as a possession that the Chinese have a right to enjoy.

Besides its picture-perfect Shangri-la imagery, Lijiang has another unique point that distinguishes it from other heritage towns in China. As mentioned in Chapter 3, Lijiang is said to be an ancient town that does not have a city wall. This point has been highlighted in many news reports and tourism brochures coming out of China. However, this unique trait is given more credence because an international NGO has chosen to highlight the exceptional difference. According to Global Heritage Fund (GHF), a non-profit international conservation organization based in Palo Alto, California,

> Lijiang is one of the few ancient towns in the world not to be surrounded by city walls, and common folklore has it that the Mu family name might be the reason for this. To have *Mu* – a Chinese word meaning wood – surrounded by a frame or wall would be *Kun*, which in Chinese means predicament or siege; therefore, the town was left without a protective wall.
>
> (GHF n.d.:1)

The distinction has helped Lijiang to become "China's top domestic tourist destination" since 2001 (GHF 2004:1). People flock to see this unique characteristic, which, by itself, is not inordinately attractive, but when coupled with the Shangri-la myth, is inviting as it beckons all to "enter" and share in its solace from the hectic world.

Showcasing Naxi "lived" heritage

The second strategy to attract tourists draws on the rhetoric that Lijiang Ancient Town still has a practicing and vibrant Naxi culture: not only do officials play up Naxi cultural splendor but they also promise its social continuation. There is some concern that tourism development has driven out so many local residents that many wonder whether Naxi culture still exists in the town. Xuan Ke,[2] a local interested in preserving Naxi music, claims that "Lijiang Ancient Town is dead." The mouthpiece of the local authorities challenged this by carrying stories that portray "aboriginal residents in the town demonstrating their genial Naxi culture to outsiders" (*Lijiang Daily* 22 May 2004). The Bureau of Culture (Downtown District in the City of Lijiang) also emphatically pointed out that the "Naxi people reside in this place for generations. They work and live here. Therefore the town is a living site" (Respondent G06).

Evidence of a lived culture comes in the form of visual elements that help formulate the tourist gaze. They include the still-inhabited old buildings, people using the three-eyed wells, Dongba hieroglyphics on the signboards of shops and adorning the entrances of houses, a daily "religious" ritual performed by the shamanistic priests in Dongba Gong, women in Naxi traditional costume, and daily dance performances in Sifang Square. These elements easily facilitate the focused gaze (Urry 2002) and discourage tourists from digging deeper into the reality of local society. The intense and sophisticated aestheticization of material landscapes is definitely partial, fractured, and selective, but effective (Ateljevic and Doorne 2003; Jackson and Thrift 1995).

The ease of "finding" Naxi lived culture is also part of the project of defining the new Chinese nationalism after Mao. The flourishing of Naxi culture in the town reflects the tolerance of the minority groups by the Han majority and represents ethnic harmony between Naxi, Han, and others. Ethnic discord cannot be underestimated in China. The riots in Tibet, March 2008 for example, underscores President Hu Jintao's (2006:4) concern that "[t]he Chinese people [must] take the maintenance of ethnic unity and harmony as their bounden duty." In Lijiang, the discourse of ethnic harmony is made evident by the very existence of a flourishing Naxi lived culture.

Locals often point out that the Tea Horse Road is a historical symbol of the ability of the Naxi to live in coexistence with other ethnic groups. The Tibetans are sometimes called their "brothers." In addition, the architectural styles in Lijiang Ancient Town incorporate indigenous as well as Han elements. Even elements of Taoism and Buddhism have been embraced by the Dongba religion. The ability of the Naxi culture to thrive in Lijiang is symbolic of the central government's endorsement and promotion of "cultural diversity and multi-ethnic unity" (Oakes 1997:48). According to LTB, "the most important character of Lijiang society is multiculturalism, melting many elements of other cultures. In this sense, Lijiang Ancient Town is good example to show multiculturalism" (Respondent G04).

Hence, the juxtaposition of different cultural signs in Lijiang becomes a persuasive ideological apparatus to represent ethnic harmony and also to convey an uncluttered message to both tourists and locals that China is a united country. Also, whenever foreign national leaders visit Yunnan, the central government in Beijing arranges for them to drop by Lijiang to see China's minority groups and ethnic harmony. The leaders include Finland's then Premier Paavo Lipponen in 1998 and Singapore's then Premier Goh Chok Tong in 2003. In 2007, Jacques Rogge, the president of the International Olympic Committee, also visited Lijiang and was photographed participating in a dance in Sifang Square. The symbolic meanings endowed by the nation state, however, largely conceal the daily conflicts between the locals and migrant business persons who have settled down in Lijiang because of the many opportunities opened up by tourism. We will discuss these issues later.

"Successful" heritage preservation

The third theme that makes Lijiang attractive to tourists is the success of its heritage preservation. The dilemma between heritage preservation and tourism development has sparked heated debates in China, mainly on whether tourism as a means of development can facilitate heritage preservation or whether it jeopardizes heritage value. For instance, critics of the abuse of heritage for economic returns have targeted heritage sites such as Zhouzhuang in Jiangsu Province, Pingyao in Shanxi Province and Wuzheng in Zhejiang Province, to name a few. A commentator writing in *China Daily* (16 June 2008:4) accused local governments of being "too short-sighted"; "dictates of expediency prevent them from seeing the long-term profits that a well-protected cultural heritage can bring about." Lijiang's local government believes that the town provides a model for how to handle this dilemma. Ouyang Jian, the then Secretary of the Lijiang CCP committee, proudly claimed that "Lijiang is a model to balance conservation and development in world heritage sites" (*Lijiang Daily* 8 September 2004).[3]

The success of heritage preservation is measured by outward material manifestations of the conserved landscape and the extent of Naxi cultural revival. For instance, Dongba words inscribed on souvenirs and an increasing number of people performing Naxi music for the tourists are yardsticks of achievement. Although many houses have been readapted as guesthouses and souvenir shops, the CWHMC still maintains strict surveillance. Recently, the Yunnan People's Congress sanctioned even more regulations to guide heritage preservation and give more legitimacy to the Lijiang government's actions.[4]

More and more, heritage preservation in Lijiang is linked to the profit motive. For instance, a business person claimed that "we can support and nurture our traditional culture only if we can make profit from it" (*Lijiang Daily* 27 September 2004). Commercial benefits generated from tourism tempted many merchants to exploit heritage landscapes so that they co-work with the local government to launch a campaign of, according to Ouyang Jian, "cultural industrialization."[5] Correspondingly, some Naxi heritage resources such as music and the Dongba hieroglyphics, which had nearly vanished in the town, began to rejuvenate through tourism, "acquiring a rebirth" (Duan 2002:55). The idea of cultural industrialization in Lijiang indicates the rise of what Harvey (1989b) calls "urban entrepreneurialism" in China. The city government in Lijiang built a public–private partnership with private tourism corporations to (re)create and market "appropriately appealing" products (Salmon 1992:110) for the global tourism market.

Intellectuals, including planners, also contribute to this discourse. In 2002, the CWHMC commissioned Tongji University in Shanghai to establish a heritage preservation plan for Lijiang Ancient Town. The planners emphasize that heritage preservation can be successful only if it can propel local economic development. Their argument, as written by Shao *et al.* (2004:53), is that

> as a World Heritage Site site, Lijiang should place conservation in the framework of development. It is necessary for local society to furnish the town with decent functions, adapt it to the society under rapid transition, and let it prompt a comprehensive development in Lijiang through properly conserving and reasonably using the town.

This argument resonates with the ones made by the state and by tourism developers. All of them articulate heritage preservation as a developmental strategy and prioritize economic motives, i.e. exploiting heritage for tourist dollars. Hence, a great proportion of the town is planned as a tourism commercial zone and even the destroyed Mu Palace has been reconstructed for the tourism market. The official discourse about the "success" of heritage preservation in Lijiang rests upon selective appropriation of heritage resources for tourist consumption. The balance between heritage preservation and tourism development is thus built upon the tourist market, where Naxi heritage landscapes can sustain themselves only through their commercial exchange value.

While it is impossible to enumerate all the themes which tourism developers try to present, our intention here is to explicitly illustrate how the exercise of heritage production has been facilitated by the articulation of hegemonic discourses through the daily newspapers, the Internet, brochures, and other relevant instruments. The rhetoric definitely reflects a mixture of political consideration and economic aspirations. The next section elaborates how global forces shape Lijiang's heritage.

Globalizing Lijiang for tourism

As Chang (1999:92) argues, cities are "tied to global networks of capital flows and movements of people and technology while also serving as nodes where global processes converge." Thus, to globalize Lijiang is to facilitate the bilateral flows of capital, culture, technology, and people between Lijiang and the world. The jump-start of Lijiang's globalizing process took place when Western backpackers and Japanese group tourists visited the town in the mid-1980s. Since then, the pace has speeded up to involve many more institutions and actors.

Bringing Lijiang to the world [6]

Joseph Rock is a salient character among many in promoting Lijiang. A self-taught botanist, Rock was hired by National Geographic as a correspondent in China from 1922 to 1949. During this period, he wrote nine essays and also shot photographs of southwest China to be published in the magazine which mainly addresses Western readers. Through Rock's works, readers gained an impression of this region: "exotic kingdoms, faraway peoples, and snow-mantled peaks that [a]re little known even to geographers" (Edwards 1994:69). His most influential work is a two-volume book, *The Ancient Na-Khi Kingdom of Southwest China*, published in 1947. In Rock's (1947:viii) perspective, the Naxi Kingdom is about "a wealth of scenic beauty, marvelous forest, flowers and friendly tribes."

It is the global media that exposed Lijiang to the world after China opened its doors in 1978. Lonely Planet included Lijiang Ancient Town in its first guide book about China entitled *China: A Travel Survival Kit* published in 1984. Lijiang was dramatically written about as a must-see place: "[c]riss-crossed by canals and a maze of narrow streets, the old town is not to be missed" (Lonely Planet 1988:699). In 1992, with the support of the UK's Channel 4 and National Geographic, Phil Agland chose Lijiang Ancient Town to direct a documentary about the "real" China. The documentary captured the town's breathtaking scenery but also portrayed the harsh realities of Naxi peoples' lives. Entitled *"China: Beyond the Clouds"* the documentary, initially released in 1994 on Channel 4 in the UK and later in other European countries, received positive responses from the audience. Subsequently, it was replayed several times over due to popular demand. As such, Lijiang Ancient Town became well-known in Europe. Even if the initiative to produce the documentary was not tourism-driven, it has shaped a powerful geographical imagination that has played a significant role in enticing many international tourists to Lijiang. Visually stimulated by the scenery and Naxi life portrayed in *Beyond the Clouds*, many European tourists seek a remote but romantic town that is an enigma of Chinese daily life. To many who are eager to learn about China, this is as real as it can get when compared to the images that come out of state television and other propaganda machines.

Other international news received by the world include reports of the earthquake on 3 February 1996 (it measured 6.9 on the Richter Scale; *Reuters News* 5 February 1996). More recently, many news agencies have focused on cultural preservation in the town. They reported that many tourists (especially domestic ones) and migrant merchants have disrupted Lijiang's heritage landscapes: "The uncontrolled promotion of cultural tourism leads to the pitfalls of mass tourism, diluting its appeal and alienating the host community" (*The Toronto Star* 22 October 2004). "The town has ... suffered from cultural clashes with outsiders who came to cash in on the tourist hordes" (*Far Eastern Economic Review* 5 June 2003). Except big metropolises like Beijing and Shanghai, few cities the size of Lijiang would attract so much attention from the global media. Ironically, it is the same highly critical global media that is contributing to the promotion of Lijiang as a tourist destination.

Whereas the global media provides information and images about Lijiang to an international audience, international organizations like UNESCO directly bind Lijiang to the globe. The designation of Lijiang Ancient Town as a World Heritage Site by UNESCO in 1997 is an event that immediately elevated the town to global status and brought about a sea change. UNESCO claims that "World Heritage Sites belong to all the peoples of the world, irrespective of the territory on which they are located."[7] UNESCO's intent was to help the town withstand modernizing forces by identifying, protecting, and preserving its heritage. A cultural consultant affiliated to UNESCO's Bangkok Office and in charge of the Lijiang project maintained that "without World Heritage Site inscription, Lijiang would probably be completely gone by now, and we would only see white bathroom-tile buildings laced with cement" (*Far Eastern Economic Review* 5 June 2003).

However, we have to caution against any optimistic outlook about the World Heritage Site inscription. As Ashworth and Tunbridge (1990:30) argue, a World Heritage Site title results in the use of heritage more for "national aggrandizement and commercial advantage within the international competition," than for preservation per se. UNESCO's global call to protect Lijiang has been largely eclipsed by the massive hunt for tourism receipts. An article written in *The Asian Wall Street Journal* (23 November 2001) reported that "few cities have tried to capitalize on that brand [World Heritage] with as much zeal as Lijiang," so much so that World Heritage Site status has turned the core area of the town into "a teeming tourist zoo" (*The Asian Wall Street Journal* 23 November 2001). In this sense, Lijiang is no longer "just old, but 'olden'" (Lowenthal 1979:109), since the acts of designation and preservation give prominence to the designated sites and dissociate them from their original surroundings.

Bringing the world to Lijiang

Transnational travel agents are the main force that brings overseas tourists into Lijiang. Although agents such as American Express Travel Services and Japan Travel Bureau control a large share of the global tourism market, they have to build business alliances with Chinese partners.[8] The biggest alliance in Lijiang is between American Express and China International Travel Service (CITS). The synergy created by these alliances is propitious for China as it helps to pave the way for an improvement in the operations of several smaller travel agencies.

Transnational hotel corporations have also entered into Lijiang's tourism market since the middle 1990s. One example is Grand Lijiang Hotel, which is a co-investment by M Group from Thailand and the previous Lijiang County government.[9] Equipped with international standard services, it began to operate as early as 1995 and immediately brought considerable improvement to the service sector in Lijiang's tourism market. According to a manager in a local travel agency, the service standard at the Grand Lijiang Hotel is still a benchmark for Lijiang's hospitality sector (Respondent L14).

More hotels, either owned or operated by transnational groups, have recently emerged in Lijiang. Worthy of mention is Banyan Tree Lijiang, owned and operated by Singapore's Banyan Tree Corporation. Opened in May 2006, Banyan Tree Lijiang is alleged to be the most luxurious resort in China. Although the resort is located several miles away from Lijiang Ancient Town, it still claims a certain spatial and cultural affinity to the town. On its website, Banyan Tree Lijiang advertises that its luxurious villas "reflect the rich fabric of this locale through their design and furnishings."[10] The buildings follow the Lijiang architectural style and are one-storey structures in keeping with Lijiang Ancient Town's overall landscape. The local government warmly embraces the entry of Banyan Tree Lijiang, as shown in the rhetoric (Lijiang Ancient Downtown Government 2006):

> The management model that Banyan Tree operates resorts successfully all over the world and its huge brand value can propel Lijiang's tourism development. The resort [Banyan Tree Lijiang] will enhance Lijiang's economic diversity and foster a helpful tourism environment to configure Lijiang's new international image and transform Naxi culture.

It is, however, difficult to measure how far Lijiang can benefit from Banyan Tree Lijiang and other international service powers. Undeniably, tourism TNCs realize the huge value of Lijiang Ancient Town in the global tourism market and have strategically planned to shape and influence Lijiang's heritage production for a high-profile tourism/leisure market. Because tourism TNCs have a proven record of success and a great deal of experience, the local government is easily persuaded to change heritage landscapes in Lijiang Ancient Town to suit the big players.

Other non-profit international organizations have also given their attention to Lijiang. Working closely with the local government, organizations such as the World Bank, UNESCO, GHF, and Nature Conservancy bring capital and "advanced" ideas about heritage tourism to Lijiang. These ideas and capital reflect the dominance of global forces in influencing Lijiang's heritage tourism. After the earthquake in 1996, under the request of the Yunnan provincial government, the World Bank immediately sent a special bank credit note to provide loans to Lijiang and other places in Yunnan suffering from the natural disaster. Required by the World Bank, these special funds went to infrastructure restoration, house repair, and the rehabilitation of public services. In addition to the loans, the World Bank provided necessary guidelines for reconstruction techniques and sustainable tourism since "local project staff need expertise and support in the area of heritage conservation" and "in planning for adaptive reuse of historic buildings" (Ebbe and Hankey 2000:46). After the earthquake, GHF, in conjunction with UNESCO, established a joint partnership with Lijiang's local government to formulate the first master conservation plan. The organization also helped establish China's first Preservation Incentive Fund in Lijiang to "authentically restore the most endangered ancient residences" (GHF 13 September 2007).

Some organizations bypass local governmental agencies and individually implement their projects in Lijiang. For example, the Global Naxi Culture Conservation Society (GNCCS), founded in 1996 in California by a Naxi offspring living in the United States, has as its mission the preservation and promotion of the culture of the Naxi people by disseminating the Naxi experience as an integral part of Chinese culture and also by interacting with ethnic Chinese around the world (GNCCS n.d.). GNCCS's current project in Lijiang is to donate thousands of Chinese yuan to Lijiang No. 1 Senior High School per year. These special funds are used first, to encourage students to learn Dongba culture, including its dances, paintings, and hieroglyphics, and second, to aid the tutors in compiling textbooks about Naxi culture.

The Lijiang representative of GNCCS (Respondent L18) related that the local government only cares about profit and therefore only invests in lucrative projects. Hence, money is required for more meaningful projects on Naxi cultural preservation. GNCCS prefers to deal directly with the local schools it supports as "it is very troublesome to contact the government" (Respondent L18). Nevertheless, the representative still has to obtain permission from the government body in charge of education before gaining access to the middle school. The very purpose of this project is to, as Respondent L18 remarked, "let them [Naxi students] not forget they are from Lijiang" so that they "tell other people proudly that they know Dongba words." In Lijiang, several other global NGOs like GNCCS are also passionate about protecting local culture from external exploitation and from internal corruption. However, pressure from local government and various tourism developers who are primarily interested in courting economic returns from heritage tourism provide major obstacles to NGOs' ability to realize their goals.

Global forces in Lijiang operate through global mass media, global organizations like GNCCS, and global capital, and have different, even conflicting, agendas on Lijiang's heritage tourism. Although they are very powerful, they have to find a compromise with national and local forces. They rely heavily on their local collaborators and thrive on local forms of knowledge. Rather than "place-less" global forces, they have to be "territorially embedded" (Yeung 1998:303). International organizations have to co-work with the Lijiang government or their local representatives if these global players want to establish a foothold in Lijiang. The way that these global forces "globalize" Lijiang is by going local on some of their products and projects. The next section discusses the influence of *national* forces in the production of Lijiang's landscapes.

Hanization as a national force in the production of Lijiang

The story of remaking Lijiang Ancient Town commenced when a key primary organ of the Chinese state, the State Council, moved to award the town National Historic and Cultural City status in 1986. By emphasizing its quaintness and long history, Lijiang effectively became a "national star" that has contributed to the "reinforcement of socialist ideological and ethical progress ... through the development of the tourism sector" (The State Council 1986:1). To the central government, the success of Lijiang can serve as a role model for how the economic gap between the developed coastal areas of China and the peripheral inland undeveloped areas can be reduced. During his visit to Lijiang as Vice Premier in 1995, Zhu Rongji expounded Lijiang's tourism resources: "Lijiang does not only own natural landscape and historic relics, but also minority culture. It is very unique.... Lijiang has great potential of becoming an important international destination in the future" (LTB n.d.:2). His remark was followed soon after by action. When the Lijiang local authorities applied for a World Heritage Site title in 1996, the Ministry of Construction went behind it and acted like a patron for the Lijiang officials. Without the strong recommendation of the central government in Beijing, Lijiang's status would not have risen to be what it is today. In this sense, two authoritative bodies gave credence to Lijiang's legitimacy as a valuable asset in the Chinese tourism landscape: the Chinese central government and UNESCO. Whereas UNESCO never directly discussed the great potential that exists for tourism development, nevertheless, its recognition of Lijiang raised many expectations of economic gains that can presumably be brought in by tourism (Lew *et al.* 2003). The titles of World Heritage and National Historic and Cultural City effectively made Lijiang Ancient Town into "a highly sought-after prize" (Drost 1996:481).

Several problems had to be overcome, including the inefficient transportation service linking Lijiang and Kunming, the capital and hub of Yunnan province. In 1985, there were only 435 foreign tourist arrivals, mostly backpackers and explorers (Duan 2002). Domestic tourism was non-existent except for a few official visits. In an email interview, a tourist said that "when I first went there in 1991, Lijiang was a dirty, undeveloped place with a handful of Western backpackers sitting in some primitive cafes" (Respondent IT9). Obviously, this has to change.

Hence, the Yunnan provincial government and the Lijiang government office co-invested 120 million Chinese yuan to build Lijiang airport to make Lijiang more accessible (*Shenghuo Xinbao* 9 June 2006). The opening of the airport on 9 June 1995 allowed tourists to reach Lijiang from Kunming in about 40 minutes, as compared to the previous 16-hour ride by bus. Following that, the Yunnan provincial government sought to improve land transportation by investing in a highway to link Dali to Lijiang. The highway opened on 18 December 1998 and cuts down the traveling time between Kunming and Lijiang by 6 hours (*Lijiang Yearbook* 1999). In 2006, the State Council announced an investment of 4.1 billion yuan to build a railway linking Dali and Lijiang as one of the key projects of the great western development plan (*Xinhua News Agency* 20 August 2006). All these investments from the central government and the provincial government helped tremendously to improve Lijiang's accessibility and enhance its tourism sector.

The selling of built heritage and minority culture has become ubiquitous for once peripheral regions of China (Oakes 1998). Many successful stories, including Lijiang, have been established as models for the economic and cultural development of minority groups and also as examples of how ethnic harmony can be built. A recent report in *Xinhua News Agency* (4 April 2006), for instance, claims that tourism helps more rural people to become wealthier, especially in the provinces of Guizhou and Yunnan where minority groups' customs and cultures are well preserved. In addition, spotlighting Lijiang as a successful example in tourism development has clearly spurred other areas in western China to refashion themselves as potential tourist attractions targeting the global tourism market. Tourism is thus seen "not simply as a propaganda and marketing tool" for propelling tourist arrivals in regions like Lijiang, but also serves as a mechanism to forge Chinese nationalism, as it can integrate minority groups and peripheral regions into a united nation (Oakes 1998:126). However, this seemingly neutral depiction of tourism and nationalism in China does not preclude the disparities between Han and Naxi that continue to exist, requiring a further Hanization of Lijiang Ancient Town.

According to Oakes (1998:84), Hanization is a form of "inner colonialism." It can be seen as a process to "civilize" the peripheral people to be on a par with the Han majority people. The nature of the inner-colonial enterprise rests upon what Harrell (1995:36, emphasis added) calls "the assumption of cultural superiority by the politically and economically powerful centre and the use of that superiority, and the supposed benefits it can confer on the peripheral peoples, as an aspect of *hegemonic rule*." In the case of Lijiang, the process of Hanization was blatantly driven by the Chinese state. Now it is taking effect through a delicate mechanism underpinned by a combination of aggressive Chinese capital and veiled political administration.

Tourism serves to intensify Hanization as Lijiang becomes more and more immersed in global tourism. Chinese and global capital, with strong support from the local government, fashion Lijiang Ancient Town into "an exotic place of exile, of escape" (Oakes 1998:8) for metropolitan tourists seeking nostalgia lost to urban modernity. Lijiang's heritage, both material landscapes and vernacular landscapes, effectively supports the construction of "otherness" as an attractive feature. Table 4.1 shows the top nine investment projects in Lijiang City in 2003 and in 2002, respectively. Apart from Gaomeigu Observatory and Sino–British Arboretum, invested in by the central government for non-tourism purposes, the rest of the projects were tourism related and were invested in by tourism developers from the coastal regions and from Kunming. These investment projects rapidly changed the city of Lijiang and forced it into a mode of urbanization similar to other coastal cities in China.

We discuss capital investments and commodification more, in the following chapters. For now, we stress that domestic capital accelerates the pace of Lijiang's immersion into the tourism market and renders it lucrative for profit making. As we will show in Chapter 5, domestic Han tourists also wield their capital to shape Lijiang's heritage landscapes into a space of authentic separateness. As Harvey (1989a:343) aptly argues,

> Its [capital's] internalised rules of operation are such as to ensure that [there] is a dynamic and revolutionary mode of social organisation, restlessly and ceaselessly transforming the society within which it is embedded. The process masks and fetishises, achieves growth through creative destruction, creates new wants and needs, exploits the capacity for human labour and desire, transforms spaces, and speeds up the pace of life.

It is Chinese capital and its owners that impose their dominance and commodify Lijiang's heritage landscapes. They shape the town as a representation of Han capitalism and convert Naxi culture and heritage in the town into various symbols for consumption. As a powerful ideology operating in shaping Lijiang's heritage landscapes, Hanization has remained an ideological instrument for the Chinese state to maintain its hegemony in places where the minority groups inhabit.

Table 4.1 Top investment projects in Lijiang, 2002–03

Contractual projects in 2003	Investment amount (Chinese yuan, million)	Projects under construction in 2002	Investment amount (Chinese yuan, million)
Jinkai Shopping Mall	130	Gaomeigu Observatory	30
Southern Business District	200	Liyuan Hotel	33
Dianxi Resort	250	Lijiang Home	34.9
Qixing Business Street	270	Sun Garden	40
Yuhe Ecologic Lodge	320	Longyaoxiang Resort	50
Ancient Town Golf Club	500	Yuliang Garden	50
Shuhe Chama Town	500	Sino–British Arboretum	80
Lijiang Tourism Cultural City	2200	Liguang Ecologic District	150
Xianghe Town	6000	Baisha International Art District	370

Source: Zong (2005).

Through tourism, Hanization becomes more subtle and effective, proven in many heritage sites in Guizhou and Yunnan, and recently, in Tibet.

Besides commodification, tourism development in Lijiang Ancient Town shows that the central government tolerates the uniqueness of its peripheral peoples. As a result, the great flow of domestic Han tourists into Lijiang is viewed as bringing supposed benefits to the Naxi people. These benefits entail economic revenues (tourism contributes over 60 percent of Lijiang's GDP) and cultural fusion, which are assumed to mold Lijiang and many other peripheral places into a condition of common affluence with the coastal areas.[11]

Tourism facilitates the reproduction of power relations between the powerful and the less powerful, a condition which has existed in China's society historically and contemporarily. In Lijiang, the compromise reached for developing heritage tourism is an outcome of negotiations in which the locals can improve their quality of life in the face of the intrusion of domestic and transnational capital and cultures and where the government can make money. This compromise condition is very transient, as both sides are always eager to overlook it to negotiate for a better advantage. These endless negotiations nourish the hegemony of heritage tourism. As Oakes (1998:38) puts it, the affinity between tourism and nationalism needs emphasis: "national governments ... found that tourism could be effectively deployed not simply in attracting foreign exchanges, but in prompting a vision of national unity built upon a selectively sanitized representation of multicultural diversity." This argument has two implications.

On the one hand, the nation state has a strong intention of, in the words of Wood (1997:6), "asserting and creating unique national cultures" by constituting different ethnic cultures under a united label. In reality, the national cultures are little more than an authoritative abstraction of Han Chineseness. On the other hand, "the most evident and most easily marketed forms of cultural uniqueness are often lifestyle and artifacts (heritage) of sub-national ethnic groups – which are often considered 'backward' by the dominant ethnic majority." (Wood 1997:6).

Various tensions between unity (national integration) and uniqueness (ethnic diversity) are present. The state has to resolve these tensions to attain the moral hegemony of nation building. This is generally achieved by domesticating the minority groups in some way (Wood 1997). According to Wood (1997:7), the state's attempts "may inadvertently empower ethnic groups to assert their interests and identities in new ways." Therefore, tourism provides a medium to link state-sanctioned ethnic identity and heritage attributes with Chinese nationalism in China; it also, however, engenders a set of resources and agendas that reinforce and challenge this ambiguous link as locals strive for the command of their fate.

Heritage tourism and local authorities

Functions of local authorities

At the local level, two statutory boards, CWHMC and LTB, play significant roles in Lijiang's tourism development. Heritage preservation in Lijiang Ancient Town can be traced back to the 1950s. However, it did not receive adequate attention from the local government until the master urban plan of Lijiang County was formulated in 1983. After the mid-1990s, a special agency to supervise urban conservation and heritage management was set up, which later became the CWHMC in 2001. CWHMC is headed by the top leader of the Prefecture government and the committee includes officials, professionals, scholars, and residential representatives. The Mayor of Lijiang City became the nominal head of CWHMC after Lijiang Prefecture was transferred into Lijiang City in 2002.[12] Table 4.2 shows the evolution of the heritage agencies of Lijiang Ancient Town.

CWHMC was initially designed to alter the desultory situation where many governmental bodies participated in heritage management. Since CWHMC was formed, the Mayor has a very strong control. The voices of non-governmental committee members are too faint to be heard. A scholar who was such a member points out:

> What we can do is to try to take our responsibility. If possible, we want to provide our advice and assistance. But we are very helpless! The current political mechanism is that local government leader makes the final decision .... If he thinks your advice is compatible with his, he says the advice is professional; if incompatible, it becomes another story.
>
> (Respondent O2)

When even the professional elite cannot influence the local government's decision, it is much more difficult for local ordinary residents to participate in

Table 4.2 The evolution of the heritage agencies of Lijiang Ancient Town

Period	Agency	Responsibility	Official in charge
Before 1998	Construction Bureau of Lijiang County	Conservation; maintenance	Director of Construction Bureau
	Dayan Town Government	Administration	Head of the Town Government
1998 to May 2000	Office of Heritage Management	Control the vehicle influx into the town; renovate the canals	Head of the Office
June 2000 to January 2001	Conservation Committee of Lijiang Ancient Town	Conservation; management	Head of Lijiang County
February 2001 to July 2002	CWHMC	Conservation; management	Head of Lijiang Prefecture
August 2002 to September 2005	CWHMC	Conservation; management	Mayor of Lijiang City
From October 2005 onwards	Authority for World Heritage Conservation and Management	Conservation; management	Director of the Authority

Source: authors' interview data.

heritage management. It is not surprising to find that all residents interviewed revealed that they were never consulted by CWHMC, although they would like to share their concerns with the government. Even UNESCO has no authority to intervene in Lijiang's heritage management. Respondent O4, a senior consultant of UNESCO's Bangkok office said that:

> There is also other agenda which quite actually is part of [local] leadership concern for development and modernization which may conflict with some [of] UNESCO's issues. But we can't do more anyway because, after all, it is their town, it is their country .... It is not for us to tell China what to do. The role of UNESCO is to offer advice. [If p]eople take it, that's great; [if] they don't want it, that's their decision.

It is Lijiang's local government that monopolizes heritage management and excludes other groups from decision making. The local authority does not allow others to challenge its political hegemony and, if necessary, it coerces because it can legally enforce discipline on those groups who do not "consent" (Gramsci 1971:12).

CWHMC's responsibilities cover the implementation of urban planning, drafting the Act on heritage preservation, collecting maintenance fees, and supervising construction projects. However, the agency gradually extended its functions to include the regulation of tourism businesses, providing daily security for tourists, and leasing public houses to private investors. Many take the view that CWHMC abuses its power as it is profit centered. For instance, CWHMC not only restored the architectural façade in Dongda Street but also tried to direct the commercial activities within the street. In 2002, there were many shop houses along the street selling fashion attire with popular brands like Adidas. These catered to the locals. CWHMC ordered these shops out of Dongda Street in 2003. G02 elaborated CWHMC's considerations:

> We wiped away many modern commodities, like Adidas, out of the town last year [2003]. Why? These commodities are not compatible with the town's value. The commodities which are allowed to exist in our town should be in relation to [Naxi] culture and ethnicity .... Actually, our purpose is to maintain the town's culture-related commercial environment rather than to eliminate all business.

Through controlling Dongba Street and the rest of the town, local authorities can build a "perfected image of a well-ordered city" (Boyer 1994:11) that will appeal to tourists but which lacks the vibrancy of activities for ordinary people.

In the face of any critique, the agency takes the position that its policies and instructions are vested in cultural preservation and urban conservation. One shop owner commented that CWHMC always engaged in "passive management" and lacked "the ability of comprehensive deployment" (Respondent OM11) that would incorporate the residents' voices.

Another important statutory board responsible for heritage tourism is LTB. The main duties of LTB include tourism planning, sector management, tourism employer training, tourism promotion, and the design and development of tourism products.[13] Although it is not accorded the same authoritative influence on the town as CWHMC, LTB can inscribe its agenda on heritage landscapes through affecting tourism corporations like travel agents and hotels. Whether LTB can effectively manipulate the tourism market is, however, another question.

An example to highlight LTB's influence is the promotion of the "Naxi cultural route." In May 2005, the Lijiang Tourism Association, as an agency affiliated to the LTB, pressed that all travel agencies operating package tours to Lijiang Ancient Town should sell tourists the "Naxi cultural route," a product combining several attractions and a tourism commercial district within and around the town. The purpose was allegedly to "diversify Lijiang's tourism products and enhance Lijiang's tourism image and brand" (Lijiang Tourism Association 2005:1). The association threatened that those disobeying the order would be heavily fined by the LTB. After the notification was released, overseas and domestic travel agents expressed such strong discontent that the Yunnan Tourism Bureau and the CNTA, as the superior of the LTB, had to step in to appease the angry agents. In December 2005, the Yunnan Tourism Bureau formally ordered the LTB to stop Lijiang Tourism Association's hard sell (*China Youth Daily* 23 December 2005). Obviously, it is the tourism corporations that could mobilize economic and political resources to stop the "Naxi cultural route." Both sides eventually reached a compromise. Compromise here means that travel agents neither refuse completely this tourism product nor destabilize the prevailing structure of the tourism industry. They maintain their autonomy to deal with tourism products in terms of what the tourism markets want rather than sell according to an administrative order.

With regard to LTB's intervention in the tourism market, different groups hold different views. An official of LTB's market division responded that "now our intervention is so deficient that Lijiang's tourism industry becomes very difficult. Why? LTB does not have authority to intervene in the market" (Respondent G7). The official complained that other government agencies such as CWHMC have dissolved LTB's authority to supervise tourism firms and attractions. However, a tourism agency manager had a different opinion: "Government should do well in planning and regulation, instead of intervening in tourism market. LTB's guidelines definitely disrupt the whole market, destroy the previous patterns, and result in more chaos" (Respondent L14). He emphasized that LTB's intervention would lead to chaos in Lijiang's tourism market. Apart from direct intervention, another way by which LTB influences the market is through government-linked corporations. Owned by Lijiang City government and led by LTB, CITS Lijiang, as the biggest travel agent in Lijiang City. It controls the majority of packaged tourist inflows and plays a dominant role in Lijiang's market. Thus, complaints arose from other travel agents:

It is CITS Lijiang who earns all money. It's at the top of the hierarchy and controlling the tourism market. A small agent like ours absolutely has no power to bargain with CITS. Several agents in the top like CITS Lijiang use and even exploit local tourism resources and manpower [to earn money].

(Respondent L14)

These two typical interpretations of the role of government in the tourism market reflect the tensions between government and tourism firms to compete for priority in the production of heritage tourism in Lijiang. The reality is that tourism corporations admit the local government's authority in regulation and planning and hope it can foster a healthy market from which many local people can benefit from tourism. Meanwhile, the local government does not settle for this position, but instead endeavors to equip itself with entrepreneurship so as to operate tourism businesses on its own. The multiple roles that the local government plays inevitably trigger tensions between government and capital. These tensions, however, have not been strong enough to damage their unwitting alliance in producing heritage tourism.

The evolution of the heritage tourism authorities in Lijiang indicates a systematic transformation from sporadic management to organized governance. The history of the authorities for heritage management is a history of ongoing control and rationalization exerted by the local government on Lijiang Ancient Town, all having the direct objective of establishing absolute governance over the production and consumption of heritage landscapes. The more important the town is in Lijiang's economic and social development, the tighter is the surveillance that heritage authorities wield on heritage tourism. It is clear that the state fully seizes authority in heritage management and inscribes its values on heritage representations, expecting that the town can generate huge economic and political returns.

The preservation and reconstruction of heritage landscapes

Lijiang's heritage preservation started in the early 1990s. In 1992, Lijiang's People's Congress formally sanctioned the Conservation Plan for Lijiang Ancient Town after it became a "national star." The Plan demarcated the boundary of Lijiang Ancient Town. The core area with strict conservation accounted for 51.7 ha and the buffer zone, to retain its continuation as a historical site and withstand the intrusion of Lijiang's new city occupied 70.1 ha (Figure 4.1) (Lijiang County Government 1992). According to the Plan, the purpose of this urban conservation is to retain the holistic value of the town and protect material landscapes, including the urban form, the canals, and clusters of buildings, and lived ethnic culture from being disturbed. CWHMC commissioned the latest plan by Tongji University in Shanghai, which was completed in 2003. Through conservation, Lijiang Ancient Town was made into a place for displaying what Naxi people's lifestyle is like and also what a repository to contain Naxi culture should have.

Two points can be raised regarding heritage preservation in Lijiang. First, the preservation of the entire town has frequently been on the coat-tails of architectural conservation and more often than not, the primary attention is given to individual buildings rather than the Naxi lived experiences. The result is the creation of an idealized past with an accurate replication of architectural façades, but the separation of Lijiang's vernacular landscape. Second, the priority on *development* encouraged the formation of a tourism-driven commercial district within the town. This district is dotted with various heritage icons and constrains space for the Naxi. Motivated to run Lijiang Ancient Town for economic returns, the local entrepreneurial government and many tourism developers consciously utilized Lijiang's well-conserved material landscape as a way to attract tourists (Bao and Su 2004; Wang 2007). It is likely that the irreplaceable cultural heritage resources are promoted for tourism revenues and conservation awareness is eclipsed by development.

If conservation plans aim at technical protection, a series of laws and regulations attempt to offer extra legitimate guards. Since June 1994, the People's Congress of Yunnan Province, the highest legislature in this province, has enacted two special regulations for Lijiang's heritage preservation, i.e. the Conservation and Management of Lijiang Historic City and the Preservation of Dongba Culture. These regulations authorize the watchdogs of conservation (CWHMC and the Dongba Cultural Museum, respectively) to wield lawful means to ward off any damage to the town and to Dongba culture. Moreover, they placed Lijiang's material and vernacular landscapes under the jurisdiction of the local authority and weakened any force to challenge the authority.

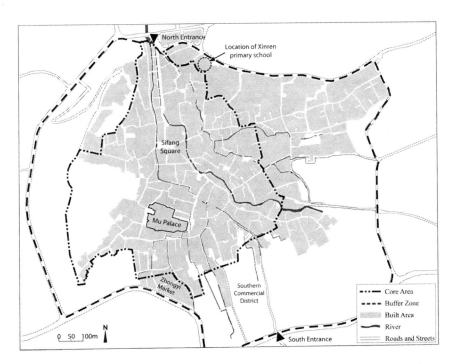

Figure 4.1 The conserved area of Lijiang Ancient Town. Source: redrawn from Lijiang Country Government 1992.

Apart from preserving the existing material and vernacular landscapes, another strategy is heritage reconstruction. After demolishing many inappropriate "modern" concrete buildings that have polluted Lijiang's heritage value, local authorities constructed new buildings, but with a traditional look, in order to maintain the integrity of Lijiang Ancient Town. Dongda Street is a good example. This street did not exist before the 1990s. In order to integrate the ancient town with the new city, local authorities planned to build an avenue through the heart of the town (Sifang Square) in the early 1990s. This plan received fierce resistance from residents in the ancient town because they were not satisfied with the compensation they would be paid for demolishing their houses, which have stood for many generations. The residents' struggle against their relocation was so strong that, in the end, the new avenue stopped short at Sifang Square. The unfinished avenue was later named Dongda Street. It was lined on either side by concrete buildings for offices and businesses, which broke up the original landscape of Lijiang because they were tall, modern, and ugly-looking. The application for World Heritage Site title changed the fate of Dongda Street. The earthquake in 1996 resulted in the collapse of most of the concrete buildings along Dongda Street. The government took this opportunity to remove all the concrete buildings since they "were inappropriate constructions and their structures and features violated the value of the town" (Lijiang County Government 1997). New buildings were erected that had many of the distinguishable features of the traditional buildings and helped to maintain the continuity of the traditional townscape (Ebbe and Hankey 2000). Albeit new, Dongda Street was in keeping with the rest of Lijiang Ancient Town. Now most tour guides make a short stop in Dongda Street and introduce the genres of Naxi buildings to tourists.

The second way was to reconstruct buildings which were demolished. In varying degrees, Lijiang Ancient Town was obviously not as reflective of high culture as the Great Wall or Forbidden City in Beijing are; instead, it embodies abundant information about the mundane life of Naxi people. However, the local government was determined to alter this situation, since Lijiang's material landscape lacks monumental imagery to bedazzle tourists. The biggest project of restoration was the Mu Palace. Historically, the Mu Palace contained a cluster of buildings for the Mu clan to live in and handle official affairs in their reign of the Naxi people (see Chapter 3). After suffering numerous political upheavals, these buildings were eventually destroyed during the Cultural Revolution when Mao Zedong called for a nationwide movement to demolish the 'four olds' (*sijiu*) – old thought, old culture, old custom, and old tradition – in order to establish a new socialist China. Ironically, this destruction left space for the local government to reconstruct and reinvent a new Mu Palace to cater for a competitive tourism market.

The government-orchestrated project to reconstruct Mu Palace ended in 2000. The World Bank provided a huge loan for this project. Learning from the Forbidden City in Beijing, the new Mu Palace acquired monumental meaning (Figure 4.2). By contrast with the less-adorned look of original Naxi buildings, the new buildings boast grand size and glitzy appearance. According to a staff working in Mu Palace:

> To reconstruct Mu Palace is to enhance Lijiang Ancient Town. If Sifang Square represents the mundane aspect of the town life, then Mu Palace signifies the high culture of Mu clan. Frankly speaking, the cluster of current buildings cannot be viewed as an authentic relic since they are totally reconstructed.
>
> (Respondent G13)

The new Mu Palace was immediately endowed with new meanings. The largesse of the new Mu Palace reflects the clan's power and wealth in Lijiang's past. Once regarded as a representative of the evils of feudalism and anti-socialism, the Mu clan stronghold is now an integral part of Naxi society (*Lijiang Daily* 29 January 1999). Currently, tourists pay 35 Chinese yuan for admission. More recently, local government announced plans to reconstruct the Confucian temple and yamun, which had served Han officials during the Qing Dynasty, as yet another emblem of authenticity.

When the government disassembled the anti-socialist symbolism given to the buildings during Mao's regime, the reconstructed Mu Palace became a spectacle landscape which can "inspire positive feelings of admiration and wonder" (Kong and Yeoh 1997:216) of the Naxi elites among visitors and residents. These feelings would help or even educate tourists and locals to understand CCP's discourse on ethnicity since Mu Palace "represents a flourishing national spirit and contributes to the renaissance of ethnic culture" (*Lijiang Daily* 29 January 1999). In this sense, the reconstructed buildings in Lijiang become symbolic landscapes.

Figure 4.2 Frontage of Mu Palace: a mini Forbidden City? Source: author's photo.

On the one hand, these buildings do not have historic meaning since they are totally reconstructed. But they denote recreated pasts to facilitate the presentation of the developer's values. As Yeoh and Kong (1999:142) argue, "the recreation of the past in a place gives the state the opportunity to filter out what it deems undesirable and to retain what it considers beneficial to cultivating a sense of cohesion and national identity." The reconstructed buildings in Mu Palace symbolize not only a triumph of successful architectural replication but also present a radically new interpretation of ethnicity and "a particularly effective medium of official communication between governors and governed" (Tunbridge and Ashworth 1996:16).

The success of tourism in Lijiang

Having the support of the central government and UNESCO, the local government's capital tie-ups ranged from the global (e.g. Grand Lijiang Hotel) to the national (e.g. with business persons from Beijing, Zhejiang and Guangdong) (Table 4.1) and locally (within Lijiang). For example, *Lishuijinsha* (literally, beautiful water and golden sand) is a variety show developed for tourists by a company from Shenzhen in Guangdong province. The company employ many choreographers from Beijing and Hong Kong to incorporate Broadway-styles into Yunnan ethnic dance so that the spectacular show can attract many more visitors.

The efforts made by local government have paid off. The town has witnessed an exponential increase in visitor arrivals (Table 4.3). From 1.05 million domestic tourists and 102,000 international visitors in 1996, by 2005, Lijiang City boasted

Table 4.3 Tourist arrivals and receipts, Lijiang Prefecture (City), 1996–2007

Year	Domestic tourism		Inbound tourism	
	Tourist arrivals (million)	Receipts (yuan, billion)	Tourist arrivals (thousand)	Receipts (US$, million)
1996	1.05	–	102.0	9.66
1997	1.69	0.84	108.1	12.43
1998	1.96	–	54.6	12.83
1999	2.48	–	120.0	19.00
2000	2.91	1.64	91.9	27.54
2001	3.12	1.79	105.0	30.38
2002	3.23	1.99	148.7	41.87
2003	2.93	2.22	82.4	22.67
2004	3.51	2.95	92.1	26.63
2005	3.86	3.45	182.8	49.31
2006	4.29	3.89	308.7[a]	88.20
2007	4.91	5.82	400.7	119.00

Source: Lijiang Tourism Bureau (2004), Lijiang Bureau of Statistics (2006; 2007; 2008).

[a] For the first time, Lijiang Bureau of Statistics showed the components of inbound tourism. Among 308,700 inbound tourist arrivals in 2006, 28 % came from Hong Kong and Macau, 22% from Taiwan, and 50% from other foreign countries.

that its domestic tourist arrivals reached as high as 3.9 million and overseas tourist arrivals rose to 182,800. In 1996, domestic tourism receipts were 0.16 billion Chinese yuan. This rose to 3.45 billion Chinese yuan by 2005. Whereas international tourists brought Lijiang US$9.7 million in earnings in 1996, this number rose to US$49.3 million in 2005 (Lijiang Bureau of Statistics 2006; LTB 2004). In 2005, tourism revenues accounted for 63.9 percent of the local GDP. The ambition is for tourist arrivals to reach 7.4 million and for tourism revenue to rise to 8 billion Chinese yuan by 2010 (Lijiang Chinese Communist Party Committee 2006).

The legitimacy of tourism is not only in the number of jobs it has generated and the income it has brought to Lijiang. Whereas there is certainly a drive for tourism-induced modernization in Lijiang, it is also acknowledged that the built heritage and Naxi culture should be closely monitored. In 2003, He Zixing, the Lijiang CCP leader, stressed that the purpose of preservation of the town is to "ensure the sustainable development of ethnic cultural industry" (*Lijiang Daily* 29 March 2006). As he argued, appropriating ethnic culture is a way to "display the infinite charm of the excellent culture of Chinese nationalities to the whole world and advertise Lijiang's cultural image as a vivacious and burgeoning city" (*Lijiang Daily* 29 March 2006). In the view of the local government, all efforts about planning, regulation, commodification, and promotion aim to increase the fame of Lijiang's rich heritage while simultaneously, conserving it for sustained tourism interests.

By many measures, the success of tourism in Lijiang can be evaluated economically. Nevertheless, there are also some "social" successes, such as a better quality of life for many and heritage revival and preservation within the ancient town.

Conclusions

This chapter has analytically discussed the hegemonic discourse of Lijiang's heritage tourism. Premised on the notion of *development*, the government focused on three things to help it realize its goals: Lijiang's image as a lost horizon, Naxi lived culture, and planned urban conservation to preserve its physical heritage. This discourse of development permeated the whole history of Lijiang's immersion in heritage tourism. We have also discussed how global capital has to ally with national government and at the local level to facilitate Lijiang's tourism development. Various representations of Lijiang's heritage landscapes were also discussed – images at the global and national levels that will appeal to tourists. It seems that, at the end of the day, "globalization is mediated by local agencies and locally constituted relationships – in particular, cultural traditions, power relationships which are played out at a specific location, and the emotional ties of people to places" (Teo and Lim 2003:302). In Lijiang, the forces to mediate globalization derive from both the nation state and the local society.

National forces play an important role in Lijiang's tourism development. On the one hand, the central government and Yunnan provincial government put in huge investments and enhanced Lijiang's visibility in order to accelerate its tourism development. Domestic capital from the coastal regions like Fujian and Zhejiang and international capital from Singapore and elsewhere actively harness Lijiang's heritage landscapes to increase tourism revenues. On the other hand, any tourism promotion on Lijiang cannot contradict the national goals and Lijiang's tourism has to contribute to Chinese nationalism.

By linking capital and politics, the process of heritage production in Lijiang achieves two goals. First, Naxi ethnic culture and the town's physical attributes have been conserved and sanitized for tourists and investment. In other words, according to Britton (1991:475), heritage production becomes "a predominantly capitalistically organized activity driven by the inherent and defining social dynamics of that system." This can turn the town into an important avenue for capital accumulation. Second, the producers in a dominant position inscribe their values on the production of heritage landscapes. These values entail not only economic incentives as mentioned earlier but also political symbolism, serving to convince the masses to comply with dominant values so as to facilitate the construction of a hegemonic leadership. For instance, the authority of Lijiang's heritage selection and promotion resided in the hands of the powerful elite as they are able to decide "what constitutes heritage and what of the past is worth conserving" (Teo and Huang 1995:599).

In the next chapter, we analyze and discuss the consumption of heritage landscapes. The emphasis is on how tourists consume Lijiang's heritage and exert their influence on the representation of heritage landscapes. We argue that tourists use their buying power and cultural dispositions to consume Lijiang's heritage. They build their own identity and justify the dominant discourse(s) about tourism landscapes.

5 Consuming heritage

Tourists' expectations and influence on Lijiang

> The material practices and experiences entailed in the construction and experiential qualities of place must be dialectically interrelated with the way places are both represented and imagined.
>
> (Harvey 1993:17)

Chapter 4 illustrated the power of capital and bureaucracy in the production and reproduction of tourism images consumed by the masses. This chapter concentrates on the consumption of heritage by tourists. We take the position that tourists not only purchase and use tourism products but also engage in "the production of meaning, experience, knowledge or objects" through their photography, sightseeing, and other activities at a site (Mansvelt 2005:7). Through these aspects of consumption, tourists build their own identity (called "cultural capital" by Desforges (2000)) and justify or deconstruct the dominant discourse(s) about tourism landscapes.

Tourism used to be described as hedonistic consumption. This is far from the truth. Consumers are never passive. Zukin and Maguire (2004:173) argue that consumption involves "a project of forming and expressing identity." Thrift (2006:290) echoes, "[consumers] generate value by fostering allegiance, by offering instant feedback and by providing active interventions in the commodity itself." Arguments such as these may lead readers to believe that consumption entails free choice. Research, however, tells us that consumption is a practice subject to internal constraints such as purchasing power and personal preference, which are conditioned by a variety of social forces and institutional arrangements managing the options open to the consumers (Warde 2005; Williams *et al.* 2001; Zukin 1998). As such, in line with the proposition made by Ateljevic and Doorne (2003), we also maintain that tourists constitute an important part of the dialectics that determine tourism outcomes.

This chapter will examine how tourists imagine and consume heritage and explore the meanings they give to the ancient town. The importance of imagination has been detailed in Arjun Appadurai's work (1996). According to him, in today's information society, imagination has become a necessary part of mental work for ordinary people to mediate the world in the practice of their everyday life. In the case of tourists, their imagination of a destination has already taken shape before they visit it, as a consequence of their consumption of the mass media. Appadurai (1996:7) further contends that imagination provokes actions: "the imagination is today a staging ground for action, and not only for escape." Thus, imagination in tourists' minds can inspire them to visit a place and to consume it according to their predisposed values about it. As Lash and Urry (1994:260) point out, "consumption becomes more skilled as in a sense [that] everyone becomes a hermeneutis [capable of] reading and interpreting the extraordinary rich and diverse array of signs and images." Tourists' imagination and their actual practices of consumption come together at the site of consumption and become central to the generation of meanings and knowledge about the destination.

In the case of Lijiang, we argue that tourists attempt to read authenticity from a number of landscapes in search of the "other" that will separate them from everyday encounters they have to deal with in their real world. Furthermore, where commodification is evident, we will argue that tourists are capable of expressing their *consent* or *dissent* when they consume the destination. In this chapter, we also highlight the point that consumption can complicate the production of landscapes because of the different purchasing powers and preferences of the international vis-à-vis domestic tourists. For now, we argue that the predominance of domestic tourists has seen tourist spaces in Lijiang make way for the consumption preferences of this group, whereas international tourists find themselves marginalized.

Consuming heritage: knowledge and practice

The imagination of Lijiang

Domestic and international tourists were observed to have explicitly different ways of getting information about Lijiang Ancient Town (Table 5.1). For domestic tourists, visual media (videos/television/radio) (cited by 50.8 percent of respondents) and print media (books/magazine/newspaper) (cited by 46.5 percent of respondents) were the two top information resources. Numerous reports in newspapers of China typically portray Lijiang as an "Oriental Venice" with "a unique culture and a long history of over 800 years" (*China Daily* 4 January 2006). Touristic imagination of Lijiang centers on tradition, sublime landscapes, a unique Naxi culture, and a slow pace of life:

> Lijiang's uniqueness lies in the harmony between human being and nature in the town. Its environment is very congenial and the town is full of scenic and poetic landscapes.
>
> (*People's Daily* 17 October 2002)

Table 5.1 Information sources[a]

	Domestic tourists (n = 303)		International tourists (n = 180)	
	Number	*Percent*[b]	*Number*	*Percent*[b]
Books/magazine/newspaper	154	50.8	62	34.4
Videos/television/radio	141	46.5	7	3.9
Friends or family members	139	45.9	65	36.1
Internet	90	29.7	37	20.6
Brochures/travel guide	35	11.6	115	63.9

Source: authors' data.

[a]More than one answer may be given by each respondent.
[b]Percent of total respondents rather than percent of total answers given by respondents.

It [Lijiang Ancient Town] is characterized by many narrow waterways, cobblestone streets, canals, trees and old houses with small shops and cozy guesthouses.

(*China Daily* 3 April 2006)

The Old Town is a warren of narrow streets and intricately decorated low wooden buildings, many used as shops selling traditional medicines and a variety of teas. Yet, even with marvels such as one of the few remaining Ming Dynasty stone bridges, there is a sense that it is all part of a show, a show aimed at giving wealthy Han Chinese and Western visitors a taste of a rarefied past.

(*The Times* 7 October 2006)

Television has also played an important role in popularizing Lijiang to potential domestic tourists. Several television series such as *Yimi Yangguan* (literally, One-meter-long sunlight) are filmed in Lijiang. As a romance drama, it has made Lijiang famous as a good destination for celebrating Valentine's Day (*People's Daily* 10 February 2006). Television (fiction and documentaries) and the visual media directly capture the "truth" of the immediate moment (Lefebvre 1991). Consumption of this helps in the generation of meanings about the place which in turn "regulate social [and spatial] practices ... and consequently have real practical effects" (Kim and Richardson 2003:219; see also Urry's (2002) argument on tourist gaze). It is hence not surprising to find that domestic tourists would seek to verify this romantic imagery of *Yimi Yangguan* when they visit Lijiang. In an Internet blog, for instance, a tourist (Anonymous 2006) penned this: "I visited Lijiang two years ago and I followed the footprints in *Yimi Yangguan* to look for something. I went to the guesthouse, Sifang Square and the bar [as seen in the series]. [In the end, t]he only feeling I have is that I don't want to leave [Lijiang]."

By far, the most popular imagination is Lijiang as a historical city frozen in time. As an antithesis of modernity, Lijiang is described by a Beijing tourist

(Respondent DT1) as naively unreal. This tourist frankly admitted that he did not oppose the "locals owning refrigerators and television sets" but what he preferred was backward and poor people leading fulfilling and happy lives:

> Before we came here, we imagined how minority groups look like. We imagined that Lijiang had a peaceful life. [It's] not like Beijing, not much commercialized. We really wanted to experience a normal [Lijiang] life, one in which a man is farming and a woman weaving .... Well, I mean, I don't want to see a very primitive life. But it has to be very *natural*.
>
> (Respondent DT1)

> Lijiang is a place to completely rest my soul. Many people come to Lijiang for relaxation, but I come here to pursue a spiritual substance. The life in big cities, such as Shanghai and Beijing, generates high work stress and forces you to move ahead. You cannot stop for a while to share and to enjoy. But in Lijiang, you are in no hurry and you can enjoy the sun and the life, without considering other things.
>
> (Respondent DT6)

Including the above respondents, 9 out of 11 domestic tourists in the interviews spoke of a need to experience tourism landscapes quite the opposite of their hectic routine lives in modern cities. In their minds, Naxi vernacular and material landscapes are symbols of tradition, of authentic rurality that is pure, simple/ unadulterated, and appealing. "In the pursuit of modernity ..., our cities have been paying a high price for erasing an important part of their own history. And such change is irreversible." (*China Daily* 29 December 2007). This malaise spawned a search for tradition and nostalgia, making Lijiang an attractive place to visit.

Unlike domestic tourists, however, international tourists relied more on brochures and travel guides for information. Notably, it is Lonely Planet that popularized Lijiang to the overseas community (Table 5.1; see also Chapter 4). Some international tourists say their imagination of Lijiang is that of a "small village" (Respondent IT3). "So you read books. They say [Lijiang is]... beautiful, historic, beautiful rivers, trees, water and you think, oh, it looks very beautiful. And then you say, oh, it is a World Heritage Site. And you go. It *must* be good" (Respondent IT6). In Lonely Planet's Internet discussion page called the Thorn Tree Forum, a tourist (Anonymous 2007) commented that "Lijiang to me was like 'Disney does China'. [I] imagine a quaint old Chinese town with every last building converted into a souvenir shop, utterly drained of all authenticity." These tourists described the landscapes they expected to encounter and experience in Lijiang. Different from domestic tourists, they seem to prioritize authenticity over an escape from the humdrum of modern life.

When asked for reasons why they visited Lijiang Ancient Town, over half of the domestic and international respondents ranked the town's heritage landscape as their main draw (Table 5.2). The World Heritage Site title was the third most

Table 5.2 Reasons for visiting Lijiang Ancient Town[a]

	Domestic tourists (n = 303)		International tourists (n = 180)	
	Number	*Percent*[b]	*Number*	*Percent*[b]
Enjoy its unique urban form and local architecture	181	59.7	96	53.6
Experience its rich cultural diversity and local practices	175	57.8	114	63.7
Lijiang Ancient Town is a World Heritage Site	144	47.5	67	37.4
Many people recommended Lijiang Ancient Town to me	90	29.7	62	34.6
Visit the nature parks nearby	84	27.7	67	37.4
Visit family/friends who reside in Lijiang Ancient Town	9	3.0	4	2.2
Attend local festivals	8	2.6	3	1.7
Business	8	2.6	1	0.6
Others	28	9.2	21	11.7

Source: authors' data.

[a]More than one answer may be given by each respondent.
[b]Percent of total respondents rather than percent of total answers given by respondents.

important motivating factor, as cited by 47.5 percent of domestic respondents and 37.4 percent of international visitors. Famous *natural* spots around the town, like Yulong Snow Mountain and Tiger Leaping Gorge, also attracted the tourists (between a quarter of the domestic to a third of the international tourists).

Consuming heritage

In this section, we will concentrate on how tourists consume through *gazing, touching and listening*.[1] According to Crouch *et al.* (2001:254), "actions, movements, ideas, dispositions, feelings, attitudes and subjectivities the individual possesses and uses in being a tourist" comes together in the tourist space of consumption. It is through these practices of consumption that heritage spaces are socially constructed in relation to the imagination of the place vis-à-vis the tourists' identities. Through their consumption, tourists can discursively make *sense* of the place they visit and generate meanings for the landscapes they encounter. As we clarified in Chapter 2, peoples' activities are usually conditioned by the extent of external socioeconomic constraints over them and their own philosophic dispositions. Tourists' consumption is no exception. In Lijiang, tourists are far from a homogeneous group and, therefore, their consumption would generate many different spatial outcomes. We mainly focus on the differences between the domestic and international tourists.

Table 5.3 summarizes the main activities of international and domestic tourists in Lijiang Ancient Town. Domestic tourists favor sightseeing (cited by

Table 5.3 Main activities undertaken by tourists[a]

	Domestic tourists (n = 303)		International tourists (n = 180)	
	Number	Percent[b]	Number	Percent[b]
Gazing				
Sightseeing	260	85.8	154	85.6
Photography	201	66.3	153	85.0
Touching				
Shopping	225	74.3	115	63.9
Dancing	148	48.8	9	5.0
Dining	141	46.5	155	86.1
Living in a guesthouse	113	37.3	80	44.4
Visiting Mu Palace	85	28.1	32	17.8
Drinking or eating in a bar	83	27.4	114	63.3
Town tour via horseback	32	10.6	3	1.7
Listening				
Attending Naxi concert	46	15.2	61	33.9
Others	5	1.7	6	3.3

Source: authors' data.

[a]More than one answer may be given by each respondent.
[b]Percent of total respondents rather than percent of total answers given by respondents.

85.8 percent of respondents), shopping (74.3 percent), and taking photos (66.3 percent), whereas the top three activities of international tourists are dining (chosen by 86.1 percent of respondents), sightseeing (85.6 percent), and taking photos (85.0 percent). The results affirm that sightseeing and taking photos are the two main components which constitute the "must" in Lijiang. They are what de Certeau (cited from Jackson and Holbrook 1995:1928) describes as "exercise[s] in ubiquity."

Sightseeing is *gazing*. Tourists come to the site of Lijiang to gaze at precisely the heritage landscapes mentioned in the brochures, guidebooks, and other media they have read/seen. They consume artifacts, including buildings and bridges, vivid symbols of Naxi culture like attire, and Dongba hieroglyphics. These elements confirm their romanticized imagination of local heritage and society. Sightseeing not only exemplifies tourists' willingness to glimpse, see, or stare at the objects with their eyes but also enables tourists to collect sights to daydream and contemplate "an 'artefactual' history, in which ...[real] *social* experiences are ... ignored" (Urry 2002:102, original emphasis). Through sightseeing, tourists affirm the visual against their original imagination of Lijiang so that they can give meaning to the space they encounter. Terkenli (2002) calls this "staging." The "stages" the tourists encounter have to comply with their own expectations and to satisfy their "unequivocal taste" (Terkenli 2002: 242) for an immediate (even if superficial) Naxi heritage.

If sightseeing allows tourists to fulfill their daydreams and imagination, photography gives them a chance to capture and freeze these imaginations and claim them as their own possessions. Many scholars have researched the close relation between photographing and the tourist experience. For instance, Edensor (1998:129) remarks that "photography is a strategy to recode and enframe experience." The snapshots help tourists collect visual signs for remembering and to inscribe their feeling and identity in time and space in relation to Lijiang Ancient Town. A tourist highlighted the importance of photography:

> Although I am alone, I don't feel it bothers me. I take my camera everywhere, no matter it is attractive or not. If my feeling comes, I just take a picture. Later on I go back to my home and see the pictures and still enjoy them. As I told you, I have taken more than five hundred pictures.
>
> (Respondent IT4)

Here, Respondent IT4 makes a connection between the practice *in* and *after* his Lijiang visit and how his geographical imagination of Lijiang has been eternalized. Photographing Lijiang was, for him, the main way to remember the objects he encountered.

As Crang (1997:367) aptly argues, the pictures tourists like Respondent IT4 take are reflective of "not just picturing a landscape, nor representing places – it is seizing a moment in a place" and more importantly, they are "communicating some point about [the] experience in one particular place and time to an audience or viewer in another place and time." For instance, one of the international tourists whom we guided during our fieldwork sent us pictures he took of Lijiang and added in his letter: "I have some great pictures of the day we spent together …. Enjoy the photos from our trips! The China photos are my favorite. You are in some of them. We have to thank you for spending the time with us" (Respondent IT5). For him, the pictures can build a spatial connection between Lijiang Ancient Town and himself and strengthen the social connections between himself and us.

This form of consumption should not be taken lightly. Tourists' photos actually help to mold Lijiang's heritage landscapes into iconic images. In particular, those that depict nostalgia (historic buildings), nature (water, mountains, trees, and gardens), and the exotic (Naxi ethnic group) have circulated around the world and become reference points for potential consumers to look out for when they eventually visit Lijiang. A browse through the websites Tianyaclub.cn,[2] xitek. com,[3] and travelchinaguide.com[4] will reveal a wealth of such iconic images. Thus, photography completes what Albers and James (1988:136) call the "hermeneutic circle," starting with tourists' imagination of place and ending with their productions of the very "same" images by snapshots in situ.

Figure 5.1 shows tourists jostling each other as they attempt to "document" their visit with their cameras. Their practice of photographing also feeds back into the production of heritage landscapes. In order to engender the "repertoire of actions" that involves photographing and the reproduction of these images

Figure 5.1 Remembering Lijiang Ancient Town. This is a popular spot for photography. The backdrop is an enlarged version of ex President Jiang Zemin's handwriting and says, "World Heritage Site – Lijiang Ancient Town." Source: Authors' photo.

(Crawshaw and Urry 1997:183), CWHMC has beautified the architectural facades along the main streets of Lijiang and clearly marked spots which are appropriate for tourists to take photos. The authority even requires all female employees in the tourism sector to wear colorful Naxi attire, which has inevitably become a popular subject for snapshots. Private enterprise is complicit in this goal. *Lishuijinsha* (see Chapter 4) is a visual treat of colorful costumes and "actions" (dance) which tourists happily capture with their cameras. All these operations help to reduce Lijiang's heritage landscapes into a large homogeneous tourist space that is devoid of real people and social reality and replaced instead by sanitized symbols of Naxi heritage. Many people in Lijiang are just stage props for the tourist gaze. As part of global consumption and reproduction of tourist images, the practice of photography in Lijiang "reinforces hegemonic understandings in the economy of signs" (Edensor 1998:129). These images are put up and circulated by the external organizations such as UNESCO, world-renowned tour book publishers such as Lonely Planet, and travel agencies. The consumers, namely the tourists, both domestic and international, in their turn, help to perpetuate the hegemonic discourse of what Lijiang is by reaffirming their consent of these imaginations.

Among the many ways of *touching* Lijiang Ancient Town, shopping is probably the most popular. Every day, hundreds of tourists patronize the shops in the town and purchase souvenirs. They mainly buy trinklets, key chains, silverware, local specialties like Yunnan tea, and the Naxi costume (authors' observation). Tourists purchase these souvenirs either for themselves to help them remember their Lijiang trip or for their friends and relatives as a gift, as shown by the following tourists' comments:

> We bought some souvenirs with Dongba pictographic words. We will give them away. Well, it is not good you don't buy anything after you visit a place. The Dongba souvenirs I give at least signify my sincerity. My friends will appreciate this novelty.
>
> (Respondent DT2)

> [The souvenirs I bought were] just for my girl friend … buy something for her.
>
> (Respondent IT4)

> I bought many souvenirs. Some are gifts for other people; some are for myself.
>
> (Respondent IT7)

For these tourists, the incorporation of shopping into their consumption results in a socio-spatial connection between themselves, the people around them, the traders and locals in Lijiang, and their friends and family back home. First of all, shopping provides tourists many opportunities to be in close touch with the townspeople. As Respondent DT2 mentioned, it is her *duty* to shop. Through shopping, she can discover what Naxi heritage is, learn how to move around Lijiang, know the local commercial and cultural environment, and meet the locals who live in Lijiang. In other words, shopping helps many tourists to garner intimate knowledge about Lijiang.

Second, the souvenirs they purchase in Lijiang are mementos to remember a place that is far away from where they come from and these souvenirs evoke good memories. Tourists can bring the souvenirs back and, by looking at them, remember their visit to Lijiang and imaginatively touch Lijiang for a temporary "escape." Thus, souvenirs should be distinctive and should convey strong "local" meanings. As Respondent DT2 complained, "what I really want to buy is some unique souvenir relevant to Naxi ethnicity, which … cannot be found in other places. But the choice is very limited." A tourist from Macau (Respondent IT4) marveled at the similarity between the souvenirs in Lijiang and those in Thailand and other Southeast Asian countries. The global network of souvenir production tends to homogenize tourist space because the products they make for purchase by the tourists are the same. Many tourists felt "extremely disappointed since the town has become a modern supermarket, [holding] an illusory fame as an ancient town."[5]

Third, shopping is not a purely economic transaction between tourists and traders. Instead, it is "a social activity built around social exchange" (Shields 1992:102). Souvenirs given to friends are a means of asserting tourists' identity through their personal taste in selecting souvenirs and their economic ability to afford them. They also constitute cultural capital because the souvenirs help tourists show others what they have acquired of foreign places for themselves.

A visit to Lijiang becomes a fashion accessory that tourists can show off (*People's Daily* 17 October 2002).

Apart from shopping, other activities involving touch include dancing, dining, visiting Mu Palace, a town tour via horseback, and so on (see Table 5.3). Tourists want to touch either material landscapes such as the Mu Palace and the traditional guesthouses, or the vernacular landscapes such as local Naxi dance, food, and horseback transport. For instance, many independent tourists, regardless of their nationality, preferred to stay in a guesthouse in the ancient town. As Respondent IT1 mentioned, "the building is beautiful. I am staying in a courtyard guesthouse, very *traditional*, and it is a good experience. I feel that I experience the authentic ancient culture of Lijiang." For tourists like Respondent IT1, the tactile experience of sleeping and living in a guesthouse makes Lijiang more authentic.

Both domestic and international tourists regard the social interaction with the Naxi as an important part of their experience of Lijiang (Table 5.4). Indeed, when asked whether they had contact with local people, 48.9 percent of international respondents and 51.8 percent of domestic tourists reported that they actually did during their trip. Although these tourists could have mistaken Han merchants for indigenous residents, the fact that personal encounters mattered is significant, as social interaction with locals would help them to understand Naxi culture better. To tourists, Harrison (2003:69) argues, "the experience of connecting across time, space and social hierarchies ... [i]s deeply meaningful." Thus, it is not surprising to find tourists saying: "I want to interact with locals and know their life. This is a *sincere* interaction. This interaction is what we long for since we no longer find it in the cities" (Respondent DT5).

Some tourists consciously avoided the highly touristic areas of the town and endeavored to venture into more "local" places. A couple from France stepped into the alleys and streets where mass tourists are rarely found. They observed how local people lived every day. They also asked for permission to take photos of locals and thanked them. Both guests and hosts seemed happy by the encounter despite the language barrier. The gap between tourists and locals is narrowed by such meetings; the photos and the gesticulation become the "means of communication"

Table 5.4 Tourists' contact with locals

	Domestic tourists (n = 303)		International tourists (n = 180)	
	Number	Percent	Number	Percent
Yes	157	51.8	88	48.9
Would like to but I had no chance	116	38.3	73	40.6
No	2	0.7	10	5.6
Don't care	28	9.2	9	5.0
Total	303	100.00	180.00	100.00

Source: authors' data.

(Giddens 1991:196) through which tourists attach meaning to their encounter with "real" Lijiang inhabitants.

The final consumption practice is *listening*. Tourists attend music concerts to listen to Naxi music. As reported by the respondents, 15.2 percent of domestic tourists and 33.9 percent of international visitors did this (see Table 5.3). Respondent IT6 had the following response: "the music is very interesting. I think it is very important although we cannot understand what we hear all the time. It is a very good cultural experience." Because Naxi music is unique, the music performances in the town attract hundreds of tourists every night.

Although it would be difficult to deny that there are some tourists who can appreciate the music, for most, even domestic tourists, catching a performance is merely for the purpose of increasing cultural capital. It becomes a conversation piece among the tourists for when they get home. This was confirmed by Respondent LP1: "many tourists, as far as I observe, actually fail to understand it [Naxi music]. More than 80 percent don't understand it. Nevertheless, they *must* listen to it once they visit Lijiang. They just want to listen to it"; "I like the Naxi music show. It is very good and the artists too. To me, it is a part of the World Heritage Site. I came to watch the artists and hear the music, and meet the traditional people" (Respondent IT1). Through listening, tourists come closer to consuming authentic Lijiang culture.

Through their consumption and the meanings they attach to specific attractions, tourists play a role in determining which attractions are viable and which are not. What is popular among the tourists will become the justification for tourism planners and private enterprise to invest more money, thereby strengthening their hegemonic position of influence in landscape developments. Table 5.5 presents tourists' evaluation of different heritage elements that purportedly represent

Table 5.5 Mean importance of heritage elements

Heritage elements	Domestic tourists (n = 303)		International tourists (n = 180)	
	Mean[a]	SD	Mean[a]	SD
Local buildings and canals	1.4	0.75	1.5	0.71
Naxi traditional music	1.2	0.94	1.1	0.92
Traditional costume	1.1	0.87	1.1	0.83
Naxi language (dialect and pictography)	1.1	0.99	0.7	1.10
Dance	0.9	0.87	0.9	0.82
Mu Palace	0.9	0.86	0.4	0.86
Dongba religion/spiritual life	0.8	0.95	0.5	1.10
Handicrafts (carvings, silverware, etc.)	0.7	0.98	0.9	0.94
Folk tales, myths, and legends, etc.	0.6	0.89	0.5	0.94

Source: authors' data.

[a]Respondents were asked to indicate on a five-point scale, whether they thought the items represent Naxi culture. A maximum value of +2 was given to "very representative" and –2 to "very unrepresentative."

Naxi culture. Generally, all nine elements scored a relatively high mean. However, material landscapes obtained a higher score than vernacular landscapes. Tourists find Lijiang's built heritage to be more indicative of a historical city: "The designed architecture, the canals, the stone, how old they are! Very, very old, a lot of history ..." (Respondent IT6); "What impress me in Lijiang are the buildings, canals, and water. I like Lijiang's buildings. They look like handmade. The buildings in Kuala Lumpur are too modern" (Respondent IT7). For all of these tourists, the well-preserved material landscape in Lijiang accords with their imagination of a historical city.

Not all the buildings in Lijiang are attractive to the tourists. Newly-rebuilt Mu Palace obtained a low score of 0.9 from domestic tourists and 0.4 from international ones (Table 5.5). Respondent IT7 felt that Mu Palace is not in keeping with his expectations of a historical city: "I did not enter because it is reconstructed. I have no interest in it. In the old town, I just want to experience an authentic ambience." To tourists, Mu Palace is not part of Lijiang's "authentic" heritage in spite of the expense spent on it and its promotion by tour agents and the state authorities. Those in power try to strengthen their position by controlling the design of buildings within the ancient town but there is dissent from discerning consumers who challenge their actions.

Other elements with high scores included Naxi traditional music and costume (see Table 5.5). These can be easily touched and sensed and they can be found in the front region of the town. Intangible elements such as folk tales and religion, however, are harder to find as they remain in the back regions of Lijiang and tourists do not have enough time to dwell deeper into Naxi culture.

From the data on consumption, it is evident that the tourists are far from what an explorer should be (Smith 1977). By all counts, the appreciation of Lijiang for most tourists is only skin deep. They neither have the time nor the desire to go beyond the surface/front region of Lijiang.[6] With a highly aesthetic environment that is well conserved, Lijiang Ancient Town is inauthentically authentic. Just a step behind a theme park, tourists' gaze and their consumption (of staged events such as the Naxi music performances, of kitsch souvenirs, of stays at guesthouses which go the full throttle in replicating a traditional house, etc.),[7] are not far from what Feifer (1985) expects of "post-tourists." They know that they are not time-travelers when they visit historical sites and that they cannot evade their condition as outsiders. Hence, "the tourist increasingly accepts the commodified world and therefore does not seek authentic values," eliding any potential reservations about visiting sites that are unabashedly "themed," "staged," and commodified (Blom 2000:31).

Tourists were also asked in the survey to evaluate heritage preservation in Lijiang. With regard to the preservation of the material landscape, both domestic and international tourists agreed that the state had been successful in restoring traditional buildings (67 percent of the domestic respondents and 68.9 percent of the international tourists, respectively) (Table 5.6).

However, the respondents were less than happy with cultural preservation. The international tourists surveyed were more skeptical than domestic visitors with

Table 5.6 Evaluation of government's effort in successfully restoring traditional buildings[a]

	Domestic tourists (n = 303)		International tourists (n = 180)	
	Number	Percent	Number	Percent
Strongly agree	56	18.5	36	20
Agree	147	48.5	88	48.9
Neutral or no comment	83	27.4	46	25.6
Disagree	12	4.0	8	4.4
Strongly disagree	5	1.7	2	1.1
Total	303	100	180	100

Source: authors' data.

[a]Respondents were asked to indicate agreement with the statement that "The government has done an excellent job in restoring historical buildings."

regard to the statement that the government has balanced tourism development and the protection of Naxi culture (Table 5.7). Less than a quarter of international respondents strongly agreed or agreed with this statement, whereas 37.8 percent strongly disagreed or disagreed. The separation between vernacular and material landscape triggers many critiques: "culture will be completely lost and the town completely made for tourists" (Respondent IT2) and "without the Naxi, the town would lose its identity" (Respondent DT6).

Many tourists disagreed with the statement that Lijiang is a good show-case of heritage preservation and tourism development. The government's claim that Lijiang has a win–win situation in the relationship between conservation and development is hence unfounded. Tourists felt that although Lijiang's material landscape had been well preserved, its vernacular landscape has been

Table 5.7 Evaluation of government's effort in preserving Naxi culture[a]

	Domestic tourists (n = 303)		International tourists (n = 180)	
	Number	Percent	Number	Percent
Strongly agree	36	11.9	7	3.9
Agree	128	42.2	35	19.4
Neutral or no comment	106	35.0	70	38.9
Disagree	27	8.9	52	28.9
Strongly disagree	6	2.0	16	8.9
Total	303	100	180	100

Source: authors' data.

[a]Respondents were asked to indicate agreement to the statement that "Government has balanced tourism development and the protection of Naxi culture."

threatened or even damaged by tourism development. The reappropriation of the past has become an entrepreneurial strategy for profit making. However, this development is at the sacrifice of its vernacular landscape, which was once rooted in the town. As a result, "the town is worthless nonsense without lived culture inside" (a female tourist from Guangdong, comment made in questionnaire). Whereas the consumers may not have undermined the influence of the state authorities and private enterprise in their onward plow to further touristify Lijiang, the challenge posed to the authorities by the tourist consumers remains part of the dynamics that will figure into how Lijiang's tourism development will evolve.

Finding a balance between the old and the new in consumption

Tourists often graft their personal standard of consumption in their place of origin onto their destinations. Many tourists in our survey admit that Lijiang's tourism infrastructure is acceptable. The various choices of accommodation, food, and transportation facilitate their trip although some may complain that the price is steep: "You needn't worry about accommodation and food in the town. You can have more time to enjoy local culture" (Respondent DT6); "There are advantages too. For instance, to go out to Tiger Leaping Gorge is much easier because agents set up here [in Lijiang] and I can change currency conveniently [than at the gorge]. So, those kinds of things …" (Respondent IT2).

For many international tourists, especially those from Western countries, their enjoyment depends on the presence of some of the familiar. To enter a purely local environment could mean risk or an uncertainty.

> I just came through Laos where washrooms are very primitive. Well, for me, you know, it is not a huge problem. But I came here, [it's] with so modern and clean washrooms; it just goes back to life [sic]. I don't have to think so much about, you know, taking care of myself when I'm walking around. It is very nice.
>
> (Respondent IT1)

> A lot of tourists can say I don't want to change the culture. But when tourists come in ….they expect people [locals] to be able to speak English. They want to be able to find pizza …. There are more Westernized restaurants [in Lijiang] than Chinese restaurants.
>
> (Respondent O5)

Even domestic tourists have standards:

> This afternoon we cooked supper in the guesthouse …. The food in the town is not suitable for us. You see, we cannot become part of local life. It is a conflict, isn't it? To the foreigners, they might feel uncomfortable without

Western food. It is not authentic Western food.[8] Therefore, I believe authenticity is relational.

(Respondent DT4)

These quotes speak of an ambivalence frequently experienced by the tourists. They want to enjoy high-quality facilities and services, yet they also desire landscapes different from their daily lives. As a Canadian tourist said, "we are tourists and culture is what we are looking for. But at the same time, we need a comfortable 'home'" (Respondent IT5). These requirements have implications: What the tourists want, they get. Such feedback from the tourists has become justification for the local government and tourism developers to push for improvements in Lijiang's tourism infrastructure such as the expressway, the airport, more luxury hotels, and a clean urban environment that meets international standards. As one of the stakeholders in Lijiang's future, the tourists have inadvertently contributed to the hegemonic discourse about more and faster tourism-driven change for Lijiang.

At the same time, the pursuit for difference and authenticity remains unaffected. Caught between "utopia and dystopia" (Meethan 2004:23), tourists want to experience "authentic" Lijiang, which tourism authorities feel is in their vested interest to deliver. If satisfied, tourists themselves will reproduce this meaning and bring about more visitors to Lijiang. Thus, Lijiang Ancient Town has been molded into an extension of modernity, on the one hand, and a deliberate display of cultural and visual difference, on the other hand. As a consequence, one of the most fascinating aspects of Lijiang (and probably many other tourist destinations in this global era) is that it has "become more homogenous in some ways and more heterogeneous in others" (Zukin 1991:12).

Whereas it would do well for Lijiang to pay attention to the standard of services it provides, heritage remains central to why tourists come to Lijiang. Many tourists have realized that the current situation in the ancient town is becoming less than ideal. A tourist from Shenzhen complained: "[The town] is boring... It is completely impossible for me to find local people to have a chat with, although the streets are filled with people" (Respondent DT5). In addition, local people, especially the elderly, resist visitors' overtures of friendship:

Today we came across a group of old Naxi people in a street far away from the town centre and felt that it reflects well, real Naxi life. So we tried to photograph them, but they closed the door immediately.

(Respondent DT4)

Naxi residents do not want to be "stage props" for tourists and will avoid crowded tourist spaces. This withdrawal is covert resistance to the staging of Naxi life in Lijiang. When the interaction with the host becomes hostile, how can tourists make sense of Naxi lived culture and vernacular landscape?

Since they cannot see any signs of quotidian life or enter in the back stage, tourists insist that they have not experienced authenticity. For example, some tourists complained that the Naxi costume was a "uniform" since "everyone wears it in a very similar way" (Respondent DT2). The dance they witnessed at Sifang Square was viewed as a contrived activity to "attract tourists" rather than "a part of their everyday life" since "I don't think in the normal daily life, they dance every afternoon" (Respondent IT4). In fact, local dancers affirm that the dance is *really* part of their daily life since they come to Sifang Square regularly for practice (Su and Teo 2008). The above tourists' interpretation is largely derived from their own observations and readings, without verification from local people. In their eyes, the authenticity of Naxi heritage is downgraded by what they think are staged arrangements.

In the view of domestic tourists, the most serious problem is Hanization of Naxi vernacular landscape: "The influence of the Han is high here. I cannot find Naxi cultural forms like language, food and more importantly, tradition in the town" (Respondent DT3); "It is impossible to understand what Naxi lifestyle is like if you stay in the town because what you experience here is not much different from home" (informal interview with a university student from Beijing). Their critiques express their discontent of the influence of Han culture on Naxi heritage (see also Chapter 4), on the one hand, but highlight their desire to seek for an escape through precisely this culture, on the other. Domestic tourists, particularly those from big cities in China, thought highly of Lijiang's slow pace of life, its simplicity, and its strong traditions: "I seek for serenity in Lijiang, a sense of peace .... I want to escape from a life full of business [sic]" (Respondent DT5); "I believe people come here for a lifestyle, which cannot be enjoyed in big cities. Everyone wants to find a place to stay quietly for a while" (Respondent DT4). These tourists wished that the short time they spend in Lijiang could alleviate them from the considerable noise, pollution, pressure, and indifference they have to tolerate in the big cities. Lijiang's heritage can provide them with a reprieve. Indeed, many people mentioned that they came to Lijiang for an escape:

> Actually, everyday you are very busy in big cities. Everyone expects to find [in Lijiang] a place to stay peacefully. Even if this peace is temporary, it can lessen some of our pressure. Lijiang is different from modern society and provides the peace we need.
>
> (Respondent DT4)

Nevertheless, this desire for an escape entraps them in Lijiang's tourism modernity, which only promises an illusion about peaceful life, tradition, and authenticity. According to Wang (1999b:105), "[r]outinised work in industry or a bureaucracy impose[s] a constraining, compelling, rigid tempo and rhythm, a situation in which individuals become automated, robot-like, de-individualized, repetitively doing Sisyphus-like wearing tasks .... Under such conditions workers experience temporal alienation." Tourists in Lijiang make a determined effort to give meaning to Lijiang according to their own imagination and desire. To escape from "the routine, the mundanity and the boredom of their everyday lives"

(Tucker 2003:61), domestic tourists who constitute the main consumers in Lijiang Ancient Town search for the exotic, not only in the sense of the "other" as different (e.g. Naxi culture) but also the "other" as in a place which has stood still. The historical landscape, the rich traditions, and the simple life are part of the tourist imagination of Lijiang Ancient Town and tourists come seeking for this. Once their imagination cannot be fulfilled, tourists express anger and discontent.

As Ateljevic and Doorne (2002:662–663) argue, tourists "increasingly attempt to construct their identities by articulating consumption preferences and lifestyle practices that signal their taste and position in society." This articulation may generate conflicts. For tourism planners and developers, the internationalization of Lijiang falls in line with their desired goal of turning Lijiang into a world-class attraction. This hegemonic discourse is not without problems. Tourists also want a Lijiang that is not encumbered by change (what they deem "a 'live fossil' of authenticity" (Wang 1999b:139)), which requires a different strategy for tourism development. Some negotiation is required. The next section explores some of these tensions and their implications.

Tension among the consumers

This tension is most pronounced between the domestic group tourists and the rest. For many domestic middle-class tourists, who are mainly *group* tourists, their experience of Lijiang is one of conspicuous consumption (Veblen 1934 [1899]), i.e. there is lavish spending on services and goods in order to show off their wealth or to pamper their appetite for luxury. We term them "conspicuous tourists." In Lijiang, many domestic tourists were found to order expensive food and alcohol, especially in places like the bars and restaurants along Cuiwen Lane. The space of tourism consumption becomes an imaginary space where they can feign wealth. Even if the tourist does not actually belong to the upper class, he/she can use consumption to redefine his/her identity, even if it is only short-lived.

In contrast, the fewer but nevertheless present *independent* domestic tourists differentiate themselves from the conspicuous tourists.[9] One tourist clarified: "I am not interested in the Lijiang under the flag of a tour guide. I want to know Lijiang and locals as soon as possible, an authentic and original Lijiang."[10] However, domestic cultural tourists are not favored by the tourism market. As noted by Respondent DT2:

> The town caters for the tourists who are seeking luxurious consumption and fun. Therefore, the town becomes more and more commercial. People like me who come here for culture are disappointed at the town; but people could feel comfortable if they come here to enjoy luxury. In their opinion, the town is 'perfect'. Different people have different ideas of what 'perfect' means.

Cultural tourists like Respondent DT2 are not happy that Lijiang permits banal consumption, which waters down the authenticity of the "natural simple life"

(Respondent DT1). However, to those visitors seeking conspicuous consumption, the town is a perfect place, as it offers an exotic getaway containing many restaurants, bars, and hotels.

There are different spatial outcomes arising from the different consumer needs of the tourists. Cultural tourists identify themselves as different from conspicuous tourists staying in the modern hotels in the new city. For example, one of the independent domestic tourists talked about why it was worth choosing a guesthouse with a courtyard in the ancient town rather than a star-ranked hotel in the new city:

> This guesthouse and its courtyard are very peaceful although Lijiang Ancient Town is itself chaotic and noisy. I lived at the Yulong Garden Hotel, the venue of our conference which is quite near to the ancient town. But I moved out from the hotel into this guesthouse as soon as the conference was over. Why? I want to have a chance to enjoy the town more intimately.

Without the guesthouse stay, he is articulating that his experience of Lijiang would not be complete. Unlike the modern hotel, the courtyard of the "traditional" guesthouse he lived in embodies a space for self-contemplation that helps him to escape the "busyness" omnipresent in Lijiang's main streets and his place of origin, which is Beijing. The divisions between the "new city" and the "old town," the "modern hotel" and the "traditional guesthouse" are more than metaphorical: for him, they are real and meaningful.

Many international tourists accepted the contrived construction of Naxi culture in the town:

> I told you that I know [Lijiang] is not a real place. But it is not a Hollywood cinema set [either]. I still feel comfortable.
>
> (Respondent IT8)

> It didn't really disappoint me because I still see a lot of ancient architecture here. And I learned a little bit about traditional culture here. I don't think the things I see are real but I find I enjoy it.
>
> (Respondent IT4)

> Yes, it is commercialized, and we realized that. But at the same time, it gave us a look at what the culture is.
>
> (Respondent IT6)

> Let me tell you something about this old town. [It's] very cool! The water has fish. That is great. I just find … it is very cool.
>
> (Respondent IT3)

For these tourists, their visit in Lijiang is not a way of gaining authentic experience of Naxi heritage; rather, it is a way of "gaining pleasure" (Desforges 2001:362). As post-tourists (Feifer 1985), they do not care much about the *difference* between the real and the fake. Or in Cohen's (1988) words of describing diversionary tourists, they consider touristic products contrived in nature, but still appeal to them. For these tourists, tourism is "a form of play" (Cohen 1988:383) and the realistic way to experience Lijiang is to find novelty and to enjoy it.

A close observation on international tourists can verify this point and show the difference between them and domestic cultural tourists. We had guided many international tourists during our fieldwork and all of them were intrigued by Zhongyi Market, which is a marketplace bordering the new city and the ancient town. This market serves local residents who buy their daily necessities here (Figure 5.2). The foreign tourists cheerfully photographed the daily transactions taking place in the market and repeatedly walked through a labyrinth of stalls. Some even asked us to explain things they found interesting. Tourists commented on the market: "It is really China. I like it" (Respondent IT8); "It is a good market because it consists of all kinds of people, *local* people. No tourists! It is their everyday life" (Respondent IT6). For these tourists, the market is a truly vernacular landscape that is completely undisturbed by mass tourism.

However, the domestic tourists we interviewed expressed no interest in the market, partly because it lacks spectacle and "othering" and partly because they are reluctant to dig deep into Naxi society. Instead, they superficially and

Figure 5.2 Foreign tourists at Zhongyi Market. For the foreign tourists, the market is not staged but real. Source: authors' photo.

superciliously focused on the symbols of Naxi heritage that have been carefully put together by the local government and tourism developers.

The difference between tourists' preferences has bearings on how Lijiang is to be consumed. As domestic tourists form the predominant market of Lijiang's tourism industry, they inevitably command the most spaces of consumption in the town. Cuiwen Lane is a good example to uncover the competition for space between domestic and international tourists. Before 1997, Cuiwen Lane was a gathering venue for Western backpackers to share their experiences during beer-drinking sessions. Thus, several bars (such as Figure 5.3) provided Western food to satisfy this market group. When mass domestic tourists entered into Lijiang after 2000, the bars became a draw as anything associated with Western consumption was deemed de riguer. The domestic tourists started to colonize the drinking holes of the backpackers and forced them to bars on the outskirts of the core area.

As yet, not many Chinese tourists have the financial means to visit Western countries. But many are willing to enhance their social status by a taste of "something Western." Here in Lijiang's Cuiwen Lane, a replica is provided and they have a chance to engage in an imagined Western lifestyle. The fascination with the West does not necessarily translate into a Western-centric landscape. Instead, a hybridized space of consumption emerges that synthesizes the West, Han culture, and Naxi heritage. For example, the bar owners decorate the walls

Figure 5.3 A typical café along Cuiwen Lane. Source: authors' photo.

with posters that have a Western theme (e.g. Casa Blanca posters and Budweiser posters), play Western pop music, and provide a bilingual (English and Mandarin) menu of food and wine. However, Chinese food and local alcohol are still available. For scholars writing about homogenization and hybridization of space under globalization (Appadurai 1996; Bryman 1995; Ritzer 2004), Cuiwen Lane is a good example.

As a result, there is an obvious separation of space for tourists in Cuiwen Lane. In the morning, some international tourists come to the bars for Western breakfast, including coffee and sandwiches. By noon, international tourists start to withdraw and domestic independent tourists start to fill the spaces in the bars. They take up the tables for lunch or to have tea (drinking Yunnan tea has been imagined as a part of Naxi leisurely daily life). At night, Cuiwen Lane becomes a space of consumption for conspicuous tourists, who gather on the ground floor and push the independent domestic tourists and the international tourists to the second floor. It is economic power that determines the use of space in Cuiwen Lane. Owing to the flow of domestic tourists, the lane is under transformation from a space for Western backpackers to a space that is separated and contested by the domestic group tourists. The implications of this contestation are not lost on tourism entrepreneurs. So long as domestic group tourists continue to be a big market, the bars and restaurants will respond by putting up more tables and signboards to attract the tourists.[11] The tourists benefit, as does private enterprise and the state. As for the Naxi, how effective they will be in negotiating the protection of their homes is something that will become more and more contentious.

As more and more tourism services in Lijiang cater to the large domestic market, international tourists feel marginalized. There are some complaints from foreign tourists concerning the lack of translation in Lijiang's attraction sites. A Canadian tourist expressed her discontent:

> We had … a lot of concerns …[There was a lot of …] personal talking, making jokes, having fun in Chinese. We were a part of …[the performance but w]e cannot understand. Everybody was laughing. … Chinese [language] makes things difficult. Because we are tourists, we want to try new culture. But because it doesn't cater to us … it becomes frustrating.
>
> (Respondent IT6)

What Respondent IT6 pointed out is that she failed to appreciate Naxi music because of insufficient language facilitators. Another independent tourist from Canada (Respondent IT1) also admitted that "the language is a problem to a degree" and "a big challenge" in Lijiang. Domestic tourists have entrenched the dominance of Mandarin in this tourist space of Lijiang. International tourists are marginalized, as little space is left for them to make sense of Lijiang's vernacular landscape. Whereas the state desires for more translation to cater to international tourists, other stakeholders such as the restaurants, the music hall, and the shops, are only interested in the domestic tourists because they form the biggest group.

Consequently, Lijiang Ancient Town has emerged as more of a domestic tourist enclave than an international world-class attraction as spelt out in the rhetoric adopted by the state authorities such as the CWHMC and the LTB.

Accommodation as spaces of consumption have also been affected by the influx of domestic Chinese tourists. Prior to their arrival, Westerners were happy to live in the guesthouses within the ancient town. Many were dorm-like, as they were also residences. Today, many guesthouse owners have upgraded their accommodation from common rooms and dorms to hotel-like standard rooms. Unlike Western backpackers who prefer to stay in common rooms or dorms because of their limited budget and their desire for an authentic experience, Chinese tourists favor standard rooms.[12] The direct result is that Western backpackers find it difficult to find cheap rooms within the ancient town. An Australian independent tourist (Respondent IT9) had this to say:

> In 1991 there might be 20 Western tourists in the town at any time. Now it feels like there are probably 30 to 40 Western tourists and 3,000 to 4,000 Chinese tourists! This is due to the explosion in Chinese domestic tourism and tourism from Hong Kong .... Ironically, many young Western visitors find the place too popular and spoiled by tourism, and instead aim for more unspoiled areas such as Deqin.[13]

The different purchasing power of the domestic and international tourists has helped determine spatial usage in Lijiang Ancient Town.[14] A majority of guesthouses, restaurants, bars, souvenir shops, and other tourism facilities have become spaces of domestic tourists' consumption; international tourists are not the main target in Lijiang's tourism market.

International tourists start to withdraw from the space of consumption in Lijiang as a way to contest the dominance of domestic tourists. They choose other destinations like Shangri-La rather than Lijiang when they visit Yunnan. Many international tourists simply treat the town as a gateway to other attractions nearby and pay little attention to the town itself. Asked if she would recommend Lijiang to her friends, Respondent IT2 replied:

> I would like to tell people the best thing about Lijiang is Tiger Leaping Gorge. For sure! This is pretty, I like Lijiang but it is nothing compared with the Gorge. Because I like natural beauty and adventure experience, I get out of Lijiang to see people in a more natural land.

Locals also have tense relationships with domestic tourists. Many Naxi confide that international tourists, mainly from Western countries, behave more politely than Chinese visitors. Edensor (1998) claims that tourists from underdeveloped countries do not know well how to be "good" tourists. *International Herald Tribune* (23 October 2005) also claims that Chinese tourists have built a notorious image for being noisy sightseers and ostentatious shoppers wherever they go in the world. For what it is worth, the Naxi have also complained that domestic visitors do not "respect" local culture and do not behave appropriately. Some Naxi locals critiqued that many domestic tourists lacked courtesy to Naxi people and have little regard for Lijiang's urban environment. For instance, a town resident commented:

> In the town, *laowai*[15] want to learn more than Chinese tourists. They are interested in everything, regardless of the old or the modern. Quite differently, Chinese people only care about their own interest. If there is no benefit, they don't want to learn .... In comparison to *laowai*, Chinese people have a low interest in learning our culture. *Laowai* love studying Naxi culture much more.
>
> (Respondent LP13)

Respondent LP13's comment suggests that tourism should go beyond the economic relations between tourists and the local culture. Hence, she and many other locals are more willing to share Naxi culture with international tourists than domestic tourists because they believe the former are genuinely interested in studying their heritage. In their view, domestic tourists only want a superficial understanding of Naxi culture and they fear that Lijiang will become no more than a museum (see Chapter 6).

Tensions between the international and domestic tourists do exist and consumption is far from homogeneous. As the groups tug in sometimes divergent directions, depending on their preferences, their priorities, and their economic ability, the hegemonic discourse about Lijiang has to shift to take into account these variations. Hence, to understand Lijiang's tourism landscape is to take into account not only structures such as the state and capital but also the agency of the consumers and the locals (discussed in Chapter 7), and that the outcome is a compromised equilibrium of the dynamic interaction between all.

Conclusions

This chapter has been concerned with how tourists consume Lijiang's heritage landscapes and how their consumption is fed back into Lijiang's heritage production. Tourists imagine Lijiang as a destination with a nostalgic tradition and with nature that is not threatened by human existence. Their imagination plays an important role in instructing their consumption. It was found that tourists gaze, touch, and listen to fulfill their imagination. Through gazing, they capture the beauty of Lijiang's historic buildings and the customs and traditions of the Naxi people; through touching, they build economic and social connections with Lijiang's inhabitants; and through listening, they develop more engagement with local culture and can verify that Lijiang is indeed unique. To satisfy tourists, the local government and tourism businesses stage Lijiang's heritage landscapes to conform to the imagination of the tourists and to the advertisements/guidebooks. Whereas some tourists applauded the success of this preservation of Lijiang, many were also unhappy about the current condition. This chapter argues that both groups have the economic and cultural power to influence the project of (re) presenting Lijiang.

Tourists can, by their consumption preferences, create contradictions. Their expectation for a high-quality tourism infrastructure has led to a globally homogenized landscape in Lijiang, but their desire for authenticity has also helped to raise awareness in Naxi heritage that will assist in its battle against commercialization. Tourists can assist the state in persuading Lijiang residents to accept that development is inevitable but tourists also play the role of subverting this message. In Lijiang's tourist space, the state and tourism developers will obviously woo the domestic tourists, since they have higher purchasing power that will assist the state and capital in securing their hegemonic dominance. But the analysis should not stop at highlighting the power of government and capital in forming and shaping tourist space. This chapter has also shown that the dominance of the conspicuous tourists is frequently contested. Through their spatial practices of withdrawal, both international and domestic independent tourists can resist hegemony. Domestic cultural tourists find their own spaces of consumption in the town (e.g. the guesthouses) and avoid the dominant spaces of the domestic group tourists. Resistance feeds back into production, and spaces that cater to the more discerning tourist, albeit limited, still make a presence in the deliberations of capital.

In the next chapter, we will extend our examination of the socio-spatial outcomes of heritage production and consumption by exploring the commodified landscapes through which hegemony is anchored in the tourism space of Lijiang Ancient Town. Three forms of heritage landscapes will be discussed: material, vernacular, and symbolic. These socio-spatial outcomes are incorporated into the interplay of production and consumption, and offer a tangible way to structure the representation of heritage landscape in Lijiang within the wider context informed by the commodification and politicization of tourism.

6   Landscapes of hegemony

Commodification and the
socio-spatial transformation
of Lijiang

This chapter examines the commodification of Lijiang's heritage landscapes and the socio-spatial transformation of the town. Our intention is to provide an analysis of how heritage landscapes in Lijiang Ancient Town are commodified as tourism development progresses, and how the resulting socio-spatial transformations lead to a museumization of heritage. We argue that hegemony is strong because the commodified landscapes are not only the outcomes of policymakers' visions of turning Lijiang Ancient Town into a thriving tourist attraction but also they have the consent of the majority of the locals who have been persuaded to embrace this same goal. As we will show in this chapter, commodification can bring about substantial economic returns to investors and satisfy tourist consumers. For in-migrant Han private enterprise (that runs many of the shops and guesthouses) and the indigenous Naxi, this state of affairs is acceptable and, in some cases, viewed as an inevitable outcome of modernization as Lijiang Ancient Town's contact with the global economy becomes more entrenched. As Lijiang transforms, the hegemony of the state authorities at the national/provincial levels and private enterprise at the local level strengthens.[1]

The socio-spatial transformation of Lijiang is evident in the material, vernacular, and symbolic landscapes of the ancient town. Daily commerce in Lijiang has almost totally given way to tourist-oriented businesses. Hundreds of residential buildings have been adaptively reused as souvenir shops or tourism services. Many elements of Naxi vernacular landscape such as attire, Naxi music, and Dongba hieroglyphics have acquired exchange value and are being sold in the tourism marketplace. What commodification has done to Lijiang is to effectively separate the contents of the ancient town (the people, their way of life, and their history) from the forms (how these are represented). Since hegemony entails a dialectical outcome (see Chapter 2), we also discuss how locals buck this trend and how they have become marginalized as a result. Since tourism is so pervasive, we argue that the socio-spatial transformation in Lijiang may, in the end, lead to a museumization of heritage.

This chapter commences with a documentation of the trajectory of the town's commercial change to show how spatial transformation occurred over time, providing an analysis of the mechanisms that account for the current shop distribution in the town. Subsequently, the chapter explores the commodification of three forms of heritage landscapes – material, vernacular, and symbolic – to reveal the power of capital and to show how Lijiang residents are brought into line. The final part discusses how Lijiang Ancient Town is "museumized."

The scope of commodification in Lijiang

Historically, Lijiang Ancient Town was a commercial venue for town residents and peasants who live in the vicinity. Many peasants gathered at Sifang Square to sell agricultural products such as eggs, poultry, or firewood and charcoal, and buy necessities such as salt, sugar, salted vegetables, and wine. The humdrum of daily commerce at Sifang Square was captured in celluloid by Joseph Rock in the 1920s. Figure 6.1 presents a glimpse of the daily buzz at the square. Goullart (1955:19) described Sifang Square shops in the mid 1940s as "rather dark and mean" and that they "had no plate-glass windows but only wooden counters, facing the street, with shelves below for the display of goods." He also mentioned that "the market-place began to function only in the afternoon. In the morning both the market-place and streets were deserted" (Goullart 1955:20; see also Guo and He 1999; Mu 1997; Lijiang Office for Editing Local History 1997). A survey carried out in 1987 (Yunnan Institute of Designing 1987:10) indicated that the square had not changed its function: "Sifang Square was a market for primary products. The total number of fixed stalls in the market counted on December 8, 1987 was 147, among which the vegetable ones were majority." Apart from Kegong Pavilion on the square, the residential houses around the square were utilized for shops on the ground floor and for residence on the upper floor.

Figure 6.1 Sifang Square in the 1920s. Source: Rock (1947), with permission from Harvard University Press. Every effort has been made to contact all copyright holders but please contact the Press if you have any queries.

It was very much a lived space of the Naxi people, a core for the people to congregate.

Beginning in 1990s, dramatic changes took place. Data collected for 2000 (Yamamura 2004), 2002 (Bao and Su 2004), and 2004 (our site survey) indicate an increasing number of tourism-oriented shops in the square and throughout Lijiang. In 2002, among the 901 shops along the main streets of the ancient town, as high as 75.7 percent, i.e. 682 shops sold tourist products such as souvenirs (Bao and Su 2004). The number of shops serving a mixed clientele of locals and tourists was 195 and that of resident-oriented shops 24, the proportion being 21.6 percent and 2.6 percent, respectively (Table 6.1). Considering the commercial transformation in the town between 2000 and 2002, Bao and Su (2004:431) argued that:

> the number of shops rose sharply (in the town) and the shops added served only tourists; resident-oriented shops gradually withdrew in the main streets in accordance with the rapid expansion of tourist-oriented shops; the houses in well-located Dongda street and Sifang Square were carefully divided into different units to accommodate increasing tourism businesses.

This tourism-oriented commercial environment further intensified. By 2004, the total number of shops had increased to 1,215, i.e. 34.8 percent higher than that in 2002. As shown in Table 6.1, the main increase was in shops selling souvenirs,

Table 6.1 Types of shops, 2002 and 2004

Shops	2002	2004
Tourist-oriented shops		
Souvenir	367	575
Ethnic costume	101	167
Local specialties	79	105
Bar	44	51
Guesthouse	37	49
Book/CD shop	23	15
Tourism service	22	23
Hotel	7	9
Naxi Music Hall	2	2
General shops		
Clothing	90	73
Restaurant	59	65
Grocery	34	45
Clinic	12	7
Resident services	24	29
Total	901	1,215

Source: authors' data, Bao and Su (2004).

ethnic costume, and local specialities. Put together, these three types of shops accounted for 69.7 percent of all the shops surveyed in 2004, in comparison with 60.7 percent in 2002.

Figure 6.2 further shows that the shops that are popular with tourists are in the main tourist thoroughfares like Sifang Square and Dongda Street.

A typical case of Lijiang's development can be found in Bayi Street. In 2002, 80 percent of the buildings along the street were used as residences. By 2004, the Southern Commercial District had been completed, incorporating many hotels (see Figure 4.1). As a key route linking the Southern Commercial District to Sifang Square, Bayi Street saw more than 80 percent of its buildings switch to tourism businesses. The transformation of Bayi Street is a macrocosm of the radical changes in Lijiang as a result of the tourism boom.

CWHMC and LTB were also responsible for the touristification of many side streets in Lijiang. In order to ease the tourist jam around Sifang Square, the

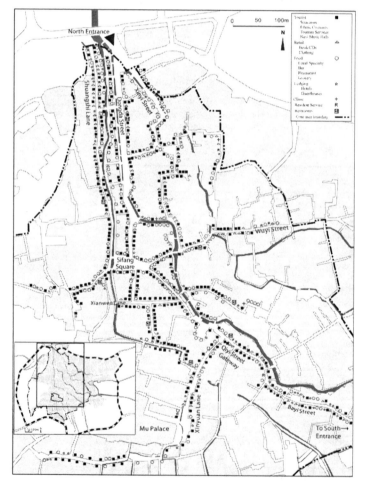

Figure 6.2 Shop distribution in Lijiang Ancient Town. Source: authors' survey.

town entrance and Dongda Streets, CWHMC turned 10 courtyard houses into "working units" to display Naxi ethnic culture, architectural wisdom, and craft skills. Called the "entering Naxi family" program, the houses were dispersed across different corners of the town in order to siphon off the tourist traffic from the main attractions. As a result, tourists who want to visit these houses have to leave the core area. As Respondent GO2 explained,

> The main purpose of this program is to invite true Naxi cultural practitioners and craft persons into the town. In these houses, they can display Naxi culture. Another purpose is to scatter tourist flows. After they enter into the town, tourists mainly gather in Sifang Square. It is too crowded. When tourists head for these working units, they need to pass over some [Naxi] living areas. Only by this way [sic] can tourists really and slowly experience Naxi people's ancient town and ethnic culture.

A close look at the shop distribution of Lijiang will show how economics shapes the town's commercial landscape. Table 6.2 provides details about shop distribution in six main streets of Lijiang Ancient Town. Clearly, souvenir shops outnumber the rest. There are very few shops serving the residents. This has caused much inconvenience to the residents, as they have to travel miles to the new city in order to do their daily shopping.

In the town, rent is an important economic mechanism to shape shop distribution. A dense flow of tourists translates into high rents. Cuiwen Lane, Sifang Square, Dongda Street are some examples of high rentals. As a businessperson (Respondent OM5) mentioned, "a shop at the town entrance is leased at a rent of 400,000 [Chinese yuan] per year. What a whopping price! If it were in

Table 6.2 Shop distribution on the main streets of Lijiang, 2004

	Dongda Street	Sifang Square	Shuangshi Lane	Qiyi Street Gateway	Xianwen Lane	Xinyuan Lane
Souvenir	46	21	55	78	71	42
Ethnic costume	30	14	21	28	5	7
Local specialties	22	7	8	25	8	8
Bars	0	12	0	0	0	2
Guesthouse	3	1	11	1	2	3
Book/CD shop	2	2	0	1	0	3
Tourism service	4	0	4	1	1	2
Hotel	0	0	0	0	0	0
Naxi Music Hall	2	0	0	0	0	0
Clothing	4	0	5	5	2	5
Restaurant	4	3	1	3	0	0
Grocery	7	3	3	6	2	0
Resident service	3	1	9	9	1	0
Habitation	0	0	4	3	13	2

Source: authors' data.

another location, the rent could be less than 40,000 [per year]." Respondent OM6 recounted the story of a shop in Sifang Square:

> [I]ts rent is now 200–250,000 [Chinese yuan] per year. Previously, it was not so high. Initially, we took the shop at an annual rent of 40,000. Later on, the owner changed and the rent rose to 120,000. Some investors speculated on the shop so that the rent jumped up to the current amount.

As rents rise, many shops have become displaced: "the big shops can make huge profits and the small shops like ours can generate very limited returns" (Respondent OM2). The shop owners who cannot earn enough profit have to sell or transfer their license to others.[2]

Apart from the number and distribution of shops in the town, we also investigated the license ownership of these shops.[3] Most of shops in the main tourist streets are controlled by individual or corporate investors from outside of Yunnan, such as from Fujian Province and Zhejiang Province, rather than by the locals: "along this street (Xinhua Street), only *this* shop is run by me and the rest [are] by outsiders" (Respondent LP9); "now very few locals are running business in the town. It's easy to differentiate them by their accents. Almost all of business persons are speaking Mandarin. Hearing their accents, you know they are not locals. Many actually speak Hokkien or Zhejiang dialect" (Respondent OM6). Official data from CWHMC showed that in 2005, over 70 percent of shops in the town were operated by outsiders (*Yunnan Daily* 9 June 2006).

Lijiang's case is not very different from Kenya (Rosemary 1987), Gambia (Thompson *et al.* 1995), or Fiji islands (Britton 1982). Colonization by external capital is also common in many heritage sites in other parts of China, such as in Yangsuo in Guangxi (Zhang, W. 2003) and Pingyao in Shangxi (Huang 2006). In these cases, the booming local community-based tourism businesses in the initial stage of tourism development were gradually replaced by external ownership when tourist flows became large scale (Shaw and Williams 1998). Rather than live in the houses in the ancient town, Lijiang's residents are benefiting *financially* from tourism when they rent their residences to these in-migrants. This economic benefit, as discussed below, is crucial to further commodification of Lijiang.

How space is maneuvered in the ancient town is dependent on the power of capital, and the spatial outcomes illustrated so far indicate that the discourse of tourism development is hegemonic:

> Commodification is inevitable. Actually, Lijiang is commercialized. However, a lot of people are still willing to visit Lijiang.
>
> (Respondent OM11)

> What can you rely on without tourism businesses? You cannot say, enjoy the sun in the doorway. Without income, how can I do that? Everyone has their pursuit. Through tourism businesses, I can enhance my quality of life

and Lijiang can develop its economy and improve its social environment. It is the only way.

(Respondent LP12)

If you don't commercialize the town, ... tourism businesses [will go] into the new city.

(Respondent LP27)

It [commodification] is inevitable. Tourism sector includes eating, shopping, sightseeing, and transportation. Shopping is a main component. Tourists also hope to buy something in the town. It is very normal.

(Respondent DT6)

It [the town] is very much commercialized. But it is not wrong to be commercialized because people have to make money to live by and the government has to make money to promote tourism attractions. There is nothing wrong...

(Respondent IT4)

Thanks to the commercial performances, Naxi music can be well preserved and attract many people, especially young men to learn. Actually [in my view]... no one cares about commodification after a few years.

(Respondent DT3)

These respondents agree that commodification is necessary to preserve Naxi heritage and make the tourism industry possible. For them and many others, commodification is expected.

Owing to tourism, residential homes and Naxi lived culture have acquired exchange value. The local government benefits financially; tourists enjoy themselves and, most of all, for the people of Lijiang, tourism as a means to alleviate poverty is very appealing. Economic benefits generated through commoditizing Naxi culture can help the peripheral places such as Lijiang catch up with the pace of *development* in China's coastal region. In this sense, tourism commodification spawns a remarkable coalescence of consent from the majority and gains legitimacy for both the producers of Lijiang's heritage tourism and the people who are living or lived in the ancient town.

The commodification in/of Lijiang Ancient Town thus naturalizes the discourse of development in the everyday tourism of Lijiang and becomes a hegemonic control of tourism space in the town. On the one hand, commodification allows the state, through a public–private partnership with tourism corporations, to employ the power of bureaucracy, and capital to "secure the economic foundations of its hegemony through promoting the economic interests of subaltern classes and thereby consolidating their support" (Jessop 1982:151). For the Chinese state, "development" has mainly been a hegemonic project of economic gains and rising GDP. Lijiang's speedy growth in tourist visitorship and its flourishing tourism businesses act as affirmation that tourism-driven commodification makes the project of development a reality and not merely rhetoric. Nevertheless, who really benefits from and loses in this project is veiled in Lijiang's official discourses. On the other hand, commodification also offers tourists a chance to consume and invest their imagination and meaning into the representation of heritage landscape (Chapter 5). Therefore, it is not surprising to find that Lijiang Ancient Town is beginning to look like a theme park or a themed shopping mall, with the heritage landscapes commodified to meet tourist preferences.

Before we analyze how three types of heritage landscapes – i.e. material, vernacular, and symbolic – are commodified, we qualify that hegemony is never complete, as there still exist groups of people who resist it. Disjunction will always occur among different groups, which we will elaborate in Chapter 7.

Commodified heritage landscapes

In Chapter 2, three forms of landscapes were used to categorize Lijiang's heritage landscapes: they are material, vernacular, and symbolic landscapes. Britton (1991:462) explained that the commodification of place can take two routes: the legal transfer of commercial property rights from other uses to tourism facilities or the transformation of the attributes of the place into tourism commodities. In Lijiang, the commodification of material landscapes consistently follows the first form, whereas that of vernacular and symbolic landscapes follows the second.

Material landscapes

Adaptive reuse is an effective approach in reconstructing Lijiang's material landscape. It is an entrepreneurial strategy to manage urban heritage resources and the aim is to "foster and encourage local development and employment growth" (Harvey 1989b:3). Moreover, it is "not just a practical solution to the problem of what to do with obsolete or redundant structures," but "a clear and powerful ideological statement" (Markus and Cameron 2001:139). In Lijiang, the ideological statement is profit. The houses are but well-preserved architectural shells; the ambience and functions of the conserved buildings are completely different from before because of adaptive reuse following urban conservation. Lijiang's material landscape has undergone a significant transformation into a landscape of spectacle catering to tourists' gaze and consumption (Figure 6.3). While the façade is beautiful to gaze at, Naxi daily life in the buildings has all but disappeared and the ancient town has become a sanitized place that masks many social conflicts with regard to the Naxi community.

To maintain architectural attractiveness, CWHMC has enacted strict codes so as to tidy up the façades of buildings in order to highlight unique Naxi architecture. This is to the exclusion of modern architectural styles. In addition, CWHMC regulates the use of the houses, especially those along the main streets which tourists use frequently. For instance, shop owners cannot place advertisements and goods outside of their shops because this will efface the beautiful architecture or hide it from view. When an official in CWHMC required a shop owner to remove an awning, her reason was that the shield could adversely affect tourists'

Figure 6.3 A landscape of spectacle in Lijiang Ancient Town. The very high wall has been inscribed with Dongba pictographic words. It was built by the local government so that tourists would have a good photograhic spot to capture their visit to Lijiang. Source: authors' photo.

enjoyment of Naxi architecture. Local authorities deploy aesthetic design codes to instruct and regulate architectural construction and restoration. The outcome is that the material landscape becomes disciplined and homogenized and hides away its variegated origins by selectively incorporating certain features that make up a coherent visualized display. These local features, which "are always staged to appear remarkable rather than being a part of space around which everyday activities revolve," have eliminated its links with the Naxi so as to serve tourists (Edensor 1998:52).

Whereas the controls are fairly strict, shop owners still manage to advertise their ware within the building codes. Their signboards are in the Han language of Mandarin, in English, and in indigenous Dongba. In addition, shop owners will delineate their proprietary space very clearly and will chase away those whom they do not think are customers. Naxi people who used to socialize and chitchat under the eaves of the houses along the main streets are no longer able to do so. Lijiang's main streets are now commercialized public passages devoid of meaningful social interaction.

Apart from residential houses and streets, other forms of Lijiang's material landscape have also been commercialized. In Lijiang's history, canals facilitated the local residents' everyday life by being the main water source for daily usage. The intermingling of canals and streets yields "space for locals to enjoy public activities which encourage harmonious interpersonal relationships" (Yan and Li 2002:3). However, scenes of residents socializing beside the canals have gradually disappeared as tourists crowd along them to take photos or to dine *al fresco*. For instance, the bars in Cuiwen Lane and Shuangshi Lane line the banks of the West River and the small canals. Although the canals cannot be literally sold, they are commercialized in that they add aesthetic value to the bars so as to attract tourists.

Although historically canals are "culture carriers," this characteristic is gradually waning in Lijiang. For example, residents in the town were accustomed to releasing lanterns into the canals as a way to commemorate their ancestors during the Zhongyuan (Hungry Ghost) festival in mid June of the lunar calendar. In May 2000, the government-owned Naxi Cultural Development Company decided to package this festival as a tourism product in order to fully harness Lijiang's cultural resources and encourage tourist participation. The company arranged for dozens of employees to sell papier-mâché lotuses fitted with candles for a price of 10 Chinese yuan per piece. The flowers were to be floated in the canals by the tourists after they had made a wish. As a result, the Xinhua Street Residential Committee ceased to organize this annual activity for local residents after 2004. A staff member of the committee pointed out: "there is no need for us to organize this kind of activity any more since the company operates this activity every day" (informal interview). A local resident (Respondent O2) commented that "now every day is Zhongyuan festival; the cultural atmosphere is destroyed." However, a manager of the company (Respondent L8) held a different viewpoint:

> This problem is not about the concept of the festival, but how you understand it. ... We are only concern how to encourage tourists to take part in our traditional activities in the long term.... If we didn't embark on this project commercially, no one would have the chance to see it any more. In my opinion, the cultural industry is to preserve the culture by using economic means.

To the local residents, the event does not have cultural significance any more. As Respondent O2 pointed out, "we don't celebrate the traditional festivals [in the town] any more." By commercializing the annual ritual into an everyday practice for tourists, tourism has adulterated tradition and rendered the cultural values attached to the canals meaningless.

Even central public spaces are not spared. As we stressed before, Sifang Square was a meeting point for town residents and villagers around the town to buy and sell daily necessities. It was an everyday place for the Naxi. Described as a bazaar by some, it was a prosperous market selling local products and offered obvious convenience to the town residents. The planners in charge of Lijiang's urban conservation advised the relocation of the market because it posed a pollution threat to the town's environment (Yunnan Institute of Designing 1987). Following this advice, the local government forced all vendors and hawkers in the market to move away so that the square would not be "dirty" any more. Now it has become a clean and vacant area for the tourists to gather to watch traditional dances, take a ride on a peasant workhorse through the ancient town's streets, and to buy their souvenirs (Figure 6.4). In the evenings, tourists can sit at the cafes around the square and take in the view of the historic landscape, which is enhanced by strategically placed floodlights. The shops around the square have also changed their wares in favor of tourists' expectations rather than the local residents' needs and wants.

This change has made the locals unhappy. A young Naxi (Respondent LP5) commented:

> I feel Sifang Square possesses all the characteristics of an ancient town ... almost ideal, like those towns projected in movies and on television. Now it is too commodified and the current architectural decoration [the lights that enhance the beauty of the buildings makes the town] quite different from the past .... I feel a little lost right now.

If the younger generation feel "lost," the elderly feel worse. They say they feel displaced. The square has become "elsewhere." It is tourists who have replaced the Naxi as the main users of the square. When the elderly would sit at the square to chitchat and commune, tourists would come with their cameras to take pictures.

Figure 6.4 Sifang Square in 2004. This photo was taken on 1 July 2004 and the angle is similar to that taken by Rock (1947; see Figure 6.1). The square was congested, but most people are not of Naxi origin. Most are tourists. Source: authors' photo.

Unhappy that they are zooified, the elderly have moved to more peripheral locations in order to have some privacy.

The space of Sifang Square is also highly disciplined as it comes under surveillance by CWHMC. Security guards hired by CWHMC deter vendors and thieves from harassing tourists in the square and along the main tourist streets. During our fieldwork, we witnessed several instances of security guards chasing after thieves within the square. In the view of the local authorities, Sifang Square should be free from social disorder. As the focus of Lijiang Ancient Town, it should give the image of a utopia that is peaceful and ordered so that tourists can enjoy heritage in comfort, albeit as a utopia filled with commercial transactions.

The meanings of Lijiang's material landscape are not tied to Lijiang Ancient Town; they are floating signifiers of a hybridized culture which embodies both the signs of Naxi heritage and elements of global consumer culture that seeks after pleasure, nostalgia, and enjoyment. For instance, some real estate developers from Zhejiang and Kunming started to invest in commercial districts (including Yuhe Lodge and Southern Commercial District) nearby the town after 2003. To ensure that the tourism business would be minimally affected, the developers went out of their way to create a compatible heritage ambience to the ancient town. They incorporated three important heritage symbols – i.e. canals, bridges, and flagstone streets – into the projects.

Architectural façades in these districts also replicate those in the ancient town. The deliberate imitation conveys a continuation of the ancient town and synthesizes the town's symbolic heritage value into a new development in order to persuade tourists to accept the imagined landscape. In one advertisement, the developers propose that Yuhe Lodge is the rebirth of Lijiang Ancient Town (*Lijiang Daily* 8 April 2004). Ironically, many indigenous residents in this area were displaced to the new city as new simulated buildings replaced their traditional houses. These simulated landscapes are a product of "capitalist enterprise that cater to demands for goods and services that serve as instruments of entertainment, … self-cultivation, ornamentation, social positionality, and so on" (Scott 2000:12). Thus, Naxi heritage can be converted into commodified signs and Lijiang's material landscape is no more than a mythical invention construed by the practitioners of a dominant mass culture.

Vernacular landscapes

Apart from the material landscapes, tourism developers have also converted many Naxi cultural elements into tourist products. These include the vernacular language, Dongba hieroglyphics, Dongba ritual worship dances, the horse-drawn caravan along Tea Horse Road, Naxi costume, and Naxi music.

Since the adoption of Mandarin as the medium of instruction in schools during Mao Zedong's time, the Dongba language has been slowly disappearing. Only a few dongbas (priests) can speak the language. However, because it is unique, it has been revived. Scholars who can still read Dongba pictography have laboriously copied religious scripts to keep the language alive for the Naxi. Many work with the Dongba Cultural Institute. As a distinct emblem of Naxi culture, Dongba pictographic language is one of the first to be commodified. It can be found on many souvenirs such as T-shirts and silver trinklets to remind tourists of the uniqueness of Lijiang Ancient Town. For instance, shops selling silverware offer to inscribe Naxi words on demand. Translated from Mandarin proverbs, they mostly express greetings: "People come here mainly to seek for memorabilia. If the silverware shows the sign of local culture through Dongba pictographic words, they are happy. They buy it for a memory" (Respondent OM2). Ironically, silver is an import. Historically, Lijiang was known for its copper. Now the copper industry in the town has been replaced by silver because of higher profits. In November 2004, 96 silver souvenir shops could be found in the town, more than 80 percent of which were operated by in-migrants from Dali, Fujian, and Kunming. Although Naxi people seldom use silver ornaments, tourists are told that Naxi society uses silver to protect babies from bad luck and brides traditionally wear silver if they desire a happy marriage (Respondent OM2). This invented cultural meaning is so persuasive that even young local people believe that Lijiang once had a silver industry in its history.

In Lijiang, religious dance is used in worship in the Dongba religion and was totally banned during Mao's reign. In 2000, the managers of Dongba Gong (the Dongba Temple) invited a group of dongbas to stay in the town to perform the dance for tourists. Since then, the dance has been modified for stage performances. Its form has been simplified and shortened so that the dongba and his apprentices can perform in front of tourists every night. Although people in Dongba Gong insist that their performance is authentic, the religious meanings of the worship dance are gone: "I tell our audience it [the performance] is authentic and original. It is not true. But I have no choice. I have to adapt the original to attract tourist. We have no choice" (Respondent LP16). Dongba Gong may be the only place in the world where the religious dance is practiced but even this, as part of Naxi vernacular landscape, has been commoditized.

While the ritual dance is still a popular attraction, it has come under threat from other performance shows. Realizing the huge potential in Lijiang's tourism market, a tourism company from Shenzhen in Guangdong Province produced *Lishuijinsha* to provide tourists with a comprehensive enjoyment of Yunnan ethnic cultures. The show is a spectacle and purely a product for tourists' entertainment. As Respondent OM7, a manager of the dance show said,

> We mainly focus on ethnic dance. *Lishuijinsha* is an entertainment activity. It doesn't have deep historical responsibility or any duty with regard to propaganda [for CCP]. It is culture for tourist pleasure and relaxation. It tells tourists something about ethnic tradition, attire and culture. We hope tourists feel pleased and enjoy it. That is our aim.

Because of its attractiveness, *Lishuijinsha* has become the top earner of tourism revenue in Lijiang. It also exerts great pressure on Dongba Gong, as most tour guides prefer to recommend *Lishuijinsha* to their customers. No matter how much people applaud the performance in Dongba Gong as authentic and culturally significant, Lijiang's tourism market still favors *Lishuijinsha*. The real forms of ethnic culture in Lijiang and the rest of Yunnan are condensed into a shallow and superficial performance show akin to a product manufactured in an assembly line. The distinct cultural lines of the many ethnic groups in Yunnan are lost to the tourists who are there to be entertained. If the ritual performance in Dongba Gong, as a form of tradition invented and staged to present Naxi unique culture to tourists, still embodies historical components, the glitzy show of *Lishuijinsha* is a pure commodity.

Many locals, especially intellectuals, have realized the potential of the tourism market in spurring people to actively learn local culture. Naxi music is one example. Before the establishment of the PRC, Naxi music was a daily entertainment, enjoyed and played by local intellectuals for the village people. After 1949, the local government suppressed local music in favor of a socialist identity. Accordingly, the authorities discouraged them from playing Naxi music. As a result, Naxi music was only used for accompaniment in funerals. The musicians were marginalized and no one wanted to take up the art. It is Xuan Ke who discovered the huge value of Naxi music in attracting tourists. He packaged the funeral music into a successful tourism attraction and earned millions of Chinese yuan from tourists. An increasing number of young people are following suit. A local (Respondent LP1) said, "young people definitely refuse to learn it [Naxi music] if there are no economic returns." The successful story of Naxi music convinces many locals that tourism commodification can revive Naxi culture in the town and awaken a sense of pride among the local community when millions of tourists recognize the uniqueness of Naxi culture.

Not only are various elements of Lijiang's vernacular landscape highly commercialized inventions but also the bodies of Naxi women have gone under the tourist gaze. To display Naxi culture, the local government ordered all female tourism employees working in the town to wear Naxi-style attire. The rationale is that those benefiting from tourism have to contribute to heritage production. The most popular attire they wear has gone through several improvements to highlight the original cultural elements *and* fit contemporary appreciation standards. Without doubt, the distinctive design and color of the costume catches many tourists' attention; the omnipresence of the costume in the town verifies that Naxi culture does exist in situ. The order to wear the traditional costume has now become normative for the female workers. Respondent OM2 commented,

> [Wearing Naxi attire] is the government's order. You would be fined if they find you don't wear. Initially, I felt very uneasy. Now I feel uncomfortable if I don't wear it. I got accustomed. Take the headband as example. You will feel cold without it. It can keep me warm actually .... I certainly refuse to wear it when I am home. I wear Bai costume.

It is worth considering two facets of moral hegemony in this quotation. On the one hand, the state tries to persuade those female workers to accept its order.

The consent from this special group is seemingly achieved as some unwittingly get accustomed to Naxi attire. Foucault (1979) calls this the cultivation of a docile body among the governed through the enforcement of discipline and punishment. Female workers' Naxi attire, together with their body, perpetuate women's subordination to the masculine tourism gaze and eroticizes native women. As Waitt (1997:57) puts it, "patriarchal power relations are ... reinforced by the mode of gender representation." On the other hand, these workers boycott this gendered hegemony after they return to their personal space outside of the scope of tourism discipline. They dress either in their own ethnic costume or casual apparel like jeans and T-shirts. The alternative attire is a way to separate them from the disciplined spaces of tourism commodification and to express their identity through the body as a contested space. It is a covert means of resistance to the dominant ideals of the local authorities and international and domestic male tourists.

Writing about the tourism-driven commodification of culture, Cohen (1988:382) argues that commodification does not suggest that all "meaning is gone"; "new meanings may be added to old ones, which persevere into the new situation." There is some truth in these statements. Nevertheless, we suggest that Cohen neglects some important questions about "new meanings": namely, who invents them and for what purposes. In Lijiang, we observe that the local government and tourism corporations add new meanings to various Naxi cultural forms and invent traditions, less to enable the locals to "maintain a meaningful local or ethnic identity," as Cohen suggests, than to persuade the locals to accept a scenario of commodification because of the economic benefits they can derive from it. This observation resonates with the work by Hobsbawm and Ranger (1983) on the invention of tradition. They argue that states engage in invention though "a process of formalization and ritualization" to establish relations of authority and legitimize political elites' power (1983:4). The invented traditions in Lijiang, such as wearing silver, playing music, releasing lanterns into the canals, writing Dongba hieroglyphics, performing religious dances, and other cultural activities, aim to give the commodified vernacular landscapes "social continuity and natural law as expressed in history" (Hobsbawm and Ranger 1983:2) so that the locals and tourists may accept that these landscapes are still meaningful. Furthermore, these invented traditions help the state and corporations to maintain hegemony, along with suitably tailored discourses in heritage preservation.

Another point about the commodification of vernacular landscapes is the strength and adaptability of living traditions. Hobsbawm and Ranger (1983:8) argue that "where the old ways are alive, traditions need be neither revived nor invented." In other words, there is no chance to invent a tradition when it is still alive and ordinary people stick to it. In Lijiang, this is true for local Naxi food. As residents in the old town and new city keep cooking and eating traditional food at home or in the restaurants, the state and tourism corporations express little interest in Naxi food nor attempt to alter its flavors for tourists' sake. For those tourists who want to try authentic Naxi food, they can easily do so either in the ancient town or new city, leading to a limited commercial space for invented Naxi food. Whether invented traditions are created because of a wane of the old traditions is factually immaterial. Tourism provides new opportunities for entrepreneurs to take advantage of the situation. On the part of the ordinary local inhabitant, there is a genuine effort to keep alive Naxi traditions, regardless of whether they are commodified or not. Hence, it is unfortunate but realistic to say that, in Lijiang, cultural revival does not really signify a return to real Naxi culture.

Symbolic landscapes

Besides the material and vernacular landscapes of Lijiang, symbolic landscapes also help tourists to experience Lijiang. By way of aesthetic and semiotic associations, tourists can feel that their expectations about Lijiang have been met. Semiotic association is achieved by means of consumption of brands. For example, souvenir shops in Lijiang use the Bunong bell to symbolize the hardships Naxi tea-traders had to put up with in the Tea-Horse Caravan Route.[4] A manager in a shop that sells Bunong bells asserts,

> Historically, it is about the tale of Tea Horse Road; culturally, the words and devices inscribed on the bell are symbolically related to Lijiang Ancient Town. Tourists can imagine [the caravan route and the bell]... can help them to remember. Tourists will carry nice reflections of the town. The bell is about place. It's meaningless in Beijing or Shanghai. Only in Lijiang the bell has significant meaning.

> (Respondent OM13)

The Dongba hieroglyphics inscribed on the bell symbolize the uniqueness of Lijiang's heritage. The bell has been endowed with its own personality and used to articulate the place of Lijiang and the culture of Naxi people in a symbolic form. Hence, tourism firms invest Lijiang-related meaning to their brands and persuade their customers to accept these interpretations about the town and local culture.

In addition, some daily activities that have completely disappeared in Lijiang Ancient Town have been resurrected to become once again part of Lijiang's symbolic landscape. A good example is horseback riding (Figure 6.5). Although horseback riding was the main means of movement between Yunnan and Tibet before 1949 (see Chapter 4), it totally disappeared after 1950 because of modern transportation technologies. In 2002, the Naxi Cultural Development Company reintroduced horseback riding into the town and the business centered on Sifang Square as the beginning and end point of a ride through Lijiang Ancient Town. The purpose of this project, according to a manager of this company (Respondent LP8), "is not to make profit, but display the culture of the horse-drawn caravan." On the website of this company, this project is said to "depict an idea about the images of Tea Horse Road caravan and offer a chance to travel through the ages and experience the authentically rich culture of caravan created by Naxi ancestors" (Naxi Cultural Development Company n.d.:1). Without doubt, the target

Figure 6.5 Horse ride in Sifang Square. A domestic tourist wears caravan attire and holds a replica gun while he listens to the guide tell the history of the tea route. Source: authors' photo.

is tourists. Tourists have to pay 5 Chinese yuan to take photos with the horses and 35 yuan for a half-hour ride through the town. An employee suggested that "the business is not bad" (informal interview). By utilizing recognizable visual signs associated with traditional caravan culture and interpreting them in terms of indigenous meanings, the project symbolizes the ethnic harmony between Naxi and Tibet (Chapter 4) and the historical roots of Lijiang Ancient Town. By inviting tourists to enjoy it, it demonstrates "how cultural integrity and profitability can be both coexistent and interdependent" (Mason 2004:849).

Horseback riding as a tourist activity runs the risk of distorting the real caravan culture in Lijiang. Although this project can help tourists to imagine Lijiang's history through physical interaction with the horses and employees dressed like caravan members, it totally masks the torturous lives of Naxi ancestors who struggled to survive the treacherous road. The romaticization of the caravan's living conditions mirrors what Palmer (2005:16) calls a tendency in heritage tourism to "reduce the complexities of history to a kind of easily digestible shorthand."

In addition, the commodification of the horse-drawn caravan is potentially damaging for Naxi heritage. Most Naxi born after 1949 have no knowledge of the caravan route. The commodification of this part of their heritage may in fact harm local knowledge as the current generation will begin to look upon the Tea-Horse Caravan Route through rose-tinted glasses similar to the tourists.

Tourism commodification has converted Lijiang's heritage landscapes into various forms of visual expression and performance. It gives Naxi culture and Lijiang Ancient Town a new strength and legitimacy to avoid vanishing in the face of modernization and globalization. It potentially renews the Naxi cultural forms that have disappeared due to Mao's socialist regime and the intrusion of modern development. Auxiliary commodities such as gifts and souvenirs can spread the local image of Lijiang to a wide audience and entrench its distinctiveness in the mass media and in the minds of potential tourists. Commodification does not necessarily generate a new, emergent culture distinct from the original one. Rather, it prompts people – locals and outsiders – to invent traditions and incorporate them into tourism businesses (Medina 2003). However, as shown by the commodification of material, vernacular, and symbolic landscapes in Lijiang, heritage landscapes are faced with the fate that their forms and contents are separated. The expressive forms of heritage – i.e. architectural façade, dance, costume, and Dongba hieroglyphics – remain original and have critical relations with the past and with Naxi culture, but the contents of heritage are completely stylized and carefully designed for tourists. This separation leads to the depthlessness of heritage products and an easily manipulated representation of Lijiang's heritage by those who are profit minded. It also results in the museumization of Lijiang's heritage landscapes, a point discussed in the next section.

The museumization of Lijiang

Although the physical elements of Lijiang's historical landscape such as the streets, canals, and courtyards are still well preserved in the town, the lived culture – human activities – have been totally altered as a result of tourism commodification. The result is the museumization of heritage landscapes in Lijiang Ancient Town.

Relph (1976:101) points out that museumization is to preserve, reconstruct, and idealize history in heritage sites: "such places strive for accuracy of replication in their visible detail, but so long as they meet the general demand for historical atmosphere it does not seem to matter whether they are genuine relics or complete fakes and facades." Similarly, Getz (1994) argues that developers try very hard to restore the details directly visible to the eye to create a historic atmosphere for tourists instead of accentuating the authenticity of historic tradition, not to mention enhancing the tourist's understanding of the cultural and historic landscapes cherished by the locals. Commodification leads directly to the dissociation of public space and residents' social activities, resulting in the gradual disappearance of traditional cultural significance (Su and Huang 2005). The heritage landscape in Lijiang Ancient Town has thus been turned into an elite landscape disconnected from the local community by officials, planners, and developers.

The townscape under tourism commodification is clearly different from the traditional business environment in Lijiang Ancient Town. Goullart (1955:33) described the bars and open markets in the town in early 1940s, depicting the relations between the customers and the shop owners:

> Anyone could have a drink at any shop, but some villagers acquired preferences for particular shops. These regular and faithful customers grew intimate with the lady owner and always gave her the first option on whatever they were bringing to the market for sale. Similarly the lady favored them with special discounts on whatever they wanted to buy from her. Actually their relations were beyond clients and shop-owner. The lady also acted as their broker, banker, postmaster and confidante.

From Goullart's description, the social networks were informal and intimate. Perhaps it may have been romanticized by Goullart but from the accounts of the local people, the Naxi are quite tight knit. However, with the rapid growth of tourism since 1997, the town has changed dramatically under the influence of the tourism industry and foreign businessmen (Table 6.3).

Table 6.3 A comparison of Lijiang's commercial landscape in different periods

	Present situation under tourism commodification (2004)	*Tea-horse route period (around 1940)*
Number of shops	Over 1,200	Over 1,200 at the peak
Shop size	Apart from hotels, the shops are small with limited fixed capital and liquidity	Large-scale businesses and over 20 shops had branches outside the town
Main commodities	Tourism products	Daily necessities, wine, and copper ware
Main customers	Domestic and international tourists	Peasants, town inhabitants, merchants from Tibet, Kunming, and Dali
Features of customers	Lack of trust for merchants; transient customers base with strong purchasing power but limited range of purchases	Strong customer loyalty; buying goods necessary for daily use
Features of merchants	Mainly non-locals with poor credibility; poor relationship with their clients	Mainly locals with credibility; rapport with their clients
Role of the town	Tourist attraction; carrier of tourism businesses	A junction in the Tea-Horse Route; a carrier of trade
Nature of the town	Tourist city	Commercial city; suitable for living

Source: adapted from Su and Huang (2005:410–411).

The physical elements of public space like its streets, canals, and courtyards still exist in the town, but the human activities that make up Lijiang's vernacular landscape have totally altered. Local inhabitants have left the town to settle down in the new city for a number of reasons. Congestion and noise have led to the deterioration of the quality of public spaces, as tourists seem everywhere. A local resident (Respondent LP18) told us a story of his neighbor: "There is a bar directly opposite to our houses and it opens until 1 to 2 in the morning. It creates so much noise that my neighbor had to move out even though he cherished his house very much." In addition, "Previously, you could buy anything you need in the main streets. But now, all you can find are tourist things. If I need to buy daily necessities, I have to take a bus and walk for a long time" (Respondent LP3).

The number of town residents moving out is huge. In the Fourth National Census in 1990, 6,269 households or 25,379 residents lived in the town, whereas in 2000, only 13,779 residents remained (Zong 2005). Some highly touristic streets have been totally colonized by migrants. Take the district of Xinyi Street as an example. Zong (2005) reported that this district had 578 households in 1986, whereas the number dropped to less than 100 at the end of 2003. The social landscape of the town has certainly changed because of tourism. This is a tourism-driven process of demographic displacement as migrants replace the indigenous residents. We argue that the increasing flows of capital and affluent tourists escalate the value of residential houses and encourage the locals to rent their houses to migrants for tourism businesses or habitation. Many new consumption forms such as bars, guesthouses, shops, restaurants, and music hall largely exclude Naxi people's daily activities from the town and dominate the town's space of production and consumption. Lijiang Ancient Town has been transformed from a Naxi neighborhood into an exclusive enclave marked by "a proliferation of corporate entertainment and tourism venues" (Gotham 2005b:1102). In this tourist enclave, producers and consumers build an amorphous "partnership" to tacitly retain staged Naxi heritage landscapes and commodify them for profit. The staged landscapes aim to present Lijiang's heritage and please tourists. They are not different from items displayed in a museum.

As more and more residents settle down in the new city, many Naxi have expressed anxiety over the breakdown of their community space in the ancient town:

> As far as the current situation is concerned, the number of aboriginal residents in the town is decreasing. This historic town is nothing but an empty shell ....In the past we frequently came across our friends and acquaintances on the street; now we can't be sure if we can run into one another because many of them have moved out into the new city.
>
> (Respondent O2)

> Since the people moving in are total strangers with different social backgrounds, you can't trust them too easily.
>
> (Respondent LP18)

The residents may have left, but they continue to drop by the town occasionally. A former resident described the ancient city as if it were a foreign land, because, every time he went back something else had changed (Respondent LP24). Although their sentiments and nostalgic feelings may motivate them to return to the town to "visit," when they return, the former residents are like the tourists. Driven by tourism commodification, economic relations have replaced social relations in this Naxi community.

Rapoport (1982) argues that the physical environment provides cues for social behavior. People rely on these cues to justify or interpret social dynamics in order to react appropriately. Historically, urban public spaces in Lijiang Ancient Town, including the streets, canals, and the square, have significant psychological impacts on the inhabitants because they allow for socialization and enhance the peoples' sense of place. However, these spaces have been commodified and rendered "unusable." Lijiang can be said to have experienced museumization (Getz 1994), where outwardly the town is historically correct in its architecture and layout but the city is no more than an empty shell.

Conclusions

This chapter has explored commodification at length. Commodification has become "naturalized" and spontaneous, with the local residents, the state, and enterprise expecting it to happen because it is legitimate for the reason that it brings about wealth for the town. Writing about the transformation of Singapore's Chinatown, Yeoh and Kong (1994:20) argue that it was "not only perceived as a means of improving living conditions for people but as both prerequisite for the tangible proof of larger forces of socio-economic development and progress." Lijiang, likewise, can be similarly explained.

We have also argued in this chapter that with commodification, there are consequences. Spatially, local residents have to give way to commerce, which can command a higher price for the houses within the town. The amount of tourist traffic in the town and the gearing of services and goods toward tourists mean that the locals find the town unattractive as a place to live in. Community ties have disappeared in the town. In addition, the buildings have maintained their unique architecture but the physical form alone does not constitute a community. Even in terms of activities carried out by the locals, they no longer reflect daily or regular activities undertaken by the Naxi. Many of these have been commercialized for the tourists. Hence, tourists consume a constructed authenticity.

Commodification undercuts the visual expression of Naxi culture, as it converts everything in the town, and even the town itself, into tourism commodities for sale. As Harvey (1989a:102) argues, commodification destroys "all traces of production in their imagery, reinforcing the fetishism that arises automatically in the course of market exchange." The commodified landscapes lack necessary connotations about "its presence in time and space" and in "the situation of the original" (Benjamin 2001:50) although they retain their forms. The separation of forms and contents thus polarizes tourism capitalism in Lijiang and turns the town into a site that fuses an outdoor shopping mall with a Disney-like heritage theme park encrusted with many signs of Naxi heritage. The primary architects of this situation are of course the state government and private enterprise, who have persuaded the Naxi that they stand to benefit from the changes. While this hegemonic discourse about development is predominant, from this chapter, there are counter-voices. The next chapter turns to discussing local agency in Lijiang's tourism landscape. The emphasis is on how the Naxi endeavor to articulate their ethnic identity and place attachment to Lijiang.

7 Local agency in heritage tourism

'[L]ocal' situations are transformed by becoming part of wider 'global' arenas and processes, while 'global' dimensions are made meaningful in relation to specific 'local' conditions and through the understandings and strategies of 'local' actors.

(Long 1996:47)

This chapter provides a detailed analysis of local agency in Lijiang's heritage tourism. Although many Naxi now live in the new city, some still work in the ancient town and many more come back for visits. It is estimated that there are still approximately 14,000 people residing in the town (Zong 2005). This chapter examines how the Naxi respond to rapid tourism development and suggests that they are not always as disenfranchised as tourism researchers working on heritage tourism often portray (Li 2006; Nash 1996). They do not always contest tourism development, nor do they view heritage tourism as negative for local society. Instead, they can see the benefits that tourism brings and will try to balance tourism incursion into their landscape by staking claims to vital spaces so that they can continue significant and meaningful activities. Nevertheless, on frequent occasions, their claims are threatened and constrained by the economic priorities set by other groups such as private enterprise and the local government.

A large number of research papers have shown that asymmetrical power relations exist between locals and tourists, or between locals and those in dominant positions like the government and global capital (e.g. Britton 1982; Greenwood 1977; Nash 1977). These asymmetrical relations leave locals in a weak position where they have to "bear the burden of adjustment economically, socially and culturally" (Joseph and Kavoori 2001:999). This chapter, however, suggests that locals are far from passive recipients in the global interplay of tourism development. We argue that locals actually assume an active role and will mediate politically and economically powerful forces with regard to the extent to which tourism development would be embraced, especially when tourism activities begin to infringe on vernacular spaces for their everyday activities (Aitchison 2001; Ateljevic 2000; Coles and Church 2007a). The neo-Gramscian approach as developed in Chapter 2 does not regard tourism simply as an important force of nationalism (see Chapter 3) and globalization to homogenize local societies (see Chapters 5 and 6); instead, it acknowledges that "local communities are not passive, and often seize upon tourism as a means of communication in order to display their existence and to establish their own power" (Lanfant 1995:6).

This chapter has three parts. First, we examine local readings of heritage tourism to reveal whether or not ordinary citizens share the ideology of the powerful. We find that a majority of locals actually endorse the hegemonic discourse of tourism development in Lijiang. In the second part, however, we show that agreement is not tantamount to submission. In this part, we explicate local agency in heritage tourism development through a series of spatial and cultural tactics. Their purpose is to "Naxisize"/"localize" Lijiang in an attempt to strengthen and rebuild their ethnic identity. Amidst commodification of their heritage, strategies that secure place attachment, reinvigorate Naxi language education, and increase local involvement in heritage tourism development act to counterbalance the Disneyfication of the town. The final part is about the policy implications for Lijiang's tourism development. We argue that the stickiest point in Lijiang's heritage tourism is to retain the Naxi lived tradition (rather than invented tradition) in the town and to bring forth an impartial distribution of tourism revenues to the Naxi community.

Locals' readings of heritage tourism

If the intention is to develop tourism in Lijiang with support from both the state and the private sector, would commodification of the ancient town mean the alienation of local Naxi from the town? Priority given to preservation of the old buildings and of Naxi culture (religion, costume, language, and music, in particular) makes it seem like practically everyone is scripted into a heritage manuscript for consumption by the tourists. If tourism is indeed the make or break of Lijiang, do the Naxi feel marginalized in the process of tourism development? This section critically addresses these questions and explores locals' readings of Lijiang's heritage tourism.

Table 7.1 summarizes the responses of the Naxi to seven possible impacts that tourism may bring to their everyday lives. According to Table 7.1, local residents do acknowledge the benefits of tourism: for instance, improved social services (cited by 79.1 percent of the local respondents) and increased employment (73 percent). Nevertheless, they also lament the costs such as increased cost of living (83 percent) and traffic congestion (83 percent). Table 7.1 implies that the Naxi have ambivalent feelings about tourism. They know that tourism development can be both positive and negative. Relating how tourism has influenced their daily life, some responses from the locals include:

> It ... widens our horizon about the world. I know that people in USA are not evil and American tourists are very kind-hearted. At least I know it. When I was young, I was told that Taiwanese are our enemies. Taiwanese are counter-revolutionary. Now I find it is not true. Taiwanese tourists gave me

Table 7.1 The perceived impacts of tourism on locals' daily life (%)

Features	Local residents (n = 200)	
	Agree	*Disagree*
Increased cost of living	83.0	17.0
Traffic congestion	83.0	17.0
Improved social services	79.1	20.1
Increased employment	73.0	27.0
Increased safety	49.0	51.0
Increased noise and pollution	43.5	56.5

Source: authors' data.

their newspaper from which I now know they are very kind. Taiwanese are after all also Chinese people.

(Respondent LP18)

Tourism increases our salary and improves the quality of life.

(Respondent LP13)

We can exchange information. I can tell tourists Lijiang's history and Naxi culture to let them understand Lijiang. In turn, I can obtain information about many places. All of us are happy and many become my friends. This is a form of communication between people and people, place and place, nation and nation.

(Respondent LP12)

I feel quite inconvenient when I walk in the town. After I bought vegetable from market and on the way home, I had to give way to tourists. They did not let us pass; instead, it is we who make way. They spent thousands of yuan visiting Lijiang. Hence, we have to give way. It is a basic courtesy, isn't it? But I did not obtain a cent from their thousands of yuan.

(Respondent LP28)

Sometimes I feel very annoyed. Why? There are so many people. Lijiang couldn't be like this. Previously it was very peaceful and I could identify the outsiders when they entered the town. Now, it is impossible. That is why I feel that the number of Naxi people [in the town] becomes less and less.

(Respondent LP19)

The above comments about the impact of tourism on the respondents' daily life complement the results in Table 7.1. The guest–host interaction provides locals with abundant information to understand places outside of China, which has been obscured by the state for a long time. Tourism development, however, also has a negative side. According to these respondents, the troubles include congestion, noise, pollution, and the disappearance of a peaceful life.

Apart from its impact on locals' daily lives, tourism also has effects on Naxi culture and social patterns. Respondents were asked to tick, on a 5-point Likert scale, how much they agreed with a few crucial statements (Table 7.2). Positive perceptions about the impact of tourism prevailed. On average, 81 percent of the respondents agreed or strongly agreed that heritage tourism contributed to Naxi cultural revival. Without tourism, the Naxi believe that traditional culture would naturally die off. A choreographer of Naxi folk dance attached to a tourism corporation (Respondent LP16) commented:

> Tourism is a theatre stage of Naxi culture. Without this stage, it cannot be displayed or known to others. In turn, the existence of Naxi culture flourishes tourism .... The staged Naxi cultural performance can help the revival and transformation of excellent traditional culture .... But tourism [also] causes the commodification of Naxi culture and adds many invented elements to it. [In the end], you don't know which is true or false.

An average of 35.5 percent of the respondents held a negative attitude towards tourism-oriented commodification as it has caused them to lose their identity, while an equal proportion (35.5 percent) did not think so. The commodification of local performing arts for tourism consumption was considered inevitable and Lijiang is not different from the Miao in Guizhou where cultural revival has depended on the number of visitors (Schein 1989).

While tourism can contribute, it would do well to reserve giving credit until a full picture is available. As we have argued in Chapter 6, any Naxi cultural revival dwells largely in the preservation of the material landscape and the visual display of the vernacular landscape. In varying degrees, the local lived culture is waning in the town as a consequence of tourism development:

> The commodification driven by outsiders is too strong. The outside culture, brought by Fujian people and Zhejiang people, as well as fakes and imitations prevail in the town. Naxi people are forced to leave Lijiang. Inside, there are very few Naxi. The town's cultural ecology does not exist any more.
>
> (Respondent LP16)

> Destructive results emerge when more and more people move out. Many cultural phenomena disappear and Naxi culture is waning. Most shops are operated by Han people. I cannot hear Naxi language when I walk along streets. The vanishing of language is troubl[ing].
>
> (Respondent O2)

The above discordant voices express meaningful messages of resistance to the economic priority of tourism in Lijiang. They are obviously concerned about the hollowing out of their lived space by supporters of tourism development.

Hence it is not unusual to find that an average of 60 percent of the respondents agreed that tourism invigorates the town. Slightly over half of the respondents felt they were never treated less than the tourists. However, more than a third

Table 7.2 Local responses to tourism impacts on Naxi culture (%)

Statement	Local residents (p = 200)				
	Strongly disagree	Disagree	Neutral	Agree	Strongly agree
Tourism helps Naxi cultural revival	1.5	4.5	13.0	52.0	29.0
Commodification causes loss of locals identity	6.5	29.0	29.0	26.0	9.5
Locals are treated like second-class citizens in contrast to tourists	16.0	34.5	19.0	17.0	13.5
The town would be a dull place without visitors	10.0	16 .0	14.5	32.0	27.5

Source: authors' data.

(39 percent) complained that they were second class citizens in their own home-town (Table 7.2). While the center of China has arguably been Beijing, its periphery is as far stretched as Mongolia and Yunnan. Ever since Lijiang acquired World Heritage Site status and experienced a deluge of tourists, it has become de-centered not only in the minds of domestic tourists about core–periphery relations in China's geography but also in redefining Lijiang's marginalization by global forces. As Boniface and Fowler (1993:57) argue, "the attempt by minorities, often ethnic minorities, to establish a political presence through the re-creation of a group identity [is] significantly based on cultural revival." In the sample of local people, 81 percent thought Lijiang is a good international attraction. The respondents seem confident of the town's attractiveness in the global tourism market and it has also become a source of pride:

I feel proud of being Naxi. We own such a beautiful town and so many people come here to see it.

(Respondent LP13)

Lijiang is an international destination indeed. All my guests said it is worth visiting. It makes me to feel proud. As a tour guide, I visited hundreds of destinations. Among all of them, Lijiang has the highest competitiveness.

(Respondent LP15).

When I was a university student in Chengdu around 1993, my classmates felt curious once they saw *laowai* [foreigners]. But I was not curious. In Lijiang, my hometown, there are many *laowai*. I got accustomed to seeing them. It seemed that my classmates did not have the same wide horizon as I although they lived in big cities.

(Respondent LP19)

What these local respondents have pointed to is the fact that tourism development enhances locals' pride in Lijiang Ancient Town and strengthens their place attachment to their hometown. In fact for many locals, Lijiang Ancient Town was and still remains an everyday place. They have an "empathetic insideness" which is articulated by Relph (1976:51–52) as "a sense of belonging to place derived from a deep respect for or knowledge of place." This sense of place makes them confident and proud about their town, their ethnicity, and even their country. The feeling of confidence and pride emanates from both ethnic and national identification.

Before we elaborate on ethnic placeness, we look at national identity in Lijiang first. Local acceptance of Chinese nationalism, as discussed in Chapter 3, is fairly widespread. More than one-third (39 percent) of our sample believed that Lijiang is important to the central government. In-depth interviews offered more insights:

> [Naxi] music does not belong to Naxi people. It is a musical form from the Central Plain. After it was introduced into Lijiang, Naxi people incorporated our own flavor into it. Eventually, it is attached a Naxi label. However, it is a culture to be shared with the Chinese nationality.[1]
>
> (Respondent LP26)

In the view of many Naxi, they are a part of Chinese culture and Naxi culture is a sub-group of this broader Chinese culture. The pride of Chinese nationalism was evident throughout our fieldwork. We found that the Naxi identified themselves as Chinese citizens (*zhongguoren*) first before they are different from other ethnic groups such as the Han or the Bai. Similarly, many of them categorized Naxi culture as part of Chinese (*zhonghua*) culture. In other words, the nation China (*zhongguo*) comes first. Although they are aware of discrimination by Han tourists, ethnic pride is never low because their unique culture is also the pride of China, just as Bali culture is to Indonesia. LTB confirms this: "the central government values the town highly. It is a World Heritage Site, a wonderful window whereby China shows something to the global world" (Respondent GO7).

Strong nationalistic emotions ease the work of the state in persuading Lijiang residents that tourism will help the ancient town. In our questionnaire, we asked to what extent locals agree that tourism development in Lijiang should go forward? According to the respondents (Table 7.3), the local government should be *applauded* for its conservation initiatives. This finding is consistent with tourists' reactions to the well-conserved material landscape of Lijiang Ancient Town. It can be concluded that the conservation of the material landscape is successful in terms of its accurate preservation and deliberate display of visible details.

Furthermore, as shown in Table 7.3, 81.5 percent of the respondents agreed or strongly agreed that the government should enact stricter regulations for urban conservation. At the same time, a majority of them (75 percent) endorsed the

Table 7.3 The role of government in heritage tourism (%)

Statement	Local residents (p = 200)				
	Strongly disagree	Disagree	Neutral	Agree	Strongly agree
Government has done well in restoring historic buildings	2.0	3.5	22.0	51.0	21.5
Government should further encourage tourism in the town	3.0	6.0	16.0	44.5	30.5
Government should enact stricter regulations for urban conservation	3.0	4.5	11.0	23.5	58.0

Source: authors' data

view that the government should further encourage tourism development. In their minds, the importance of tourism cannot be underestimated but their heritage should also not be sacrificed for tourist consumption. The question is how to achieve a win–win situation that balances tourism development with urban conservation. It seems that most locals trust the government to find an appropriate solution (Table 7.3).

These answers provide evidential support that locals have bought into the state-proffered hegemonic discourse that the positive impacts of tourism far exceed the negative ones. In fact, most of the respondents endorsed the contribution of tourism in reviving Naxi culture, which had been kept in check during Mao's socialist regime. The local government considers tourism in Lijiang as the life force that will bring economic development to this peripheral location. Without the unique ethnic composition and building styles in Lijiang, the hurdles to growth seem insurmountable. Just bordering Shangri-la, Lijiang is indeed mysterious and this discourse is evidently shared by a majority of locals. In addition, locals' readings of heritage tourism do not simply concur with the hegemonic discourse, but rather draw on their own justification to support or reject the discourse. Even though their readings are incorporated into the discourse to contribute to the construction of the hegemony of heritage tourism in Lijiang, locals' social and spatial practices concretize their justification and help them develop their own agency in heritage tourism.

Naxization: local agency in heritage tourism

The previous chapters have analyzed how tourism development shapes Lijiang's heritage landscapes. Two prominent outcomes are the museumization of heritage and the colonization of Naxi lived space. Nevertheless, Naxi people try to modulate these outcomes in their attempts to resist the dominance of tourism capital. Specifically, their agency lies in three aspects – reclaiming space for a sense of place, Naxi language education, and through their involvement in tourism development.

The purpose is to mediate Han culture and global influences. In this process, all local forces such as the museums and schools, intellectuals, and ordinary people are mobilized in a conscious upsurge of Naxi sensibility.

(Re)claiming space for a sense of place

Although there is a common denominator that ties the state, private enterprise, and locals together, alternative readings have surfaced and this is corroborated by the manner in which locals consume the townscape and transform spaces of representation into representational spaces via their spatial practices (Lefebvre 1991).

As we have argued in Chapter 2, resistance has to go beyond verbal expression and alternative readings and enter the political and economic spheres of a society in order to effectively mediate powerful forces. Consumption is one effective form of resistance. Obviously, the town does not only serve tourists. Many tourism service outlets are also used by local residents, especially the bars. Numerous bars that provide consumers with food and alcohol are found along Cuiwen Lane (see Chapter 6). Le Petit Paris, a bar owned by an Inner Mongolian and a Frenchman, offers discounts to its regular local customers. Nevertheless, not all locals can appreciate the presence of the bars. A resident commented, "I never heard of a bar when I was young. I just knew a tea shop. The reason that bars emerge is definitely to earn money from tourists. I've never been to bars" (Respondent LP23). However, the younger generation has a different opinion. Every night, they can be observed flowing into Le Petit Paris for rest and relaxation: "Personally I love Le Petit Paris very much. You can find many locals inside at night. No matter whether you know them or not, it is easy to gather together to have a drink. It is *our* place" (informal interview with a town resident; emphasis added).

Not all the bars in Lijiang share this sentiment. In fact, spaces are segmented to give priority to the tourists. These spaces of exclusion forge what Chatterton and Hollands (2003:184) conceptualize as "a socio-spatial hierarchy of winners and losers." However, "fluid mosaic[s] of resistance, made up of countless acts of defiance and self-determination" can still be found, exemplified by locals gathering in Le Petit Paris to construct their own space of consumption (Chatterton and Hollands 2003:230). Ironically, Le Petit Paris serves Western food and plays Western music and was initially designed for Western package tourists and backpackers. At a later stage, high-earning local youth became an important market for the bar owners. They saw the potential to build a local and fixed clientele to complement the floating tourist-oriented market. Even CWHMC and other governmental boards have had to tolerate the occasional conflicts between local youths and tourists at the bars for the sake of this happy compromise.

Le Petit Paris can be called a "heterogeneous space" (Edensor 2000) of coexistence between the tourists and locals. The tourist gaze is inverted because locals use this space to moderate tourists' colonization of their lived space, effectively reconfiguring spatial exclusion (Sibley 1995). The blurred boundaries at Le Petit Paris provide a chance for the locals to add Naxi character and presence to the manicured tourism landscape of Cuiwen Lane. A full discussion of the recolonization of space along this road can be found in Su and Teo (2008).

Another example to illustrate the struggle to enlarge Naxi sense of place can be found in some residents' insistence on living in the ancient town rather than in the new city. Naxi people have developed their own building style by mixing local with Han and Tibetan architectural styles. The town's architecture is characterized by innovative adaptations that can cope with earthquakes, provide shade from the sun and shelter from the rain, and facilitate social interaction. Typically made up of adobe bricks and timberwork, the layout of the house is focused on a central courtyard around which all rooms wrap. The courtyard is integral. It is around the courtyard that family members and friends can gather to discuss events of the day or to debate issues that concern them. The eaves provide protection from the rain and sun, making the courtyard a good place to sit and relax. For those who refuse to give up their courtyard houses in Lijiang despite the advent of tourism, it has become a mission to protect their family legacy.

A common comment made by Lijiang residents is that they *enjoy* their traditional courtyard houses and dislike the modern apartments found in the new city. When asked what living in a courtyard house is like, Respondent LP27 exclaimed: "indigenous people living in peripheral regions, like us, get accustomed to living in nature. In a courtyard, it is easy to see blue sky and white clouds. If it is cold, I can stay in rooms. If I want to enjoy the cool, I can be in a corridor or in the courtyard. Sitting on a couch and sipping Naxi tea, I enjoy my life very much." This is similarly expressed by Respondent LP13: "after all, we Naxi people like courtyard. In a courtyard, you can lie on a couch, sip Naxi tea, play cards and do other things. This sense cannot be found in other places. Even a luxury house cannot convey such a sense. Never!" Although this "sense" is expressed in different ways by different local residents, the conviction is obvious. Besides a place to relax, families gather to socialize with neighbors and relatives in the courtyards and lasting bonds are established in this intimate space. These spatial practices, as conducted by many generations of Naxi people, ensure continuity and cohesion and help the town residents to develop "a guaranteed level of *competence* and a specific level of *performance*" (Lefebvre 1991:33, original emphasis). Because of these practices, the courtyard houses become the residents' representational spaces to resist the rationalization and commodification of space occurring in the ancient town and the new city. The resistance, no matter how tenuous it is, entails "more or less coherent systems of non-verbal symbols and signs" (Lefebvre 1991:39). In this case, the symbols and signs refer to tradition, peaceful life, attachment to lived space, and a sense of place, in contrast to modern lifestyle in the new city. Often, this sense is accorded with the functions of the house as a space of memory, entailing a process of growth inflected by feelings of joy and of sorrow.

Living in their courtyard houses thus denotes an important life selection, for better or worse. As Respondent LP36 pointed out,

> I have been in this house since I was born. No matter how much people afford to rent it, I don't move out. Why? I have a sense of attachment to it. Economically, my selection is not good. I can earn a rent of 60–70,000 Chinese yuan every year. Once I realize that I am old, I think it is a bad deal not to rent it out …[but] in this house, I have a sound sleep. If I live in the new city, I am not familiar with the apartment and its surroundings so that I would be sleepless. Without a sound sleep, life can be very unhappy.

Here Respondent LP36 reveals a common sentiment shared by many town residents. For those still living in the town, the assertion of attachment and familiarity is translated into a sense of rootedness and belonging that emanates from living in their own houses. This sense successfully withstands economic temptation.

This sense of place not only resides in their enjoyment of the courtyard house but also emanates from a dislike of any concrete apartment in the new city. Most of the elderly respondents said that they felt very uncomfortable when they had to live temporarily in such apartments. Utterances included: "after I live in an apartment for several days, I feel very stifled and boxed. Once you close the door, you cannot see anything" (Respondent LP23); "The apartment is like a prison. After living here for a while, I feel very uncomfortable. I always have pressure and all I see is the floor. It is not natural" (Respondent LP27); "My son bought a three-storey house in the new city. I think I can try to live there, but my wife does not want to move out. Why? She said the house is like a prison and our courtyard house is much better" (Respondent LP32); "Some time back when I asked my mother how she would feel if we sold courtyard house and move to a new apartment, she replied, 'Death on hold!'" (informal interview). Even though many respondents acknowledged that life in the ancient town has various disadvantages such as noise, pollution, and congestion, many of which are brought about by tourism development, there is nothing like home (see also Hayden 1995 and Tuan 1977). The courtyard houses bind their owners to the town, encompass the residents' life story from birth to death, and concretize the peoples' sense of place.

Apart from enjoying their courtyard houses, Naxi residents also make great efforts to maintain their property so as to retain their family legacy not only for themselves but also for their next generation:

> It is quite easy to damage the original feature if I use cement block to replace adobe. But I still find a factory producing similar adobe bricks and have made an order. It is my responsibility to protect my house. Step by step, I want to make it more comfortable, but I cannot change its structure, including its external façade and internal layout.
>
> (Respondent LP12)

Residents also maintain their houses by not renting, even if they are left vacant because:

> We don't want other people to rent our house. Once they give us money, they have the legal right to renovate our house and probably ruin the structure. It is not good for the preservation of this World Heritage Site. The town consists of many residential houses. If these houses become standard bedrooms for tourists, their architectural authenticity is destroyed and the town's value disappears.
>
> (Respondent LP23)

To tourists and tourism developers, courtyard houses are spectacular landscapes, but to town residents, these houses connote a lived space. In Lijiang, we find other more subtle maneuvers to (re)claim space, such as a dance group's recolonization of Sifang Square (see Su and Teo 2008 for details). All these practices, together with Naxi language education and locals' involvement in tourism businesses (see below), signify what Jackson (1989) terms "territorial battles" because local Naxi people have chosen to assert their agency to negotiate the hegemony of capital and bureaucracy that is changing Lijiang into a touristic town.

Naxi language education and identity building

In 1998, the local government carried out a bold experiment at Xinren Primary School. In addition to Mandarin and English, Naxi language was introduced. Language courses are generally unpopular in schools because of a shortage of teachers and materials and because students eschew work that will not help them in college entrance exams. In spite of these difficulties, several local institutions were roped in to assist in Naxi language education. They included Dongba Cultural Museum, Institute of Dongba Cultural Transformation, and Lijiang Bureau of Education. Although a laudable move, the motive was not always altruistic:

> What do tourists want to see [in Lijiang]? It is Naxi culture. Regarding this culture, the younger generation has nothing to do with it after the older one is gone. Therefore, the authorities have to "stand high and see far." They thought that pupils need learn some basic knowledge [about Naxi culture] in primary school although these kids cannot understand all.
>
> (Respondent LP25)

The education system, an ideological apparatus integral to the nation state's political machinery, has been partially appropriated by local intellectuals to build local identity to facilitate more tourism. Regarding Naxi language education, two important issues need to be raised.

First, under the pressure of Hanization and globalization, it has become a difficult problem for the Naxi to protect and oversee many aspects of their culture. Language is one of the first to give way. The use of Mandarin has a long history, as documented in Chapter 3. Although tourism has intensified such pressures by adding global influences, it has also had the reverse effect of making locals aware of the importance of their own heritage and ethnic identity. An official who was once in charge of Naxi language education advocated this proposal and felt satisfied with the achievements they made. As he pointed out:

> Previously Hanization was very serious. The situation cannot be like that. We must embark on Naxi language education. Mandarin is our national language and everyone should know it. But it doesn't mean that we can't know our own ethnic language – otherwise we forget our ancestors.
>
> (Respondent G06)

To learn Naxi language is to maintain a constant force in a rapidly changing era and helps to bind all Naxi people together under the banner of a common heritage and culture, even if it is for touristic ends.

Second, the use of primary schools to teach Naxi language means that the family is no longer the vehicle to transmit this important cultural tool. In fact, many Naxi parents believe that Mandarin will enable their children to have a better future. A typical case is Yuhua,[2] a dongba from a rural village near the town. Although the government forbade people to learn Dongba culture in the 1970s, Yuhua covertly studied Dongba culture and religious scripts from his father because he had a personal interest. He did not realize that what he learned would earn him official sanction as a legitimate Dongba priest and thus secure a stable job in a tourism corporation in the town. Ironically, he is unwilling to teach his son Dongba language. As he explained, "I have only one son who will gradu-ate this year. I never teach him as I fear its negative impacts on his Mandarin. Only when he fails to enroll in university will I begin to teach him" (Respondent OM12). Although Yuhua has himself benefited, he still urges his son not to walk down the same path. In his mind, a university degree is undoubtedly a sign of recognition in mainstream society, whereas Dongba culture and Naxi language are forms of "otherness," at best privileged only in the tourism sector.

Other than the primary schools, two government-related institutions are also involved in Naxi cultural transmission – Dongba Cultural Museum and Dongba Cultural Research Institute.[3] Both have obtained official subsidies to finance their daily operations and function as official think-tanks to fashion and interpret Naxi culture and heritage: "the Museum aims to display all Dongba culture" (Respondent GO1). Additionally, it has established a school to "foster our younger intellectuals and encourage them to learn our traditional culture" (Respondent GO1). Writing about the rationale for creating these cultural institutions in Lijiang, Chao (1996:218) argues, "the state lays claim to the once powerful fragments of the Naxi past, thus enhancing the scope of its own antiquity while simultaneously allowing the Naxi people to identify their state's history as their own." To Chao, these institutions serve the purpose of larger China and not themselves. To some extent, there is truth in Chao's evaluation of these institutions. Both these institutions stress the importance of tourism to

Naxi culture and see their efforts as an attempt to "industrialize" Naxi heritage. Hence, they influence Lijiang's tourism market by distributing their own brand of knowledge of Naxi culture, which they claim separates the genuine from the commodified.

Dongba Gong is a religious institution that is also contributing to the Naxi cultural revival. Supported by tourist dollars from performances of Dongba worship rites, which are held every night, Dongba Gong maintains a folk museum to display Naxi cultural relics and Dongba pictographic script. This display is free to locals and tourists. Its purpose is to "tell the future generation what is our culture" (Respondent LP2). Nevertheless, the motive to educate tourists through Naxi cultural display is conditioned, again, by economic motives. During our fieldwork in June 2007, we noticed that the display rooms had given away to a tourist shop that sold Naxi-related souvenirs. As a member of staff explained, the display does not make any profit and by renting the rooms out, Dongba Gong can get extra income to subsidize the performance they claim has been suffering dwindling attendance.

All the above-mentioned cultural institutions play the role of a museum, more or less. Museums are important institutions that record cultural transformation in place. As Harvey (1989a:303) argues, one way to respond to "the internationalism of modernism" is to reorganize historical tradition as a museum culture "of local history, of local production, of how things once a time were made, sold, consumed and integrated into a long-lost and often romanticized daily life." This museum culture "signif[ies] something of local identity" through "the presentation of a partially illusory past" (Harvey 1989a:303). Many of the institutions discussed in this section do exactly this. They try their best to represent Naxi culture, cognizant that culture is not static but changing in response to forces coming from many directions. Hence, we argue, that under the conditions of globalization and Hanization, these cultural institutions, including local primary schools, serve as a symbolic space for the Naxi community to resist further degeneration in Lijiang Ancient Town and also develop locals' moral hegemony in contributing to cultural transformation. Since 1997, tourism has awakened Naxi officials and scholars to the importance of Naxi identity and prompted a wave of Naxization in the community.

Local involvement in heritage tourism

The local government estimated that, in 2002, non-indigenous (referred to as migrants by the locals) merchants were operating more than 70 percent of the shops along the main streets of Lijiang Ancient Town (*Guangzhou Daily* 15 October 2002). The demographic changes occurring in the town led to the question of, "Whose Lijiang is it?" Considering the distribution of tourist receipts, the question immediately becomes one of, "Who should benefit more from tourism?"

It is not surprising to find that some locals claim priority in running tourism businesses in the town. In their mind, this priority is not based on tourism revenue alone but on the premise that the Naxi can do a better job of balancing profit against conservation since they have a stake in the town. A local respondent stressed:

> In the case of Lijiang Ancient Town, only locals can operate tourism busi-nesses. If migrants come to do business, their main aim is economic benefit. As for conservation, they definitely do not give it priority or ever consider it. Therefore, it is necessary for local enterprises and local people to oper-ate tourism. Why? Perhaps we have sentiments for the town while migrants surely have less.
>
> (Respondent LP8)

This opinion resonates with many locals. Besides profit, migrant merchants are less careful about the environment. Many shops have dumped trash into the canals because it is convenient. Last but not least, these merchants sell kitsch souvenirs to the detriment of traditional Naxi artifacts:

> The outcome that migrants bring to Lijiang is to insert external culture into the town. As a result, the town forms an impression among tourists that there is nothing especially worthwhile buying. If they don't buy crafts, the tradi-tional skills to make these crafts cannot be transferred from one generation to another. Then the culture is gone.
>
> (Respondent OM4)

These criticisms of the migrant merchants by Naxi people have established a clear boundary between them and there is a desire to limit the number of migrant merchants and to encourage locals to take over tourism-related businesses.

The locals' sentiments actually boost "localism." According to Dirlik (1996:36), localism highlights the local as a site of resistance to "the intrusion of global capi-talism" and initiates "an open-ended process of multiple social negotiations" in the global–local nexus. An official of CWHMC (Respondent G03) stressed:

> We should consider locals' interest in heritage preservation and tourism development. Locals here mainly refer to those always living in the town. It is they [and their ancestors] who create Naxi culture and the town. The outsiders coming here aim to appropriate local culture for profit.

Many strategies have been devised to raise local participation in the industry. For instance, after 2003, CWHMC stipulated that only locals can apply for business licenses to operate tourism services or sell souvenirs in the town. Moreover, all shops are required to have two items which should be related to Naxi culture and ethnicity. This aims to control the business content and provide job opportunities to Naxi craft persons. A guesthouse owner (Respondent LP23) who is a local proposed that the "government should impose less tax on those local merchants than the outsiders." It appears that the Naxi endorse CWHMC's policies to encourage local involvement in heritage tourism.

A closer examination of local involvement in heritage tourism reveals more than just the purpose of obtaining tourism income. Through their involvement in Lijiang's tourism market, the Naxi are able to exert their power in shaping heritage landscapes and retaining Naxi identity in Lijiang Ancient Town. In the town, for instance, many Naxi have converted their residential houses into guesthouses, shops, or bars. However, they would rather not rent their houses to migrant merchants:

> I really enjoy running this guesthouse. Otherwise I have nothing to do.
> (Respondent LP12)

> I believe I can easily find a job and make a living after renting this house out. But why do I turn it into a bar and run it by myself with so much effort? I don't want to live an ordinary life. I want to know what I can do for this town and how successful I can be at it.
> (Respondent LP9)

> I am still young. I want to operate successful enterprise .... I hope I can match Xuan Ke one day.
> (Respondent LP1)

For these locals, their involvement in the tourism industry goes beyond profit. They actually enjoy interacting with the guests. Without the pressure of high rent, they can successfully maintain their businesses and inscribe their own sentiments on the tourism space that they control. Hence, Naxi people have agency to contribute to competition which is not determined by foreign or Han capital alone.

As a matter of fact, many migrant merchants have expressed their discontent over the rise of localism in Lijiang. A good example to illustrate the local–migrant tension is a story told by Respondent OM10. Intrigued by Lijiang's beauty in their first trip in 2001, Respondent OM10 and her husband sold off their businesses in Hebei Province and settled down in Lijiang in 2004. They leased a house from a town resident and turned it into a guesthouse. The business license was registered in the house owner's name. She tried to get her own license but after numerous rejections from CWHMC, she gave up: "Restriction! They always restrict us! We try to obtain our business license. But they don't let migrants operate. All are for locals." Since she is paying to use the owner's business license and paying the rent for the house, she pointed out that she might as well be working for the house owner. A Taiwanese respondent (OM5) pointed out that "they [local officials] must protect locals' interests at the sacrifice of the migrant merchants. That's why house rent is rising steadily." Many migrant merchants regard localism in Lijiang as protectionism.

Whether it is withdrawing spaces from migrant entrepreneurs, re-teaching Naxi language, or reclaiming space from non-local enterprises, this section has shown that the Naxi are a force to contend with. Powerful as CWHMC, foreign, and Han capital may be, some amount of compromise is inevitable so that all can share in the tourism pie.

Policy implications for Lijiang's tourism development in the future

In the last part of this chapter, we discuss the policy implications of Lijiang's tourism development for the future. Given the many dilemmas, we do not seek for an emancipatory solution to handle the stalemate in Lijiang's tourism development, but to critically discuss the sticky points and put forward policy implications to enable a *sustained interest* of tourism development in Lijiang. This is the third objective of the book.

In the system of Lijiang's heritage tourism, Naxi lived culture (vernacular landscapes) and the material landscapes are the foremost elements. Most of the tourists who visit Lijiang experience its unique built environment and can enjoy a Naxi culture that has been adulterated by globalization but yet is appealing enough because there are signifiers enough to satisfy the post-tourist. Commodification, depthlessness, and museumization pervade Lijiang. To cite Tucker (2003:177), Lijiang Ancient Town has become "de-traditionalised and ... over-touristified." Therefore, Western backpackers argue that it is no longer authentic. More and more, tourists are saying that "once is enough" and even potential tourists have no pressing desire to visit Lijiang. However, we have to caution against any pessimistic prediction of Lijiang's tourism. As we argued in Chapter 3, the rise of affluence in China provides a huge market potential and the town is still a favorite destination for millions of Chinese consumers. Hence, new meanings are always being invented to enhance Lijiang's representational space. In this sense, the steady growth of tourist arrivals is a challenge (even a threat) to Naxi heritage.

As far as ways to retain Naxi lived culture and its material landscape in the town are concerned, two problematic issues have to be discussed. The first is that the town residents and their way of life are not given enough recognition. The locals and tourists agree that the material landscape in the town is well conserved, far exceeding the needs of the residents. They still hope that the local government can do better. However, Naxi lived culture is on the brink of vanishing from the town. Local authorities cannot prohibit the town residents from moving out to the new city, nor can they financially support the shops that only serve the town residents. We have reiterated in the previous chapters that the separation of material and vernacular landscapes, heralded by heritage preservation, can lead to the "creative destruction" of the vernacular landscapes of Lijiang (Harvey 1989a).[4] Without Naxi lived culture, a contentious endpoint is museumization.

The local authorities have attempted to take control of the demographic change in Lijiang Ancient Town. For instance, CWHMC encourages the Naxi to be involved in tourism businesses in the town. The agency also provides government-owned houses to local people who are good at calligraphy and painting to set up shops at Dongda Street. The rent is relatively cheaper than that of private shops. It co-works with other departments to upgrade the town's infrastructure. One resident commented:

> If you really want to say government does some things, you find it repaired the streets, constructed sewers, and set up street lamps. Of course, we never

know how many secret deals happen in these projects. Nevertheless, government actually did something. That's better than nothing.

(Respondent O2)

More recently in 2002, CWHMC subsidized each town resident a monthly amount of 10 yuan to be used for improving their living conditions. At the time we did fieldwork in June 2005, this subsidy had stopped. It is alleged that CWHMC used the money to recruit more guards to maintain the town's public security, which, in local government's view, is an extra public good that town residents have to pay for.

It is hard to evaluate how effective these policies are in retaining Naxi lived culture. However, the reality is that the number of Naxi residents decreased after 1997, when tourism took off in Lijiang. A local resident (Respondent LP18) observed,

> Now the town, as some say, is like a slum. The persons who have money or authority moved out to the new city. Generally, many Naxi residents in the town are poor and powerless. They cannot buy a new house in the new city so that they have to stay in the town. Some houses they live in are deplorable. Their living conditions are also very simple and crude. Their lives are very harsh. The income gap has been widened in Lijiang since 1996.

The poor and powerless residents are the losers in Lijiang's tourism development. Tourism does not contribute much to improving their quality of life. Although those residents who have settled down in the new city are reaping economic returns from tourism, the remaining poor indigenous residents are suffering the price in terms of pollution, noise, inflation, and congestion. They also have to bear the tourist gaze. A spatial divide now exists between the new city and the old town, marked by economic differences. Ethically speaking, it is unfair that the poor in the town have become the victims of tourism development in Lijiang. This issue relates to our second point – the distribution of tourism revenues – and needs to be discussed.

The distribution of tourism revenues in Lijiang is a big problem. Many groups of people, such as local authorities, town residents, migrant merchants, and local merchants, are involved in the distribution. They apparently have different abilities to adapt to Lijiang's changing tourism sector. In *Social Justice and the City*, Harvey (1973:64, emphasis added) points out:

> Differential disequilibrium in the spatial form of the city can thus redistribute income. In general, the rich and relatively resourceful can reap great benefits while the poor and necessarily immobile have only restricted opportunities. This can mean a quite substantial *regressive redistribution* of income in a rapidly changing urban system.

This regressive redistribution of tourism revenues has taken place in Lijiang and it intensifies existing social inequality and stratification. The issue of how to use the maintenance charges, for instance, is a contentious issue. CWHMC earns a large amount of money from these charges. The agency claims that the money is used for conservation projects and infrastructure improvement such as the building of public toilets and the maintenance of flagstone streets. These projects seem to favor tourists rather than residents. For instance, residents living in courtyard houses in the town are not permitted to build private toilets within their own homes. Some residents have constructed their own toilets at the risk of fines by CWHMC. Without their own toilets, residents are inconvenienced. Moreover, they are charged 20 or 50 cents per entry to use the public toilets. To poor residents, this is a financial burden. Ironically, guesthouses are permitted to build as many attached toilets as they want.

The discrimination against the Naxi indigenous residents is not uncommon in the town. CWHMC mobilizes *Lijiang Daily* to propagandize its achievements in "projects serving people" but the agency never actually says who *really* benefits from its projects. It is arguably the tourists, merchants in the town, and the government who benefit far more than indigenous residents do.

The other problem is that CWHMC is not transparent about its finances. Nobody knows how much CWHMC obtains from tourists through the maintenance charge and how much it has invested in heritage preservation.[5] Lack of transparency means CWHMC can abuse its power. Under such political leadership, equity issues are swept under the carpet and sustainability is never discussed. Without any external monitor, Lijiang's local government successfully incorporates its political and economic power into enterprise and squeezes out discontent and resistance. When we told a town resident that we planned to spend 10 years studying Lijiang, starting from 2003 onwards, he responded calmly that we would also witness the death of Lijiang Ancient Town. We hope he is wrong.

Before we discuss the policy implications for sustained interest of tourism, we will conduct a policy analysis using the principal–agent relationship to uncover the deficiencies in Lijiang's heritage tourism. This relationship is governed by "a contract specifying what the agent should do and what the principal must do in return" (Perrow 1986:224). The answer to the question "Whose Lijiang?" is that the *ordinary town residents* own Lijiang Ancient Town and should benefit from tourism development. They are the principal in Lijiang's heritage tourism. Nominally, these residents, including Naxi and other ethnic groups, vote the local government in to manage heritage tourism and urban conservation.

The above points verify that the principal–agent relationship in Lijiang's heritage tourism is very problematic. As Perrow (1986:224) argues, the principal–agent relationship is "fraught with the problems of cheating, limited information, and bounded rationality in general." Waterman and Meier (1998) go further to identify two fundamental problems about this relationship: information asymmetry and goal conflict. In Lijiang, the local authorities almost monopolize the provision and distribution of information. They use their expertise in heritage tourism and urban conservation as "a foundation of the bureaucracy's power" (Waterman and Meier 1998:183). Similarly, Bendor *et al.* (1987:797) assert that "bureaucrats rely on expertise based on … their ability to manipulate the design of policy alternatives and information about the consequences of these alternatives." Lijiang's local government undoubtedly possesses information advantages about heritage tourism and urban conservation, which far exceed that of local residents.

Moreover, conflict in goals is obvious between Lijiang's local authorities and the town residents. In the marketplace of Lijiang's heritage tourism, Lijiang's local government is forced to "expend resources both in trying to instruct the agent what to do and in monitoring and policing the agent's behavior" (Mitnick 1986:4, cited from Waterman and Meier 1998:185). The goal is to yield economic returns and attain hegemonic leadership in controlling and guiding Lijiang's tourism development. To the town residents, however, they hope to improve their quality of life whatever the means. Some rented their houses to migrant merchants for income; some turned their houses into guesthouses or other tourism facilities for profit. But for the residents who are not involved in the tourism sector, their quality of life is threatened by the negative impacts brought about by tourism development.

In the first place, we acknowledge the importance of tourism in propelling the development in Lijiang. Thus, the policy implications for a sustained interest in tourism development are two-fold. First, all stakeholders should ensure that the rights and interests of the Naxi indigenous residents are secure. Migrant merchants and tourists should respect the residents' current and future lifestyles and avoid any further takeover of their private living spaces. Lijiang's local government should prioritize the residents rather than the investors and tourists in policy making. In addition, policies should be designed with feedback from locals.

Second, an impartial distribution of tourism revenues should be incorporated to allow more indigenous residents to share in the tourism benefits. The Lijiang government should keep the residents informed of the finances in heritage preservation and in the tourism sector. Transparency in corporate governance can enhance the residents' trust in the government and improve their willingness to participate in tourism development. Furthermore, all indigenous residents in the town should receive an adequate subsidy to help them start small businesses. As more indigenous residents obtain opportunities to participate, they will want to stay in the town, making sustainability more viable for the future.

Conclusions

This chapter has detailed how tourism gives many chances to the Naxi people to rebuild their cultural roots and resurface their hidden sense of place. As Naxi language is once again practised and more residents get involved in tourism businesses, the success of Lijiang means that the ancient town will move away from a peripheral to a central position in Beijing's political vision. So long as locals continue to exercise their agency to protect their stake in Lijiang, tourist interest in the place is unlikely to completely disappear. Otherwise, degeneration will set in if power is only exercised by migrant and foreign capital or by the state whose motives are economic in nature.

8   Conclusion

Cultural politics of heritage tourism and beyond

This book explores the politics of heritage tourism in Lijiang Ancient Town by analyzing the interconnectedness of place, representation, and capital. More specifically, it investigates how stakeholders in the industry wield their power to influence the production of heritage landscapes and how the less powerful resist this dominance. How a tourism landscape is shaped does not depend on production forces alone. Consumption of tourism is also integral to socio-spatial outcomes. By teasing out the dialectical workings of forces that originate globally (namely, the international tourist, transnational tourism industry players, and international conservation organizations), nationally (the central government of China), and locally (Naxi townspeople and local provincial and town authorities) on both the production and consumption dimensions of Lijiang's tourism, a critical analysis is provided for why the hegemonic discourse supporting tourism development is sanctionable in this World Heritage Site. This chapter summarizes the key arguments and empirical findings of the book and ends with a discussion of the theoretical implications of our findings for critical tourism geographies.

Summary

This book has documented the compromised equilibrium established in the everyday space of tourism change in Lijiang. This equilibrium is the outcome of negotiations between the political aspirations of the state, global capital intent on making profit from tourism, and local agents who want to preserve their heritage as much as possible. In unraveling the mediations between these stakeholders, we analyzed not only the production, i.e. socio-spatial outcomes of their motives and goals, but also the role of consumption as a dialectic that also provides input to how Lijiang is transformed.

In Chapter 1, we identified the broad context – China's rapid transition from an isolated entity to a rising world power and the implementation of the "great western development" strategy to jettison Yunnan (where Lijiang is located) into modern society. Here, we argued that China's development was premised on the need to modernize but this requires the country to first *internationalize/globalize*. For Yunnan (and Lijiang in particular), tourism was an obvious vehicle to achieve these goals. With pristine nature that is still intact and ethnic minority groups who have a rich culture, the road to economic growth could be easily laid.

To better understand how China went about the transformation of Lijiang, we advocated a perspective that acknowledges the *non-Western* nature of our site. In addition, we also emphasized the need to extend beyond state/government and capital positionings that have been the normal fare of tourism research on cultural politics. Hence, we incorporated a study of the *ordinary* man in the street, who, we argued, has been ignored but who is a crucial part of any political process. Finally, we showed how including *time* and *space* in our analysis can add intellectual rigor, because the present and aspirations for the future are influenced by events of the past. In addition, Lijiang as a spatial entity does not function in a void. Neighboring Tibet, Sichuan, and Fujian have affected its politics, culture, and economy. In today's global economy, tourists from as far away as Australia and Malaysia similarly have an effect on Lijiang. Employing a wider brush would help studies on tourism politics to surpass the one-sidedness (blaming the West and capitalism for all its problems) of many political economy/cultural politics studies of the past.

In line with the rethinking of tourism politics, Chapter 2 offers a dialectical approach for thinking through the relational nature of power in the production and consumption of heritage: namely, a neo-Gramscian model in which heritage is analyzed within global–national–local interactions and where hegemony is ever changing as players in the industry assert dominance and resist power. Inevitably Lijiang has undergone commodification but we argue that this is not a simple or straightforward outcome.

Chapter 3 outlines the geo-historical settings of Lijiang. These settings provide the link to larger processes that reinforce and reproduce values and beliefs of the Naxi community as well as that of the Han. As much as the Naxi want to remain a linked but separate community from the Han, those from the central plains have in the past tried to draw the Naxi into their mainstream society but today find it convenient to use the "other" concept to frame a vision of unity in diversity. This latter imagery has become a strong attraction point and accounts for the rise of domestic tourism in the ancient town.

As for the empirical data, we summarize three main findings in our analysis. First of all, the power of capital and bureaucracy has shaped Lijiang into a highly touristic place as well as a political symbol of ethnic harmony (Chapter 4). For the sake of economic profit, Lijiang's city authority has established an alliance with private enterprise to package Naxi heritage landscapes so that it can compete in the world arena. Besides this idyllic imagery of a utopia that has resisted the drudgery associated with progress, the central government has also inscribed nationalist narratives into the heritage representations of the ancient town. The convivial interactions between the Naxi locals and the Han tourists endow Lijiang with the accolade of a "microcosm of ethnic harmony."

Whether international or domestic, how Lijiang is represented to the world or China, both the mass media and international organizations have had a hand to play. As shown in Chapters 3 and 4, although Lonely Planet, Channel 4 in the UK, and UNESCO may have contributed to how the world perceives Lijiang, locals have also made their mark, e.g. through local television dramas. Even if external capital wants to establish a foothold in Lijiang, they find they are mediated by local authorities insofar as having to obtain permission from the state to enter and also having to rely on local social and business networks to start their ventures in Lijiang.

Our second major finding is that tourists are not passive receivers of the heritage representations of Lijiang portrayed by capital or by bureaucracy. Tourists have their own capacities to influence Lijiang by means of their economic clout and their cultural preferences. As we showed in Chapters 5 and 6, tourists not only purchase goods and services but also endow Lijiang with new meanings. We further argue that domestic and international tourists as consumers have very different preferences. Therefore, any change to Lijiang's landscapes must take its cue from whichever consumer is more powerful.

Third, the commodification of heritage in Lijiang attests to a condition of hegemonic dominance by the state in collusion with capital. In spite of the agency of locals, we stressed in Chapter 6 that consent from virtually all the stakeholders in Lijiang Ancient Town had been given. Tourism development as good for the welfare of Lijiang has become a naturalized idea and is now socially and spatially transforming Lijiang. Because of tourism, the town is no longer an ordinary living space for the Naxi people but is almost a theme park. All this is tolerated, as the locals predominantly believe that commodification gives local culture a new strength and legitimacy to survive in the face of modernization and globalization. Hence, only cultural forms bearing highly symbolic values can survive; others with less touristic attractiveness will wane as they will not be cherished by the local people. The establishment of a "focused gaze" (Urry 2002:88) emanating from the consumers' expectations has led to a split of the material from the vernacular landscapes of Lijiang. Commodification arguably trivializes the town's cultural significance and results in the museumization of heritage.

Resistance to the dominant position nevertheless exists. We found that the Naxi do attempt to (re)claim space from tourism activities (Chapter 7). Through a revival of the language and religion, as well as turning their backs on the financially attractive proposals to rent out their courtyard houses to tourism businesses, there are underlying currents of territorial battles to reclaim space. As the number of potential domestic tourists to Lijiang remains high (more and more Chinese are becoming affluent), we raise the importance of maintaining a sustained interest in Lijiang. We have recommended more recognition for the rights and interests of Naxi indigenous residents in the town and to formulate an impartial distribution of tourism revenues so as to allow the weak to share in the tourism benefits.

Lijiang Ancient Town has evolved into an enclavic tourist space. This space is "governed by a system of ordering that materializes an ideology of consumption and regulates the performance of tourists" (Edensor 1998:52). To paraphrase Featherstone (1991:28), it is a site of "ordered disorder" where domestic tourists can release their pent-up desire for nostalgia and compete with international tourists for a space of consumption. Transnational culture has impinged on the representation of Lijiang's heritage landscapes and incorporated the town into a globally fluid space. Evidently, many groups of people are resisting these external forces and they are capable of articulating contested narratives about what Lijiang's heritage landscapes specify. In all, the representation of heritage landscapes and the development of tourism in Lijiang are filled with constant negotiations between the powerful and the weak; what we can see now in Lijiang reflects a picture of a compromised equilibrium attained by different groups of people who have given their inputs to the very existence and growth of Lijiang's tourism. This equilibrium is temporally and spatially transient, and is also a hegemonic moment as it facilitates the discourse of *development* to become normal and natural (Langman 2003).

Some useful contributions can still be made in terms of our research findings and arguments. Theoretically, we suggest that a neo-Gramscian approach can be invaluable for exploring cultural politics. Unlike structuration approaches that accentuate human agency in destabilizing social structure and postmodernist sensibilities that view the world as full of chaos and disorder, this theoretical approach highlights the dialectic of structure and agency in social relations and enunciates the idea that social structure constrains human actions but individuals have the capacity to resist these constraints. The logical application then of a Gramscian approach to hegemony draws on examining the *processes* of negotiations among the different groups in constructing social reality. This perspective offers fresh insights into understanding the world as an entity built upon a *compromised equilibrium* instead of *chaos and disorder*.

Practically, the research findings are of considerable importance as they reveal the necessity to care for the weak and/or disadvantaged in order to achieve a sustained interest in tourism development. This research does not call for an emancipatory initiative to overthrow the existing system of tourism development in Lijiang, but it does stress the urgency to lessen the dominance imposed on the weak who are already losing out from tourism development. Only when the less advantaged obtain adequate tourism benefits and feel satisfied can the powerful secure a more stable consent from them and maintain hegemonic leadership in tourism. Any policy of tourism development should not just concern itself with the winners, it has to bear the losers in mind too.

The politics of heritage tourism in China and beyond

> The key trick for cultural geography, therefore, is to begin to understand the dialectic between constant change, the ever-present flux of social relationships, and the relative permanence of reified ways of knowing, standardised 'maps of meaning' and solidified cultural production.
>
> (Mitchell 2000:294)

Heritage tourism continues to pose problems for geography. Coleman and Crang (2002:10) argue that tourism as an event is about "mobilizing and reconfiguring spaces and places, bringing them into new constellations and therefore transforming them." The recognition of and reflection upon "relational power" entails the conjunction between the prevailing logic of late capitalism and individual philosophical dispositions. Tourism politics is modeled on the compromise equilibrium embraced by the powerful and the weak and on the structure–agency dialectic. Spatial exclusion and inclusion in the process of tourism production and consumption can have dire socio-spatial consequences for heritage sites and the local community.

This book has followed on studies that transcended the realm of political economy, to interrogate the specific processes of identity building and place-making that are embedded in the cultural politics of space. Cultural politics, in the context of this book, is more than the conflicts of meanings and practices. It dwells in the interaction between the appropriation and invention of meaning and the socio-spatial transformation of landscape. The interaction is not necessarily fixed in time and space; it is dynamic. We argue that cultural politics is strongly associated with the geo-historical context of localities and rests upon economic relations as well as cultural dispositions. Drawing on this argument, we outline three theoretical implications.

First, there is a need to delve into the role of the Chinese state in a transitional period and the dynamic state–society relation in China. The transitional period in China has fostered a dramatic intersection of global–national–local forces. The peripheral people and places suffer from dual marginalization imposed by the core of China and by Western-centric and Han-centric imagination. They are geographically and economically marginalized; furthermore, their cultures are frequently linked with "otherness" to highlight their uniqueness and with "backwardness" to articulate their tradition.

The Chinese authorities ruled by the CCP still govern the nation, although their power is resisted by private enterprise and individuals and challenged by global forces. The state does indeed cautiously supervise the diffusion of power in the society to avoid its dominance being challenged and/or threatened. The state also prudently overlooks the operation of global forces in different localities. This supervision becomes more and more covert along with the popularity of consumerism. The landscape of dominance and resistance is entangled in the interstitial space between a market economy and the centrally planned model. Writing about neoliberalism with Chinese characteristics, Harvey (2005:120) specifies that China has made authoritarianism and the capitalist market compatible when the state, together with numerous social and economic forces, constructs "a particular kind of market economy that increasingly incorporates neoliberal elements interdigitated with authoritarian centralized control." In this context, tourism is used by the ruling elite to impose certain ideologies such as nationalism and patriotism upon the private space of individuals' consumption and to cultivate political socialization (Kong 1995). The CCP can persuade the governed to accept these ideologies and then attain the hegemony for developing tourism and preserving heritage. Quite different from the coercive administration implemented in Mao's regime, the state now manipulates by hegemonic control over the country. This radical change may offer opportunities to establish a new form of governance, whereby "actors regularly arrive at mutually satisfactory" situations by "negotiating with each other and co-operating in the implementation of ... decisions" (Schmitter 2002:52). This radical change calls for a concomitant change in how to understand China.

As the Chinese state is rapidly transforming from a socialist state "serving the people" (*wei renmin fuwu*) to an entrepreneurial state, the boundary of commodification and politicization in tourism and other industries is blurred.[1] For instance, under the name of "development," Lijiang's local authorities have managed to obtain the support of the central government to accelerate commodi-fication to prompt GDP growth at a pace commensurate with the coastal regions of China. Even if there is development, there is a great deal of doubt about who actually benefits. Several disadvantaged groups – such as the poor residents in Lijiang Ancient Town, the floating population in the sweatshops of the Pearl River Delta, peasants in rural China who are deprived of their land now set aside for industrialization and urbanization, and displaced urban residents who are forced to give their houses away to real estate development – are all vulnerable to the discourse of development and become marginalized and excluded in the rapid pace of economic reform. When Deng Xiaoping used the slogan "allowing some regions and some people to become prosperous before others" to motivate development, the 30-year-long economic growth testifies to the success of his reform, but at the price of increasing social inequality and stratification. The great western development strategy and many others like it only enable the power of bureaucracy and capital to grasp more economic and political fruits and deepen social stratification. In this sense, Deng's ultimate promise of common prosperity is as much a utopia as Mao's communism, depicting nothing but neoliberalization with Chinese characteristics (Harvey 2005). Yet, as we have sought to analyze throughout the whole book, it is important to problematize the discourse of *development* and the dominance of capital and bureaucracy in terms of the maneuvers of resistance in China.

The second implication is the importance of the everyday qualitative experi-ences of *ordinary* people. The terrain of cultural politics not only draws on the global space of TNCs, mobility, and capital, and the national space of state power but also gets entangled with many localities and the everyday space of life. The "everyday practices, experiences and beliefs of what have been called 'the common people'" are discussed in the book (Burgess and Gold 1985:3). This stance resonates with recent developments within cultural geography. For instance, Gilbert (1999:102) argues that "everyday life should not be treated as a backdrop to the processes that shape the city. Rather, people's everyday lives shape, and are shaped by, urban processes." Thus, studies of the cultural politics surrounding everyday space necessitate a critical engagement with the variety of meanings, values, agendas, and motivations involved in people's struggle against and compliance to the social structure. The everyday of tourism space is no exception. "Tourism involves patterns of social and cultural communication which are premised upon understanding of the function of holidays in everyday life, and mediated by meanings created by different groups of people in particular material circumstances over time" (Squire 1994:5). As Morgan and Pritchard (1998:165) speculate, "tourism manifests power and it mirrors and reinforces the distribution of social and cultural power in individual societies and in the global community." In this sense, tourism is in itself about practices of dominance and resistance in relation to the potential subversiveness of everyday life (de Certeau 1984; Mitchell 2000).

To delve into everyday space, some cultural geographers extend cultural politics into the arena of non-representational theory. According to Thrift (2000:274), this theory is "an attempt to develop a body of work that emphasizes the development of sensitivities (or disclosure), rather than knowledge *per se*, toward all of the everyday practices."[2] Similarly, Shotter (1998) pinpoints that daily practices are spontaneous and there are no casual relations between them and external forces. Many geographers relate to this idea in tourism studies and have developed some important concepts such as mobility, performance, and embodiment. Writing about cultural geographies of tourism, Crang (2004:82) accentuates "a language of script" rather than "images and representation" through which the reality is somehow distorted. While we do not deny the value of this method of analysis, we caution against the celebration of *individual* actions to escape or even overthrow the *structure* of involvements. Any practice in everyday space happens in a certain geo-historical context and draws on real social and economic relations. As Jackson (1991:226) argues, "the 'economic' and the 'cultural' are interwoven as 'economic' processes are culturally encoded, while 'cultural' processes are inseparable from the material conditions in which they take place."

In varying degrees, the politics of tourism is inextricable from economic relations. Thus, Britton (1991:451) asserts that "tourism is an important avenue of capitalist accumulation." He goes further to suggest that the geographic study of tourism requires a more rigorous theoretical core in order to "conceptualize [more] fully its role in capitalist accumulation, its economic dynamics, and its role in creating the materiality and social meaning of places" (1991:452). The cultural politics of tourism space can constitute this theoretical core, to some extent.

The third and final implication, related to the second one, is the value of dialectic thought to unveil complicated power relations in society and explore variegated spaces where individuals and groups engage in dominance, resistance, and compromise. Since the early 1990s, a new trend to redirect how cultural geography is "done" has emerged (Mitchell 2000). Increasingly, scholars in this field are paying more attention to human agency than to social structure to explore the social construction of space and the spatial construction of culture. The concept of "culture" is now thoroughly politicized (Jackson 1989). An important concept that underpins this field is dialectics. Aitchison (1999:29) summarizes new cultural geography in the following way:

> Space, place and landscape – including landscapes of leisure and tourism – are not fixed but are in a constant state of transition as a result of continuous,

dialectical struggles of power and resistance among and between the diversity of landscape providers, users and mediators.

Dialectics is useful in helping us to avoid simplistic binary categorizations and helps us transcend the divisions between consumption/production, dominance/resistance, the global/the local, to name a few. The dialectic synthesis of culture and economy enables us to understand that "the determinations of any individual signifying activity do not come from the autonomous realm of something called 'the economic', or from the contingent logic of something labeled 'the cultural'" (Peck 2006:120). They draw on "internal relations" and "contradictory processes" (Mitchell 2002:383), i.e. the interconnectedness of geo-historical conditions and internal factors.

Dialectic thought is of importance to explore the cultural politics of tourism. For instance, the dilemma in heritage tourism is the worldwide homogenization of tourist culture and consumption as well as the contrived preservation of local uniqueness (Norkunas 1993). This dilemma is the result of interminable conflicts and adjustments by which producers and consumers achieve a compromised equilibrium in tourism development. As Miller (1995:50) argues, the diversity of "local" cultures of consumption and production are "not remnants to be eliminated by a new global hegemony, but the motor behind abstracted, aggregate and finally global changes." Dialectics rejects privileging any side and highlights the contradictions of space in advancing the socio-spatial transformation of various localities (Lefebvre 1991).

To date, the new cultural geography can potentially contribute to tourism studies in many areas such as landscape, gender, sexuality, identity building, and spatial differentiation. An attempt is made to address the spatiality of tourism and embrace the everyday of tourism in the cultural politics of space. As Crang (2004:83) addresses,

> The cultural geography of tourism is not about a fixed map of destinations and peoples who are more less neatly packaged or accurately represented, but rather about a set of practices that constitute notions of what 'over there', and thus 'over here', is like and what constellations of practices and performances that recursively produce destinations and visitors.

Tourism studies focus increasingly on the interconnectedness of economy and culture, production and consumption in the global–local nexus. More and more, social theories are entering the domain of tourism research and broadening scholars' horizons to explore more fundamental social issues pertaining to race, gender, class, and ethnicity that are underlying tourism politics. Dialectical thought has thus navigated us in the cultural geography of tourism discussed in this book. In line with it, the neo-Gramscian approach has proven useful in understanding and examining the cultural politics of tourism. This could mark a powerful line of theoretical enquiry.

Notes

Chapter 1: Rethinking the politics of heritage tourism

1. In 2006, Zhang Xiqin, the vice governor of China National Tourism Administration (CNTA), highlighted Yunnan as an example of tourism development that other provinces in western China should follow. He even described Lijiang as a good role model (*Xinhua News Agency* 29 April 2006). In a national conference on reforms in cultural systems held in Lijiang on August 2008, Lijiang was again spotlighted as an excellent case of cultural industrialization (with reference to Yunnan's many ethnic minority groups).
2. In September 1999, the State Council announced the "great western development" strategy aimed at developing six provinces (Gansu, Guizhou, Qinghai, Shaanxi, Sichuan, and Yunnan), five autonomous regions (Guangxi, Inner Mongolia, Ningxia, Tibet, and Xinjiang) and Chongqing municipality in the west. Containing 71.4 percent of China's land mass and 28.8 percent of its population, the western region contributed only 17.2 percent of the national gross domestic product (GDP) in 2000 (Tian 2004). Massive infrastructure projects, restructuring of the existing economic sectors, the development of science and technology, and restoration of the environment are included in the plan (Tian 2004).
3. According to Soja (2000:19) thirdspace is "a radically different way of looking at, interpreting, and acting to change the embracing spatiality of human life." It is a strategic meeting place for "fostering collective political action against all forms of human oppression" (Soja 2000:22). Although Soja talks about the radical openness of thirdspace and its proclivity for disorder and deconstruction, the concept remains, for the most part, an abstraction yet to be fully articulated.
4. Bunnell (2004) provides a good review of modernity and the "non-West."
5. Raymond Williams (1958) contended that culture is ordinary. Although his original purpose was to dissolve the boundary between high and low cultures represented by the bourgeoisie and working classes, respectively, and to enunciate the importance of ordinary, everyday experiences in making national culture, the "ordinary" in this book involves people's everyday and quotidian life, or "immediate living experience" as termed by Williams (1977:46).
6. Material and vernacular landscapes are defined in Chapter 2.
7. *People's Daily* is the mouthpiece of the Chinese Communist Party (CCP) and comes in both Chinese and English editions. *China Daily* has a similar function but only appears as an English edition. *Xinhua News Agency* is the major source of news in China. *Yunnan Daily* is the mouthpiece of the CCP committee branch in Yunnan Province.

Chapter 2: The cultural politics of tourism: exploring the complexity of hegemony

1. An examination on the global–local nexus can be found in Yeoh (2005) and Yeoh and Chang (2001).

2. The concept of "civil society" differs from that in the West. Béja (2006:53) defines Chinese civil society as "an informally structured network of non-governmental organizations [NGOs] that have a loose relation with the party state." There is no fully *independent* NGO in China since a permit from a party-related administrative unit is required before they can operate. Even schools and churches, organisms identified by Gramsci as civil society, are under the direct jurisdiction of the Party in China. As such, autonomous individuals rather than social organizations (*shehui tuanti*) are the corner-stone of Chinese civil society. Ever since Tiananmen Square, organized collective action is still frowned upon by the Party even in a time of reform; however, control over individuals is less stifling (Seligmann 1992). This helps to avert the viewpoint that state–society relations in China are always antagonistic.
3. Cresswell (1996) provides an impressive analysis of how hegemony is imposed and maintained in space and how subordinated groups trespass boundaries to demonstrate their resistance to hegemonic power.
4. CWHMC was renamed the Authority for World Heritage Conservation and Management of Lijiang Ancient Town on 28 September 2005. In this book, we still use CWHMC to refer to the governmental board, as many of the interviewees know it by its old name.

Chapter 3: Locating Lijiang: connections and process

1. Here we prefer to use "historical" rather than "heritage" because the latter is arguably a value-laden term (see Chapter 2).
2. This book does not intend to get entangled in the popular debates concerning the economic policies formulated by Mao Zedong and Deng Xiaoping. The (dis)advantages of their policies have been well documented elsewhere (see Lin 1997; Naughton 1995; Rawski 1999). Many concur that Mao's socialist planned economy retarded economic growth between 1949 and 1978. For instance, White (1992:25) argued that Mao Zedong's economic policies served to "restrain growth in productivity by stifling initia-tive and penalising excellence." A few exceptions, such as Gray (2006), defend Mao's heritage to China, arguing that the commune and brigade factories laid the material foundation for the success of Deng's economic reform. We agree with Liu (2004:10), who emphasizes that Mao's legacy has been active and alive in contemporary China, lingering in people's everyday life and "contributing further to the paradoxes of the Deng era." China's transition from planned to market economy is a continual process of socioeconomic transformation and not a radical departure from one stage to another.
3. In a talk to a Japanese delegation on 30 June 1984, Deng Xiaoping clarified:

> The superiority of the socialist system is demonstrated, in the final analysis, by faster and greater development of those forces than under the capitalist system. As they develop, the people's material and cultural life will constantly improve. One of our shortcomings after the founding of the People's Republic was that we didn't pay enough attention to developing the productive forces. Socialism means eliminating poverty. Pauperism is not socialism, still less communism.

Deng held a very pragmatic viewpoint on the ideological conflicts between socialism and capitalism and firmly intended the liberation of productivity to achieve wealth for China.
4. An English version is available at: http://english.peopledaily.com.cn/dengxp/vol3/text/d1200.html (accessed 9 July 2006).
5. A small number of overseas Chinese from Hong Kong, Macau and other foreign coun-tries were allowed to enter mainland China to visit their relatives.
6. In China, inbound tourism refers to the arrivals contributed by citizens in Hong Kong Special Administration Region (SAR), Macau SAR, Taiwan, and visitors from any foreign country when they enter the territory of mainland China.

7. This holiday scheme was changed on 1 January 2008. The new plan shortens the May Day holiday from 3 days to 1 day but places three traditional Chinese festivals – "Tomb-sweeping" Day, Dragon-boat Festival, and Mid Autumn Festival – on the list of public holidays, each with a day off (*China Daily* 16 December 2007). The shorter holidays are likely to contribute to short-haul domestic tourism, as urbanites travel to nearby suburbs or villages rather than go abroad.
8. Chen (2005) details the reasons for this sudden switch.
9. Gries (2004) describes in detail how mainland and overseas Chinese reacted to the attack.
10. The disruption of the Olympic torch relay in Paris led to a Chinese boycott of the French giant retailer Carrefour. The Beijing government had to quell nationalist sentiments via the Internet, newspapers, and television.
11. In China's official media, public protests are described as unexpected incidents involving mass participation. According to the Blue Book of Chinese Society (Chinese Academy of Social Sciences 2005), mass incidents in China have increased ten-fold in the last 13 years, rising from 8,700 in 1993 to 87,000 in 2005.
12. For details about Kublai Khan's march into Yunnan, see Guo and He (1999) and Fang (1981). Original documents can be found in *The History of Yuan: Imperial Biographies of Kublai Khan* compiled by Song Lian in 1370.
13. A'liang A'hu was the third-generation leader of this tribal family. According to Guo and He (1999), the initial leader was a Mongolian who migrated from Gansu to Lijiang during the era of Song Emperor Hui (*c.*1100–1125).
14. The regions cover the whole of present Yunnan, Guizhou, Sichuan and part of Hunan.
15. This was probably the first time that the name of "Lijiang" officially emerged. In fact, the original name Dayechang is neglected in Lijiang's historical documents. The name Lijiang was given by a monarch of the Ming Dynasty (Zhao 1998).
16. Lijiang Fu was an administrative unit overseeing civilian affairs. In 1397, Lijiang Fu broadened its scope of work to include military affairs. Its name was changed to Lijiang Brigade (Lijiang junmin) (Gong 1988).
17. Rock (1947:62–64) provides a detailed account of the downgrading.
18. Historically, the Central Plain is known for its contrast to the peripheral regions in China. It encompasses the low and middle reaches of the Yellow River Basin, an area where Han culture originates (Tong 2002).
19. In China, all traditional cities are surrounded by walls. Lijiang Ancient Town claims that the absence of city walls makes it a unique city.
20. In dozens of historical documents, Lijiang's people were said to be made up of several groups such as the Moxie, Moxi, and Moshuo (Guo and He 1994; Rock 1947). In records written by Han intellectuals, Naxi people were referred to as "barbarians" (*man ren*). The minority groups living in Lijiang were collectively called the "Na." In 1961, however, the central government unilaterally consolidated these groups together, regardless of their size and differences, and called them "Naxi" since the majority was the Na Xi. Rees (2000) and White (1997) provide details of the ethnic identities in the Naxi community.
21. A three-eyed well is made up of three parts: the first well has the cleanest water and serves as drinking water; the second well is used for washing food items like vegetables and meat; and the third well is used for washing clothes. Although termed "wells," the water flow is continuous, as the wells are linked to the canals.

Chapter 4: Producing heritage: Lijiang's immersion into global tourism

1. Singapore's Merlion is a good example of the symbolic meaning of heritage (see Yeoh and Chang 2001). Invented in the early 1970s by the government, it is now recognized as a national symbol of Singapore.

2. Xuan Ke is a public figure in Lijiang. He is often cited in *Lijiang Daily* and other domestic newspapers.
3. Ouyang Jian was promoted to vice Minister of the Department of Propaganda on November 2005 because of his "excellent" job in using tourism to industrialize Lijiang's ethnic cultures. He is but one of many Lijiang's government cadres who have made significant career advancements because of Lijiang's successful tourism development.
4. The Regulation on the Preservation of Naxi Dongba Culture Statute and the Statute on the Conservation of Lijiang Ancient Town both took effect on 1 January 2006.
5. In the eyes of Ouyang Jian, the government is not responsible for the survival of cultural companies. Instead, its responsibility is to privatize state-owned cultural companies or encourage them to go into joint ventures with the private sector (*Xinhua News Agency* 7 September 2004).
6. This term and the heading of the next section have been adapted from similar headings used in Singapore's Tourism 21 Plan (Singapore Tourist Promotion Board 1996).
7. URL: http://whc.unesco.org/en/about/ (accessed 26 July 2006).
8. For international hotel corporations, the Chinese government has allowed them to operate directly in Chinese cities since 1978, but on the condition that they must go into joint ventures with Chinese firms. They were also expected to impart their management skills. Since China entered into the World Trade Organization in 2002, international hotel corporations are free to operate on their own. Beijing, Shanghai, Guangzhou, Shenzhen, and Xi'an were the only cities opened to international travel agencies in 2003. It was only in 2007 that these agencies could start operations in other parts of China.
9. The proper name is Lijiang Naxi Autonomous County, set up in 1961 by the State Council. The County is a part of Lijiang Prefecture. On 26 December 2002, the State Council approved the proposal to revoke Lijiang Prefecture and establish Lijiang City within the same territory. At the same time, Lijiang County was divided into two parallel administrative units: Yulong Naxi Autonomous County and Downtown District. Lijiang Ancient Town is situated in the newly established Downtown District.
10. http://www.banyantree.com/lijiang/index.htm (accessed 27 July 2006).
11. Common affluence is a key idea in Deng Xiaoping's theory of socialist market economy (see Chapter 3). The implementation of "great western development" aims to achieve this prospect.
12. In the case of Lijiang, the Mayor is nominated by the Yunnan provincial government and goes to the Lijiang People's Congress for final approval. This approval is only a stamp. The Mayor works under the leadership of the Party committee. Hence, it is the CCP secretary who has the final say.
13. From "The Main Duties of Lijiang Tourism Bureau" (*Lijiang lvyouju gongzuo zhizhe*), URL: http://www.ljta.gov.cn/dzsw/co.asp?id=55 (accessed 22 June 2005).

Chapter 5: Consuming heritage: tourists' expectations and influence on Lijiang

1. Crouch *et al.* (2001) mention three ways for tourists to make sense of destinations: looking, listening, and touching. We prefer to use "gazing" rather than "looking" since the relation between tourists and the objects they *look* at is loosely defined. The act of "gazing" embodies power relations (see discussion by Urry (2002)) and highlights tourists' purposeful intent to consume a gaze that is accumulated from both past experiences and from information gathered about the destination.

2. The website of Tianyaclub hosts 2,759 pages of Lijiang pictures taken by tourists. The most popular page, http://cache.tianya.cn/techforum/Content/49/524741.shtml (accessed 21 March 2007), has been hit 59,984 times since it was posted on 22 January 2006. The photos feature Lijiang's historic buildings, rivers, flowers, trees, and the Naxi people. The title of this webpage is "The life of a pseudo Bohemian guy in Lijiang."

3. xitek.com is the most popular website for photo enthusiasts. Entitled "For oblivious memory – Lijiang," the site similarly focuses on the ubiquitous canals, buildings, and the Naxi (see http://forum.xitek.com/showthread.php?threadid=351311 accessed 21 March 2007).

4. Travelchinaguide.com is an English website where tourists can find necessary information about Lijiang and other sites and share their experiences. In a webpage http://www.travelchinaguide.com/picture/yunnan/lijiang/ (accessed 21 March 2007), the lens trails the same objects as the above two webpages.

5. URL: http://www.tianyaclub.com/New/PublicForum/Content.asp?flag=1&idWriter=0&Key=0&idArticle=60385&strItem=travel (accessed 3 November 2005).

6. Our survey showed that 78 percent of international tourists and 55 percent of domestic tourists stayed less than 4 days in Lijiang. As we observed, group tours normally spend most of their time in attractions in the town's vicinity and less than 1 day in the town, although the town is a must-see.

7. Guesthouses not only attempt to replicate the design of traditional houses, but also hold tea-drinking sessions to create ambience.

8. When Chinese tourists mention "authenticity," they say *yuanzhi yuanwei*, which literally refers to "original taste and flavor."

9. Here we loosely divide the domestic tourists into middle-class group tourists and independent visitors. The former account for over 60 percent of Lijiang's domestic market (LTB 2005), spending less than a day in Lijiang Ancient Town. During their day trip, they shop and take many photographs. The independent tourists (less than 40 percent) stay at least 2 nights in the town. They are willing to engage with "real" Naxi culture and local lifestyle. Our purpose of segmenting domestic tourists is to show that they have different impacts on Lijiang's heritage landscapes and to allow for a more in-depth discussion of dominance and resistance. In Lijiang's tourism market, the group tourists are obviously in a dominant position, as they spend more.

10. http://www.doyouhike.net/article/797,5.html (accessed 5 November 2006).

11. During fieldwork in June–July 2007, we observed that the tables along the canal had disappeared. It was told to us that the CWHMC ordered all bar owners to remove the tables because they caused congestion at night.

12. A guesthouse owner (Respondent OM10) had this to say:

    Very few domestic tourists are willing to stay in a common room. They come to inquire whether there is standard room; if there is none, they will immediately leave. The chance to sell a common room is nearly zero.

13. Deqin is a county in the northwest of Yunnan Province. It is to the north of Lijiang and is very near to Tibet.

14. Japanese group tourists have little impact on the town as they spend only a few hours touring the town. They mostly stay in the hotels in the new city. Recently, it was noted that more and more Japanese backpackers have opted to stay in the town for a longer period in order to learn Mandarin or to enjoy the local life. Generally, they choose guesthouses as their base. However, their influence on the town is still limited when compared to Chinese tourists.

15. In China, people generally call foreigners *laowai* or *waiguoren*. Sometimes *laowai* specifically refers to Westerners.

Chapter 6: Landscapes of hegemony: commodification and the socio-spatial transformation of Lijiang

1. Since the nation state and the provincial government (Yunnan) share the same goals of development, they are treated as a single entity.
2. A shop owner has to pay a transfer fee to change/take over the operation of a shop. Investors from Guangzhou and other coastal areas have speculated heavily on these transfers and made hefty profits without even setting foot in the shops.
3. We investigated the right to operate a business rather than the ownership of the building because it is the change of hands of the licenses rather than the ownership of the building that is the more speculative.
4. Inspired by the bells widely used during the Tea-Horse Route, a business person, born in Sichuan Province, invented a new type of bell. He named the bell after himself: Bunong. Because of its unique appearance and cultural connotation, his bell has become very popular among tourists. The Bunong bell is now a must-have souvenir. Many have tried to copy Bunong's bell, but none have managed to outdo his business. Bunong operates two shops: one in Lijiang and the other in Katmandu.

Chapter 7: Local agency in heritage tourism

1. The respondent used *zhonghua minzu* (Chinese nationality), a concept encompassing Han, Naxi, Tibet, and other 53 officially recognized ethnic groups in mainland China.
2. Yuhua is a pseudonym.
3. Dongba Cultural Museum was established in 1989 by a local governmental official. The Lijiang government annually subsidizes the museum and authorizes it to collect Dongba antiques. Dongba Cultural Research Institute was founded in 1981 by a retired Lijiang Party secretary, with the support of Yunnan Institute of Social Sciences. Like the museum, the institute enjoys full sponsorship from the local government. Its main work is to rescue, collate, and study Dongba culture, especially the Dongba scripts. The current honorary director of the institute, He Zixing, is also the Communist Party Secretary of Lijiang.
4. Creative destruction not only happens in Lijiang but also in many other heritage sites in China. Recent studies on China's heritage tourism reveal that commodification has led to the destruction of Luzhi, a well-known water town in Jiangsu Province (Fan *et al.* 2008) and Zhu Jia Jiao, a historic town in Shanghai (Huang *et al.* 2007).
5. This is the reason why LTB refuses to give details on the proportion of group tourists and independent tourists. Group tourists have to pay an entry fee which is used for the maintenance of Lijiang Ancient Town.

Chapter 8: Conclusion: cultural politics of heritage tourism and beyond

1. The entrepreneurial Chinese state plays a key role in the formation of a typical mode of capitalist production, a mode which has been referred to as red capitalism (Lin 1997), Confucian capitalism (Yao and Souchou 2002), or capitalism with Chinese characteristics (Karmel 1994). No matter the different terms used, the key idea is "state regulation of a hybrid economic system with the existence of a private economic sphere that remains very close to the state system that spawned it" (Breslin 2004:1). To describe how close private capital is to the state system, we use "public–private alliance," as shown in the case of Lijiang, to depict the joint power of bureaucracy and capital not only in the arena of tourism but also in every sphere of the Chinese economy. Recently, Wu (2008) drew on neoliberalism to argue for the use of neoliberalization to characterize the trend of market-driven capital accumulation in China, contending that "the market is the dominant and leading mechanism, while the state governs the market" (Wu 2008:1096).
2. For a thorough review of non-representational theory, refer to Nash (2000).

References

Adams, K. M. (2003) The politics of heritage in Tana Toraja, Indonesia: interplaying the local and the global, *Indonesia and the Malay World*, 31: 92–107.

Adamson, W. L. (1980) *Hegemony and Revolution: A Study of Antonio Gramsci's Political and Cultural Theory*. Berkeley and London: University of California Press.

Agnew, J. A. and Corbridge, S. (1995) *Mastering Space: Hegemony, Territory and International Political Economy*. London: Routledge.

Agnew, J. A. and Duncan, J. S. (eds) (1989) *The Power of Place: Bringing together Geographical and Sociological Imaginations*. London: Unwin Hyman.

Aitchison, C. (1999) New cultural geographies: the spatiality of leisure, gender and sexuality, *Leisure Studies*, 18: 19–39.

Aitchison, C. (2001) Theorizing Other discourses of tourism, gender and culture: can the subaltern speak (in tourism)? *Tourist Studies*, 1: 133–147.

Aitchison, C., MacLeod, N. E., and Shaw, S. J. (2000) *Leisure and Tourism Landscapes: Social And Cultural Geographies*. London and New York: Routledge.

Albers, P. and James, W. (1988) Travel photography: a methodological approach, *Annals of Tourism Research*, 15: 134–158.

Alsayyad, N. (2001) Global norms and urban forms in the age of tourism: manufacturing heritage, consuming tradition. In: N. Alsayyad (ed.), *Consuming Tradition, Manufacturing Heritage: Global Norms and Urban Forms in the Age of Tourism* (pp. 1–31). London: Routledge.

Amin, A. and Thrift, N. (2002) *Cities: Reimagining the Urban*. Cambridge: Polity.

Anderson, B. (1983) *Imagined Communities: Reflections on the Origin and Spread of Nationalism*. London: Verso.

Anderson, K. J. (1988) Cultural hegemony and the race-definition process in Chinatown, Vancouver: 1880–1980, *Environment and Planning D: Society and Space*, 6: 127–149.

Anderson, P. (1976) The antinomies of Antonio Gramsci, *New Left Review*, 100: 5–79.

Andriotis, K. (2001) Tourism planning and development in Crete: recent tourism policies and their efficacy, *Journal of Sustainable Tourism*, 9: 298–316.

Anonymous (2006) I want to visit Lijiang after watching Yimiyangguan (in Chinese). Available at <http://msn.mtime.com/group/10071/discussion/29356/> (accessed 21 March 2007).

Anonymous (2007) Debating our China excursion [in] Yunnan or Lijiang and TLG? Available at <http://thorntree.lonelyplanet.com/messagepost.cfm?postaction=reply&catid=19&threadid=1312378&messid=11466324&iCountryId=84> (accessed 21 March 2007).

Appadurai, A. (1996) *Modernity at Large: Cultural Dimensions of Globalization.* Minneapolis: University of Minnesota Press.

Ashworth, G. J. and Tunbridge, J. E. (1990) *The Tourist-Historic City.* London and New York: Belhaven Press.

Ateljevic, I. (2000) Circuits of tourism: stepping beyond the 'production/consumption' dichotomy, *Tourism Geographies*, 2: 369–388.

Ateljevic, I. and Doorne, S. (2002) Representing New Zealand: tourism imagery and ideology, *Annals of Tourism Research*, 29: 648–667.

Ateljevic, I. and Doorne, S. (2003) Culture, economy and tourism commodities: social relations of production and consumption, *Tourist Studies*, 3: 123–141.

Bao, J. and Su, X. (2004) Studies on tourism commercialization in historic towns (in Chinese), *ACTA Geographical Sinica*, 59: 427–436.

Bates, T. R. (1975) Gramsci and the theory of hegemony, *Journal of the History of Ideas*, 36: 351–366.

Béja, J. P. (2006) The changing aspects of civil society in China, *Social Research: An International Quarterly of Social Sciences*, 73: 53–74.

Bendor, J., Taylor, S. and Gaalen, R. V. (1987) Politicians, bureaucrats, and asymmetric information, *American Journal of Political Science*, 31: 796–828.

Benjamin, W. (2001) The work of art in the age of mechanical reproduction. In: M. G. Durham and D. M. Kellner (eds), *Media and Cultural Studies: Keyworks* (pp. 48–70). Malden, MA: Blackwell.

Bennett, T. (1986) Introduction: 'the turn to Gramsci'. In: T. Bennett, C. Mercer, and J. Wollacott (eds), *Popular Culture and Social Relations* (pp. xi–xix). Milton Keynes: Open University Press.

Bian, Y. (2002) Chinese social stratification and social mobility, *Annual Review Sociology*, 28: 91–116.

Bianchi, R. V. (2002) Towards a new political economy of global tourism. In: R. Sharpley and D. J. Telfer (eds), *Tourism and Development: Concepts and Issues* (pp. 265–299). Clevedon: Channel View Publication.

Bishop, P. (1989) *The Myth of Shangri-la: Tibet, Travel Writing and the Western Creation of Sacred Landscape.* Berkeley and Los Angeles: University of California Press.

Blom, T. (2000) Morbid tourism: a postmodern market niche with an example from Althorp. *Norwegian Journal of Geography*, 54: 29–36.

Bocock, R. (1986) *Hegemony.* Chichester: Ellis Horwood.

Boniface, P. and Fowler, P. J. (1993) *Heritage and Tourism in "the Global Village".* London and New York: Routledge.

Bourdieu, P. (1984) *Distinction: A Social Critique of the Judgment of Taste.* London: Routledge & Kegan Paul.

Bourdieu, P. (2001) The forms of capital. In: M. Granovetter and R. Swedberg (eds), *The Sociology of Economic Life*, 2nd edn (pp. 96–111). Colorado: Westview Press.

Boyd, S. (2002) Cultural and heritage tourism in Canada: opportunities, principles and challenges, *Tourism and Hospitality Research*, 3: 211–233.

Boyer, M. C. (1994) *The City of Collective Memory: Its Historic Imagery and Architectural Entertainment.* Cambridge, Mass: MIT Press.

Brandt, L. and Rawski, T. G. (eds) (2008) *China's Great Economic Transformation.* Cambridge: Cambridge University Press.

Brenner, N. (1999) .Beyond state-centrism? space, territoriality, and geographical scale in globalization studies, *Theory and Society*, 28: 39–78.

Breslin, S. (2004) Capitalism with Chinese characteristics: the public, the private and the international. Perth: Asia Research Centre, Murdoch University (working paper No. 104).

Britton, S. (1980) The spatial organization of tourism in a neo-colonial economy: a Fiji case study, *Pacific Viewpoint*, 21: 144–165.

Britton, S. (1982) The political economy of tourism in the third world, *Annals of Tourism Research*, 9: 331–358.

Britton, S. (1991) Tourism, capital and place: towards a critical geography of tourism, *Environment and Planning D: Society and Space*, 9: 451–478.

Brown, M. J. (1996) *Negotiating Ethnicities in China and Taiwan*. Berkeley: Institute of East Asian Studies, University of California Berkeley Center for Chinese Studies.

Bryman, A. (1995) *Disney and his Worlds*. London: Routledge.

Bunnell, T. (1999) Views from above and below: the Petronas Twin Towers and/in contesting visions of development in contemporary Malaysia, *Singapore Journal of Tropical Geography*, 20: 1–23.

Bunnell, T. (2004) *Malaysia, Modernity, and the Multimedia Supper Corridor: A Critical Geography of Intelligent Landscapes*. London: Routledge.

Burgess, J. A. and Gold, J. R. (1985) *Geography, the Media & Popular Culture*. London: Croom Helm.

Burns, P. and Novelli, M. (eds) (2006) *Tourism and Politics: Global Frameworks and Local Realities*. Boston: Elsevier.

Butler, T. (2007) Re-urbanizing London Docklands: gentrification, suburbanization or new urbanism? *International Journal of Urban and Regional Research*, 31: 759–781.

Chang, T. C. (1997) Heritage as a tourism commodity: traversing the tourist-local divide, *Singapore Journal of Tropical Geography*, 18: 46–68.

Chang, T. C. (1999) Local uniqueness in the global village: heritage tourism in Singapore, *Professional Geographer*, 51: 91–103.

Chang, T. C. (2000) Theming cities, taming places: insights from Singapore, *Geografiska Annaler B*, 1: 35–54.

Chang, T. C. and Huang, S. (2005) Recreating place, replacing memories: creative destruction at the Singapore River, *Asia Pacific Viewpoint*, 46: 267–280.

Chang, T. C., Milne, S., Fallon, D., and Pohlmann, C. (1996) Urban heritage tourism: the global–local nexus, *Annals of Tourism Research*, 23: 284–305.

Chao, E. (1996) Hegemony, agency, and re-presenting the past: the invention of Dongba culture among the Naxi of southwest China? In: M. J. Brown (ed.), *Negotiating Ethnicities in China and Taiwan*. (pp. 208–239). Berkeley: University of California Press.

Chao, L. and Myers, S. H. (1998) China's consumer revolution: the 1990s and beyond, *Journal of Contemporary China*, 7: 351–368.

Chatterton, P. and Hollands, R. (2003) *Urban Nightscapes: Youth Cultures, Pleasure Spaces and Corporate Power*. London and New York: Routledge.

Chen, Z. (2005) Nationalism, internationalism and Chinese foreign policy, *Journal of Contemporary China*, 14: 35–53.

Cheong, S. and Miller, M. L. (2000) Power and tourism: a Foucauldian observation, *Annals of Tourism Research*, 27: 371–390.

China Daily (4 January 2006) Lijiang. Available at <http://www.chinadaily.com.cn/english/doc/2004-01/06/content_296124.htm> (accessed 10 March 2007).

China Daily (3 April 2006) Travel tips to the ancient town of Lijiang, p. 9.

China Daily (25 July 2006) Historical sites need protection. Available at <http://www.chinadaily.com.cn/cndy/2006-07/25/content_648343.htm> (accessed 5 June 2008).

China Daily (16 November 2007) Multi-party cooperation the historical choice. Available at <http://www.chinadaily.com.cn/cndy/2007-11/16/content_6258160.htm> (accessed 2 May 2008).

China Daily (16 December 2007) China makes 3 traditional festivals holidays. Available at <http://www.chinadaily.com.cn/china/2007-12/16/content_6324571.htm> (accessed 1 July 2008).

China Daily (29 December 2007) Urban renewal needs to respect history. Available at <http://www.chinadaily.com.cn/cndy/2007-12/29/content_6357523.htm> (accessed 17 July 2008).

China Daily (8 February 2008) China to become world's top tourist destination before 2020. Available at <http://www.chinadaily.com.cn/china/2007-02/08/content_805194.htm> (accessed 4 July 2008).

China Daily (16 June 2008) Profiting from culture. Available at <http://www.chinadaily.com.cn/opinion/2008-06/16/content_6763521.htm> (accessed 11 July 2008).

China Youth Daily (23 December 2005) Yunnan Stops Lijiang's Binding 'Naxi Cultural Route' for Sale (in Chinese). Available at <http://zqb.cyol.com/content/2005-12/23/content_1222539.htm> (accessed 15 March 2007).

Chinese Academy of Social Sciences (2005) *Blue Book of Chinese Society*. Beijing: Social Sciences Academic Press.

China National Tourism Administration (CNTA) (1997) The measurement and assessment of star hotel (in Chinese). Available at <http://www.cnta.gov.cn/22-zcfg/2j/swfd.asp> (accessed 1 May 2006).

Chinese National Tourism Administration (CNTA) (2006) *The Yearbook of China Tourism Statistics, 2005* (in Chinese), Beijing: Zhongguo lvyou chubanshe.

Chouinard, V. (1996) Structure and agency: contested concepts in human geography. In: C. Earle, K. Mathewson, and M. S. Kenzer (eds), *Concepts in Human Geography* (pp. 283–410). Lanham: Rowman & Littlefield Publishers.

Ci, J. (1994) *Dialectic of the Chinese Revolution: From Utopianism to Hedonism*. Stanford, Calif.: Stanford University Press.

Cohen, E. (1988) Authenticity and commoditization in tourism, *Annals of Tourism Research*, 15: 371–386.

Cohen, E. (2000) *The Commercialized Crafts of Thailand: Hill Tribes and Lowland Villages: Collected Articles*. Richmond, Surrey: Curzon.

Cohen, E. (2004) *Contemporary Tourism: Diversity and Change*. Boston: Elsevier.

Cole, S. (2007) *Tourism, Culture and Development: Hopes, Dreams and Realities in East Indonesia*. Clevedon: Channel View Publications.

Coleman, S. and Crang, M. (2002) Grounded tourists, travelling theory. In: S. Coleman and M. Crang (eds), *Tourism: Between Place and Performance* (pp. 1–20). New York and Oxford: Berghahn.

Coles, T. and Church, A. (2007a) Tourism, politics and the forgotten entanglements of power. In: A. Church and T. Coles (eds), *Tourism, Power and Space* (pp. 1–42). London and New York: Routledge.

Coles, T. and Church, A. (eds) (2007b) *Tourism, Power and Space*. London and New York: Routledge.

Cook, I. and Crang, P. (1996) The world on a plate: culinary culture, displacement and geographical knowledges, *Journal of Material Culture*, 1: 131–153.

Cosgrove, D. (1983) Towards a radical cultural geography: problems of theory, *Antipode*, 15: 1–11.

Cosgrove, D. (1984) *Social Formation and Symbolic Landscape*. London: Croom Helm.

Cosgrove, D. (1992) Orders and a new world: cultural geography 1990–1991, *Progress in Human Geography*, 16: 272–280.

Cosgrove, D. and Daniels, S. (eds) (1988) *The Iconography of Landscape*. Cambridge: Cambridge University Press.

Cosgrove, D. and Jackson, P. (1987) New directions in cultural geography, *Area*, 19: 95–101.

Cox, R. W. (1993) Gramsci, hegemony and international relations: an essay in method. In: S. Gill (ed.), *Gramsci, Historical Materialism and International Relations* (pp. 49–66). Cambridge: Cambridge University Press.

Crang, M. (1997) Picturing practices: research through the tourist gaze, *Progress in Human Geography*, 21: 359–373.

Crang, M. (2004) Cultural geographies of tourism. In: A. A. Lew, C. M. Hall, and A. M. Williams (eds), *A Companion to Tourism* (pp. 74–84). Malden: Blackwell.

Crawshaw, C. and Urry, J. (1997) Tourism and the photographic eye. In: C. Rojek and J. Urry (eds), *Touring Cultures: Transformations of Travel and Theory* (pp. 176–195). London: Routledge.

Cresswell, T. (1996) *In Place/Out of Place: Geography, Ideology, and Transgression*. Minneapolis and London: University of Minnesota Press.

Croll, E. J. (2006) Conjuring goods, identities and cultures. In: K. Latham, S. Thompson, and J. Klein (eds), *Consuming China: Approaches to Cultural Change in Contemporary China* (pp. 23–41). London and New York: Routledge.

Crouch, D. (1999) Introduction: encounters in leisure/tourism. In: D. Crouch (ed.), *Leisure/Tourism Geographies: Practices and Geographical Knowledge* (pp. 1–16). London and New York: Routledge.

Crouch, D., Aronsson, L., and Wahlströn, L. (2001) Tourist encounters, *Tourist Studies*, 1: 253–270.

Dann, G. (1996) *The Language of Tourism: A Sociolinguistic Perspective*. Wallingford: CAB International.

Davis, D. (2000) *The Consumer Revolution in Urban China*. Berkeley, Calif.: University of California Press.

Davis, D. (2005) Urban consumer culture, *The China Quarterly*, 183: 692–709.

de Certeau, M. (1984) *The Practice of Everyday Life*. Berkeley: University of California Press.

Dear, M. (2000) *The Postmodern Urban Condition*. Oxford, UK: Malden.

Dear, M. and Flusty, S. (1998) Postmodern urbanism, *Annals of the Association of American Geographers*, 88: 50–72.

Deng X. (1994) *Selected Works of Deng Xiaoping (1982–1992)*. Available at <http://english.peopledaily.com.cn/dengxp/vol3/text/c1220.html>(accessed 4 November 2006).

Desforges, L. (1998) 'Checking out the planet': global representations/local identities and youth travel. In: T. Skelton and G. Valentine (eds), *Cool Places: Geographies of Youth Cultures* (pp. 175–192). London: Routledge.

Desforges, L. (2000) Travelling the world: travel, identity and travel biography, *Annals of Tourism Research*, 27: 926–945.

Desforges, L. (2001) Tourism consumption and the imagination of money, *Transactions of the Institute of British Geographers*, 26: 353–364.

Dirlik, A. (1996) The Global in the local. In: R. Wilson and W. Dissanayake (eds), *Cultural Production and the Transnational Imaginary* (pp. 21–45). Durham and London: Duke University Press.

Dirlik, A. and Zhang, X. (1997) Introduction: postmodernism and China, *Boundary 2*, 24: 1–18.

Donaldson, J. A. (2007) Tourism, development and poverty reduction in Guizhou and Yunnan, *The China Quarterly*, 190: 333–351.

Dovey, K., Fitzgerald, J., and Choi, Y. (2001) Safety becomes danger: dilemmas of drug-use in public space, *Health & Place*, 7: 319–331.

Dreyer, J. T. (1976) *China's Forty Millions: Minority Nationalities and National Integration in the People's Republic of China.* Cambridge, Mass.: Harvard University Press.

Drost, A. (1996) Developing sustainable tourism for world heritage sites, *Annals of Tourism Research*, 23: 479–484.

du Cros, H. (2006) Managing visitor impacts at Lijiang, China. In: A. Leask and A. Fyall (eds), *Managing World Heritage Sites* (pp. 205–214). Amsterdam: Elsevier.

du Gay, P., Hall, L., Janes, L., Mackay, H., and Nequs, K. (1997) *Doing Cultural Studies: The Stories of the Sony Walkman.* London: Sage.

Duan, S. (2000) *A Heritage Protection and Tourism Development Case Study of Lijiang Ancient town, China.* Bangkok: UNESCO Office of the Regional Advisor for Culture in Asia and the Pacific.

Duan, S. (2002) From Lijiang Phenomenon to Lijiang Model (in Chinese), *Planner*, 6: 54–57.

Duncan, J. S. (1993) Sites of representation: place, time and the discourse of the Other. In: J. S. Duncan and D. Ley (eds), *Place/Culture/ Representation* (pp. 39–56). London and New York: Routledge.

Duncan, J. S. (2000) Representation. In: R. J. Johnston, D. Gregory, G. Pratt. and M. Watts (eds), *The Dictionary of Human Geography*, 4th edn (pp.703–705). Oxford: Blackwell.

Duncan, N. and Sharp, J. P. (1993) Confronting representation(s), *Environment and Planning D: Society and Space*, 11: 473–486.

Dwyer, O. J. (2004) Symbolic accretion and commemoration, *Social & Cultural Geography*, 5: 419–435.

Ebbe, K. and Hankey, D. (2000) *Case Study: Lijiang, China – Earthquake Reconstruction and Heritage Conservation.* Washington, DC: The World Bank.

Edensor, T. (1998) *Tourists at the Taj: Performance and Meaning at a Symbolic Site.* London and New York: Routledge.

Edensor, T. (2000) Staging tourism: tourists as performers, *Annals of Tourism Research*, 27: 322–344.

Edwards, M. (1994) Our man in China: Joseph Rock, *National Geographic*, 19: 62–81.

Erb, M. (2000) Understanding tourists: interpretations from Indonesia, *Annals of Tourism Research*, 27: 709–736.

Fan, C., Wall, G., and Mitchell, C. J. A. (2008) Creative destruction and the water town of Luzhi, China, *Tourism Management*, 29: 648–660.

Fang, G. (1981) *The History and Distribution of Naxi Ethnic Groups* (in Chinese). Kunming: Yunnan Renmin Chubanshe.

Far Eastern Economic Review (5 June 2003) China – Conservation – Shared Heritage, p. 27.

Featherstone, M. (1991) *Consumer Culture and Postmodernism.* London: Sage Publications.

Feifer, M. (1985) *Going Places: The Ways of the Tourist from Imperial Rome to the Present Day*. London: Macmillan.

Fife, W. (2005) *Doing Fieldwork: Ethnographic Methods for Research in Developing Countries and Beyond*. New York: Palgrave.

Foucault, M. (1979) *Discipline and Punish: The Birth of the Prison*. New York: Vintage.

Foucault, M. (1990) *History of Sexuality*, Vol. 1. New York: Vintage Books.

Franklin, A. and Crang, M. (2001) The trouble with tourism and travel theory? *Tourist Studies*, 1: 5–22.

Getz, D. (1994) Event tourism and the authenticity dilemma. In: W. F. Theobald (ed.), *Global Tourism: The Next Decade* (pp. 313–329). Oxford: Butterworth-Heinemann.

Ghosh, P. (2001) Gramscian hegemony: an absolutely historicist approach, *History of European Ideas*, 27: 1–43.

Gibson, C. and Kong, L. (2005) Cultural economy: a critical review, *Progress in Human Geography*, 29: 541–561.

Gibson, J. L., Ivancevich, J. M., Donnelly, J. H., and Konopaske, R. (2006) *Organizations: Behavior, Structure, Process*, 12th edn. Boston: McGraw-Hill.

Giddens, A. (1991) *Modernity and Self-Identity: Self and Society in the Late Modern Age*. Oxford: Polity Press.

Gilbert, M. (1999) Place, politics, and the production of urban space: a feminist critique of the growth machine thesis. In: A. E. G. Jonas and D. Wilson (eds), *The Urban Growth Machine: Critical Perspectives Two Decades Later* (pp. 95–108). Albany: State University of New York Press.

Gittings, J. (2005) *The Changing Face of China: From Mao to Market*. New York: Oxford University Press.

Gladney, D. C. (1994) Representing nationality in China: refiguring majority/minority identities, *Journal of Asian Studies*, 53: 92–123.

Gladstone, D. L. (2005) *From Pilgrimage to Package Tour: Travel and Tourism in the Third World*. New York: Routledge.

Global Heritage Fund (GHF) (13 September 2007) Global Heritage Fund congratulates UNESCO World Heritage site Lijiang ancient town in Yunnan, China. Available at <http://www.globalheritagefund.org/news/releases/lijiang_award_sept_07.asp> (accessed 10 July 2008).

Global Heritage Fund (GHF) (2004) GHF instrumental in transforming 1,000-year-old Chinese town into top domestic tourist destination. Available at <http://www.globalherit agefund.org/news/releases/lijiang_smithsonian_8_20_04.html> (accessed 13 June 2008).

Global Heritage Fund (GHF) (n.d.) Lijiang, China. Available at <http://www.globalherit agefund.org/where/lijiang_profile.html> (accessed 14 June 2008).

Global Naxi Cultural Conservation Society (GNCCS) (n.d.) GNCCS mission. Available at <http://www.gnccs.org/gnccs-mission.html> (accessed 10 July 2008).

Gong, Y. (1988) *A Commentary on 'the Stories of Yunnan Tusi in Ming History'* (in Chinese). Kunming: Yunnan minzu chubanshe.

Goodman, D. S. G. (2004) The campaign to 'open up the West': national, provincial-level and local perspectives, *The China Quarterly*, 178: 317–334.

Gotham, K. F. (2005a) Tourism from above and below: globalization, localization and New Orleans's Mardi Gras, *International Journal of Urban and Regional Research*, 29: 309–326.

Gotham, K. F. (2005b) Tourism gentrification: the case of New Orleans' Vieux Carre (French Quarter), *Urban Studies*, 42: 1099–1121.

Gotham, K. F. (2007) Destination New Orleans: commodification, rationalization, and the rise of urban tourism, *Journal of Consumer Culture*, 7: 305–334.

Gottdiener, M. (2000) Approaches to consumption: classical and contemporary perspectives. In: M. Gottdiener (ed.), *New Forms of Consumption: Consumer, Culture, and Commodification* (pp. 3–31). Lanham: Rowman & Littlefield.

Goulding, C. (1998) The commodification of the past, postmodern pastiche, and the search for authentic experiences at contemporary heritage attractions, *European Journal of Marketing*, 34: 835–853.

Goullart, P. (1955) *Forgotten Kingdom*. London: John Murray.

Graham, B., Ashworth, G. J., and Tunbridge, J. E. (2000) *A Geography of Heritage: Power, Culture, and Economy*. London: Arnold.

Gramsci, A. (1971) *Selections from the Prison Notebooks of Antonio Gramsci*. London: Lawrence & Wishart.

Gramsci, A. (1985) *Selections from Cultural Writings*. Cambridge, Mass.: Harvard University Press.

Gray, J. (2006) Mao in perspective, *The China Quarterly*, 187: 659–679.

Greenwood, D. J. (1977) Culture by the pound: an anthropological perspective tourism as cultural commoditization. In: V. L. Smith (ed.), *Hosts and Guests: The Anthropology of Tourism* (pp. 129–137). Philadelphia: University of Pennsylvania Press.

Gregory, D. (2000) Modernism. In: R. J. Johnston, D. Gregory, G. Pratt and M. Watts (eds), *The Dictionary of Human Geography*, 4th edn (pp. 510–512). London: Blackwell.

Gries, P. H. (2004) *China's New Nationalism: Pride, Politics, and Diplomacy*. Berkeley: University of California Press.

Guangzhou Daily (15 October 2002) Why Lijiang People escape from the Town (in Chinese). Guangzhou: Guangzhou Daily, p. 4.

Guo, D. and He, Z. (1999) *The History of Naxi Groups* (in Chinese). Chengdu: Sichuan minzhu chubanshe.

Guo, Y. (2004) *Cultural Nationalism in Contemporary China: The Search for National Identity Under Reform*. London and New York: Routledge.

Gupta, A. and Ferguson, J. (1992) Beyond "culture": space, identity, and the politics of difference, *Cultural Anthropology*, 7: 6–23.

Hall, C. M. (1994) *Tourism and Politics: Policy, Power and Place*. Chichester: Wiley.

Hall, S. (1980) Encoding/decoding. In: S. Hall, D. Hobson, D. Lowe, and P. Willis (eds), *Culture, Media, Language* (pp. 128–138). London: Hutchinson.

Hall, S. (2005) Whose heritage? un-settling 'the heritage', re-imagining the post-nation. In: J. Littler and R. Naidoo (eds), *The Politics of Heritage: The Legacies of 'Race'* (pp. 23–35). London and New York: Routledge.

Harper, D., Burke, A., and Grundvig, J. (2005) *Lonely Planet China*. London: Lonely Planet.

Harrell, S. (1995) Introduction: civilizing projects and the reaction to Them. In: S. Harrell (ed.), *Cultural Encounters on China's Ethnic Frontiers* (pp. 3–36). Seattle and London: University of Washington Press.

Harrell, S. (2001) *Ways of Being Ethnic in Southwest China*. Seattle: University of Washington Press.

Harrison, D., Hitchcock, M., and Limited, M. M. (2005) *The Politics of World Heritage: Negotiating Tourism and Conservation*. Clevedon: Channel View Publications.

Harrison, J. (2003) *Being a Tourist: Finding Meaning in Pleasure Travel*. Vancouver and Toronto: University of British Columbia Press.

Harvey, D. (1973) *Social Justice and the City*. London: Edward Arnold.

Harvey, D. (1978) The urban process under capitalism: a framework for analysis, *International Journal of Urban and Regional Research*, 2: 101–130.

Harvey, D. (1989a) *The Condition of Postmodernity: An Enquiry into the Origins of Cultural Change*. Oxford: Blackwell.

Harvey, D. (1989b) From managerialism to entrepreneurialism: the transformation in urban governance in late capitalism, *Geografiska Annaler. Series B, Human Geography*, 71: 3–17.

Harvey, D. (1993) From space to place and back again: reflections on the condition of postmodernity. In: J. Bird, B. Curtis, T. Putnam, G. Robertson, and L. Tichner (eds), *Mapping the Futures: Local Cultures, Global Change* (pp. 3–29). London and New York: Routledge.

Harvey, D. (2005) *A Brief History of Neoliberalism*. New York: Oxford University Press.

Hayden, D. (1995) *The Power of Place: Urban Landscapes As Public History*. Cambridge, Mass.: MIT Press.

He, G. (ed.) (1999) *A 50-Year-Long History of China's Tourism Industry* (in Chinese). Beijing: Zhonghuo Ivyou chubanshe.

He, H. (2001) The hereditary administration in Lijiang and 'Gaituguiliu' (in Chinese). In: G. Niu (ed.), *The Culture and History of Lijiang* (in Chinese) (Vol. 20) (pp. 12–24). Lijiang: Lijiang Prefecture Government.

He, S. and Wu, F. (2005) Property-led redevelopment in post-reform China: a case study of Xintiandi redevelopment project in Shanghai, *Journal of Urban Affairs*, 27: 1–23.

Henderson, J. C. (2003) The politics of tourism in Myanmar, *Current Issues in Tourism*, 6: 97–118.

Henderson, J. C. (2007) Communism, heritage and tourism in East Asia, *International Journal of Heritage Studies*, 13: 240–254.

Herman, J. E. (1997) Empire in the southwest: early Qing reforms to the native chieftain system, *The Journal of Asian Studies*, 56: 47–74.

Herrera, L. M. G., Smith, N., and Vera, M. (2007) Gentrification, displacement, and tourism in Santa Cruz De Tenerife, *Urban Geography*, 28: 276–298.

Hewison, R. (1987) *The Heritage Industry: Britain in a Climate of Decline*. London: Methuen.

Hilton, J. (1933) *Lost Horizon*. London: Macmillan.

Hitchcock, M. (2001) Tourism and total crisis in Indonesia: the case of Bali, *Asia Pacific Business Review*, 8: 101–120.

Hobsbawm, E. J. and Ranger, T. O. (1983) *The Invention of Tradition*. Cambridge: Cambridge University Press.

Hoffman, J. (1984) *The Gramscian Challenge: Coercion and Consent in Marxist Political Theory*. Oxford: Blackwell.

Hong Kong Trade Development Council (2001) HK vs. Shanghai: competitors or partners? Available at <http://www.tdctrade.com/tdcnews/0103/01031901.htm> (accessed 10 July 2008).

Hough, M. (1984) *City Form and Natural Process: Towards a New Urban Vernacular*. New York: Croom Helm.

Hu, J. (2006) Speech at Yale University. Available at <http://www.yale.edu/opa/hu/download/transcript_Hu_20060421.doc> (accessed 15 December 2008).

Huang, H. Y. B., Wall, G., and Mitchell, C. J. A. (2007) Creative destruction Zhu Jia Jiao, China, *Annals of Tourism Research*, 34: 1033–1055.

Huang, Y. (2006) Residents' attitude to tourism development in heritage sites: a case study of Pingyao Ancient Town (in Chinese), *Journal of Guilin Institute of Tourism*, 17: 124–128.

International Herald Tribune (23 October 2005) Chinese tourists getting a bad image. Available at <http://www.iht.com/articles/2005/10/21/business/tourists.php> (accessed 5 May 2008).

Jackson, A. (1979) *Na-Khi Religion: An Analytical Appraisal of the Na-khi Ritual Texts.* The Hague: Mouton.

Jackson, P. (1989) *Maps of Meaning: An Introduction to Cultural Geography.* London; Winchester, Mass.: Academic Division, Unwin Hyman.

Jackson, P. (1991) Mapping meanings: a cultural critique of locality studies, *Environment and Planning A*, 23: 215–228.

Jackson, P. (1999) Commodity cultures: the traffic in things, *Transactions of the Institute of British Geographers*, 24: 95–108.

Jackson, P. (2000a) Cultural politics. In: R. J. Johnston, D. Gregory, G. Pratt, and M. Watts (eds), *The Dictionary of Human Geography*, 4th edn. Oxford: Blackwell.

Jackson, P. (2000b) Rematerializing social and cultural geography, *Social & Cultural Geography*, 1: 9–14.

Jackson, P. and Holbrook, B. (1995) Multiple meanings: shopping and the cultural politics of identity, *Environment and Planning A*, 27: 1913–1930.

Jackson, P. and Thrift, N. (1995) Geographies of consumption. In: D. Miller (ed.), *Acknowledging Consumption: A Review of New Studies* (pp. 204–237). London and New York: Routledge.

Jazeel, T. (2006) Postcolonial geographies of privilege: diaspora space, the politics of personhood and the Sri Lankan Women's Association in the UK, *Transactions of the Institute of British Geographers*, 31: 19–33.

Jenkins, J. M. (1993) Tourism policy in rural New South Wales – policy and research priorities, *Geojournal*, 29: 281–290.

Jeong, S. and Santos, C. A. (2004) Cultural politics and contexted place identity, *Annals of Tourism Research*, 31: 640–656.

Jessop, B. (1982) *The Capitalist State: Marxist Theories and Methods.* New York and London: New York University Press.

Jessop, B. (1990) *State Theory: Putting Capitalist States in their Place.* Pennsylvania: Pennsylvania State University Press.

Johnson, R. (1986) The story so far: and further transformations? In: D. Punter (ed.), *Introduction to Contemporary Cultural Studies* (pp. 277–313). London: Longman.

Joseph, C. A. and Kavoori, A. P. (2001) Mediated resistance: tourism and the host community, *Annals of Tourism Research*, 28: 998–1009.

Karmel, S. M. (1994) Emerging securities markets in China: capitalism with Chinese characteristics, *China Quarterly*, 140: 1105–1120.

Kearns, G. and Philo, C. (eds) (1993) *Selling Places: The City as Cultural Capital, Past and Present.* Oxford: Pergamon Press.

Keith, M. and Pile, S. (1993) Introduction part 2: the place of politics. In: M. Keith and S. Pile (eds), *Place and the Politics of Identity* (pp. 22–40). London and New York: Routledge.

Keith, R. C. (ed.) (2005) *China as a Rising World Power and Its Response to 'Globalization'.* London and New York: Routledge.

Kibby, M. (2000) Tourists on the mother road and the information superhighway, in M. Robinson, P. Long, K. Evans, R. Sharpley, and J. Swarbrooke (eds), *Reflection* on *International Tourism: Expressions of Culture, Identity, and Meaning in Tourism* (pp. 139–149). Newcastle: University of Northumbria.

Kim, H. and Richardson, S. L. (2003) Motion picture impacts on destination images, *Annals of Tourism Research*, 30: 216–237.

King, A. D. (2003) Cultures and spaces of postcolonial knowledges. In: S. Pile, M. Domosh, and K. Anderson (eds). *Handbook of Cultural Geography* (pp. 381–397). London: Sage.

Knight, N. (2007) *Rethinking Mao: Explorations in Mao Zedong's Thought*. New York: Lexington Books.

Ko, S. (2001) China's pragmatism as a grand national development strategy: historical legacy and evolution, *Issue & Studies*, 37: 1–28.

Kolås, A. (2004) Tourism and the making of place in Shangri-La, *Tourism Geographies*, 6: 262–278.

Kong, L. (1995) Music and cultural politics: ideology and resistance in Singapore, *Transactions of the Institute of British Geographers*, 20: 447–459.

Kong, L. and Yeoh, B. S. A. (1997) The construction of national identity through the production of ritual spectacle: an analysis of National Day Parades in Singapore, *Political Geography*, 16: 213–239.

Kornai, J. (1992) *The Socialist System: The Political Economy of Communism*. New Jersey: Princeton University Press.

Lanfant, M. F. (1995) International tourism, internationalization and the challenge to identity. In: M. F. Lanfant, J. B. Allcock, and E. M. Bruner (eds), *International Tourism: Identity and Change* (pp. 24–43). London: Sage.

Langman, L. (2003) Culture, identity and hegemony: the body in a global age, *Current Sociology*, 51: 223–247.

Lash, S. and Urry, J. (1994) *Economies of Signs and Space*. London: Sage.

Latham, A. and McCormack, D. P. (2004) Moving cities: rethinking the materialities of urban geographies, *Progress in Human Geography*, 28: 701–724.

Latham, K. (2006) Introduction: consumption and cultural change in contemporary China. In: K. Latham, S. Thompson, and J. Klein (eds), *Consuming China: Approaches to Cultural Change in Contemporary China* (pp. 1–21). London and New York: Routledge.

Leask, A. (2006) World heritage site designation. In: A. Leask and A. Fyall (eds), *Managing World Heritage Sites* (pp. 5–19). Amsterdam: Elsevier.

Lees, L. (2002) Rematerializing geography: the 'new' urban geography, *Progress in Human Geography*, 26: 101–112.

Lefebvre, H. (1991) *The Production of Space*. Oxford: Blackwell.

Lew, A. A., Yu, L., and Zhang, G. (eds) (2003) *Tourism in China*. New York: Haworth Hospitality Press.

Li, W. (2006) Community decisionmaking: participation in development, *Annals of Tourism Research*, 33: 132–143.

Lijiang Ancient Downtown Government (2006) An induction to Banyan Tree Lijiang Limited Corporation. Available at <http://www.ljgczs.gov.cn/Article.asp?Id=165> (accessed 27 July 2008).

Lijiang Bureau of Statistics (2006) Statistics Bulletin of Lijiang National Economy and Social Development in 2005 (in Chinese). Available at <http://www.lijiang.gov.cn/pubnews/doc/read/tjgb/1042251549.165233465/index.asp> (accessed 7 July 2008).

Lijiang Bureau of Statistics (2007) Statistic Bulletin of Lijiang National Economy and Social Development in 2006 (in Chinese). Online. Available HTTP: < http://61.166.7.153:8080/pubnews/doc/read/tbgg/876644097.204203437/index.asp> (accessed 2 July 2008).

Lijiang Bureau of Statistics (2008) Statistics Bulletin of Lijiang National Economy and Social Development in 2007 (in Chinese). Available at <http://61.166.7.153:8080/pubnews/doc/read/tbgg/876644097.204203437/index.asp> (accessed 2 July 2008).

Lijiang Chinese Communist Party Committee (2006) The Decision about Speeding up Lijiang's Tourism Sector (in Chinese). Online. Available at <http://www.lijiang.gov.cn/pubnews/doc/read/zfwj/702375957.170765678/> (accessed 7 July 2008).

Lijiang County Government (1992) *Conservation Plan for Lijiang Historic Town* (in Chinese). Lijiang: Lijiang County Government.

Lijiang County Government (1997) *Detailed Conservation Plan of Lijiang Ancient Town* (in Chinese). Lijiang: Lijiang County Government.

Lijiang Daily (29 January 1999) The rebirth of ethnic culture (in Chinese). Lijiang: Lijiang Daily, p. 3.

Lijiang Daily (2 February 2004) Heritage preservation in Lijiang obtains attention (in Chinese). Lijiang: Lijiang Daily, p. 6.

Lijiang Daily (8 April 2004) From Dayan old town to Yuhe Lodge (in Chinese). Lijiang: Lijiang Daily, p. 4.

Lijiang Daily (8 May 2004) Solidifying and developing 'Lijiang Models' (in Chinese). Lijiang: Lijiang Daily, p. 3.

Lijiang Daily (22 May 2004) Preserving Naxi Culture (in Chinese). Lijiang: Lijiang Daily, p. 4.

Lijiang Daily (8 September 2004) Lijiang: writing a song about the harmony between conservation and development. Lijiang: Lijiang Daily, p. 1.

Lijiang Daily (27 September 2004) Market awakes the disappearing culture (in Chinese). Lijiang: Lijiang Daily, p. 3.

Lijiang Daily (29 March 2006) The practices of developing ethnic cultural industry in Lijiang (in Chinese). Lijiang: Lijiang Daily, p. 2.

Lijiang Daily (9 April 2006) Build a world-class quintessential destination through creative theory and methods (in Chinese). Available at <http://www.lijiang.gov.cn/pubnews/doc/read/fzlt/856429923.166177771/index.asp> (accessed 4 September 2008).

Lijiang Office for Editing Local History (1997) *Lijiang Almanac* Vol. 1 (in Chinese). Kunming: Yunnan minzhu chubanshe.

Lijiang Prefecture Committee for Editing Local Records (2000) *Records of Lijiang Prefecture* (in Chinese). Kunming: Yunnan renming chubanshe.

Lijiang Tourism Association (2005) *A Notification for Travel Agents on Promoting and Managing 'Naxi Cultural Route'* (in Chinese). Lijiang: Lijiang Tourism Association.

Lijiang Tourism Bureau (LTB) (n.d.) *The Emerging Lijiang Tourism* (in Chinese) (unpublished). Lijiang: Lijiang Tourism Bureau.

Lijiang Tourism Bureau (LTB) (2004) *A Basic Introduction to Lijiang's Tourism Industry* (in Chinese) (unpublished). Lijiang: Lijiang Tourism Bureau.

Lijiang Tourism Bureau (LTB) (2005). *Lijiang Tourism Master Plan (2004–2020)* (in Chinese). Lijiang: Lijiang Tourism Bureau.

Lijiang Yearbook (1999) *Dali–Lijiang Road was open* (in Chinese). Lijiang: Lijiang Yearbook.

Lim, K. F. (2004) Where love dares (not) speak its name: the expression of homosexuality in Singapore, *Urban Studies*, 41: 1759–1788.

Lin, G. C. S. (1997) *Red Capitalism in South China.* Vancouver: UBC Press.

Lin, Y., Tao, R., and Liu, M. (2005) Decentralization and local governance in the context of China's transition, *Perspective*, 6: 25–36.

Liu, D. (2002) *An Analysis and Forecast on China's Domestic Tourism Development* (in Chinese). Beijing: Shehui Kexue Wenxian Chubanshe.

Liu, D. (2005) On the beneficial interaction of the preservation and tourist utilization of ancient town (in Chinese). *Tourism Tribune*, 20: 47–53.

Liu, K. (2004) *Globalization and Cultural Trends in China*. Honolulu: University of Hawaii Press.

Lonely Planet (1988) *China: A Travel Survival Kit*, 2nd edn. Hawthorn, Victoria, Australia: Lonely Planet.

Long, N. (1996) Globalization and localization: new challenges to rural research. In: H. L. Moore (ed.), *The Future of Anthropological Knowledge* (pp. 37–59). London and New York: Routledge.

Lorimer, H. (2005) Cultural geography: the busyness of being more-than-representational? *Progress in Human Geography*, 29: 83–94.

Lowenthal, D. (1979) Age and artefact. In: D. W. Meining (ed.), *The Interpretation of Ordinary Landscapes: Geographical Essays* (pp. 104–128). Oxford: Oxford University Press.

Lv, W. (2004) Marketing orientation of tourism industry in western China (in Chinese), *Thinking*, 30: 127–132.

Ma, J. C. L. (2001) Urban transformation in China, 1949–2000: a review and research agenda, *Environment and Planning A*, 33: 1545–1569.

Ma, J. C. L. and Wu, F. (2005) *Restructuring the Chinese City: Changing Society, Economy and Space*. London and New York: Routledge.

McCann, E. J. (2002) The cultural politics of local economic development: meaning-making, place-making, and the urban policy process, *Geoforum*, 33: 385–398.

McCann, E. J. (2004) 'Best Places': interurban competition, quality of life and popular media discourse, *Urban Studies*, 41: 1909–1929.

MacCannell, D. (1976) *The Tourist: A New Theory of the Leisure Class*. New York: Schocken.

McKhann, C. F. (2001) The good, the bad, and the ugly: observations and reflections on tourism development in Lijiang. In: C. Tan, S. C. H. Cheung, and H. Yang (eds), *Tourism Anthropology and China: In Memory of Professor Wang Zhusheng*. Bangkok: White Lotus Press.

Mansvelt, J. (2005) *Geographies of Consumption*. London: Sage.

Markus, T. and Cameron, D. (2001) *Buildings and Language: The Words between the Spaces*. London: Routledge.

Marston, S. A. (2000) The social construction of scale, *Progress in Human Geography*, 24: 219–242.

Mason, K. (2004) Sound and meaning in Aboriginal tourism, *Annals of Tourism Research*, 31: 837–854.

Massey, D. (1993) Politics and space/time. In: M. Keith and S. Pile (eds), *Place and the Politics of Identity* (pp. 141–161). London and New York: Routledge.

Massey, D. and Jess, P. (1995) Place and cultures in an uneven world. In: D. Massey and P. Jess (eds), *A Place in the World: Places, Cultures and Globalization* (pp. 215–238). Oxford: Oxford University Press.

May, T. (1993) *Social Research: Issues, Methods, and Process*. Buckingham, England: Open University Press.

Medina, L. K. (2003) Commoditizing culture – tourism and Maya identity, *Annals of Tourism Research*, 30: 353–368.

Meethan, K. (2001) *Tourism in Global Society: Place, Culture, and Consumption*. New York: Palgrave.

Meethan, K. (2004) Tourism development and the political economy. In: S. Williams (ed.), *Tourism: Critical Concepts in the Social Science*, Vol. III (pp. 3–28). London and New York: Routledge.

Miller, D. (1995) Consumption as the vanguard of history: a polemic by way of an introduction. In: D. Miller (ed.), *Acknowledging Consumption: A Review of New Studies* (pp. 1–57). London and New York: Routledge.

Minca, C. (2000) 'The Bali syndrome': the explosion and implosion of 'exotic' tourist spaces, *Tourism Geographies*, 2: 389–403.

Mitchell, D. (2000) *Cultural Geography: A Critical Introduction*. Oxford, UK; Malden, Mass.: Blackwell Publishers.

Mitchell, D. (2001) The lure of the local: landscape studies at the end of a troubled century, *Progress in Human Geography*, 25: 269–281.

Mitchell, D. (2002) Cultural landscapes: the dialectical landscape–recent landscape research in human geography, *Progress in Human Geography*, 26: 381–389.

Morgan, N. and Pritchard, A. (1998) *Tourism Promotion and Power: Creating Images, Creating Identities*. Chichester: John Wiley & Sons.

Mouffe, C. (1979) Introduction: Gramsci today. In: C. Mouffe (ed.), *Gramsci and Marxist Theory* (pp. 1–18). London: Routledge & Kegan Paul.

Mu, L. (1997) *The History of Lijiang Ancient Town* (in Chinese). Beijing: Minzhuchubanshe.

Munasinghe, H. (2005) The politics of the past: constructing a national identity through heritage conservation, *International Journal of Heritage Studies*, 11: 251–260.

Munt, I. (1994) The 'other' postmodern tourism: culture, travel and the new middle classes, *Theory, Culture and Society*, 11: 101–123.

Muzaini, H. (2006) Backpacking Southeast Asia: strategies of "looking local", *Annals of Tourism Research*, 33: 144–161.

Nash, C. (2000) Performativity in practice: some recent work in cultural geography, *Progress in Human Geography*, 24: 653–664.

Nash, C. (2004) Postcolonial geographies: spatial narratives of inequality and interconnection. In: P. Cloke, P. Crang, and M. Goodwin (eds), *Envisioning Human Geographies* (pp. 104–127). London: Arnold.

Nash, D. (1977) Tourism as a form of imperialism. In: V. L. Smith (ed.), *Hosts and Guests: The Anthropology of Tourism* (pp. 37–54). Philadelphia: University of Pennsylvania Press.

Nash, D. (1996) *Anthropology of Tourism*. Kidlington, Oxford: Pergamon.

National Bureau of Statistics of China (2002) *Tabulation on Nationalities of 2000 Population Census of China* (in Chinese). Beijing: Zhongguo tongji chubanshe.

National Bureau of Statistics of China (2005) *China Statistical Yearbook 2005* (in Chinese). Beijing: Zhongguo tongji chubanshe.

Naughton, B. (1995) *Growing out of the Plan: Chinese Economic Reform, 1978–1993*. New York: Cambridge University Press.

Naxi Cultural Development Company (n.d.) Tea horse road (in Chinese). Available at <http://www.ljgc.com/chama/main.htm#> (accessed 2 July 2005).

Neuman, W. L. (2003) *Social Research Methods: Qualitative and Quantitative Approaches*, 5th edn. Boston: Allyn and Bacon.

Ngai, P. (2003) Subsumption or consumption? the phantom of consumer revolution in "globalizing" China, *Cultural Anthropology*, 18: 469–492.

Norkunas, M. K. (1993) *The Politics of Public Memory: Tourism, History, and Ethnicity in Monterey, California*. Albany: State University of New York Press.

Nyíri, P. (2006) *Scenic Spots: Chinese Tourism, the State, and Cultural Authority*. Seattle and London: University of Washington Press.

Oakes, T. (1993) The cultural space of modernity: ethnic tourism and place identity in China tourism, *Environment and Planning D: Society and Space*, 11: 47–66.

Oakes, T. (1995) Tourism in Guizhou: the legacy of internal colonialism. In: A. A. Lew and L. Yu (eds), *Tourism in China: Geographic, Political, and Economic Perspectives* (pp. 203–222). Boulder: Westview.

Oakes, T. (1997) Ethnic tourism in rural Guizhou: sense of place and the commerce of authenticity. In: M. Picard and R. E. Wood (eds), *Tourism, Ethnicity, and the State in Asian and Pacific Societies* (pp. 35–70). Honolulu: University of Hawaii Press.

Oakes, T. (1998) *Tourism and Modernity in China*. London: Routledge.

Oakes, T. (2006) Cultural strategies of development: implications for village governance in China, *The Pacific Review*, 19: 13–37.

Ohmae, K. (1990) *The Borderless World: Power and Strategy in the Interlinked Economy*. London: Collins.

Palmer, C. (2005) An ethnography of Englishness: experiencing identity through tourism, *Annals of Tourism Research*, 32: 7–27.

Parkinson, M. and Harding, A. (1995) European cities toward 2000: Entrepreneurialism, competition and social exclusion. In: M. Rhodes (ed.), *The Regions and the New Europe: Patterns in Core and Periphery Development* (pp. 53–77). Manchester: Manchester University Press.

Pearce, D. G. (1998) Tourist districts in Paris: structure and functions, *Tourism Management*, 19: 49–65.

Peck, J. (2006) Why we shouldn't be bored with the political economy versus cultural studies debate, *Cultural Critique*, 64: 92–125.

Peleggi, M. (1996) National heritage and global tourism in Thailand, *Annals of Tourism Research*, 23: 432–448.

Peleggi, M. (2005) Consuming colonial nostalgia: the monumentalisation of historic hotels in urban Southeast Asia, *Asia Pacific Viewpoint*, 46: 255–265.

People's Daily (2 February 2001) Tourism to play bigger role. Available at <http://english.peopledaily.com.cn/english/200102/02/eng20010202_61457.html> (accessed 4 October 2006).

People's Daily (9 October 2001) Qian Qichen: implement Three Representative to speed up tourism development (in Chinese). Available at <http://www.people.com.cn/GB/shizheng/19/20011009/576838.html> (accessed 6 May 2005).

People's Daily (17 October 2002) The soul of Lijiang Ancient Town is flowing water (in Chinese). Available at <http://www.people.com.cn/GB/paper464/7485/717854.html> (accessed 15 March 2007).

People's Daily (22 July 2004) 'Re-experience the Long March': China to launch 'red tourism' project (in Chinese). Available at <http://english.people.com.cn/200407/22/eng20040722_150461.html> (accessed 10 March 2005).

People's Daily (25 March 2005) Red tourist attractions post 33.26% growth (in Chinese). Available at <http://www.chinadaily.com.cn/english/doc/2005-03/25/content_428214.htm> (accessed 4 July 2008).

People's Daily (5 February 2006) Spring festival boosts China's retail consumption (in Chinese). Available at <http://english.peopledaily.com.cn/200602/05/eng20060205_240402.html> (accessed 8 August 2007).

People's Daily (10 February 2006) China's best destinations for the Valentine's Day (in Chinese). Available at <http://travel.people.com.cn/GB/41636/41644/4094042.html> (accessed 10 March 2007).

People's Daily (15 February 2008) Chinese tourists welcomed in foreign countries (in Chinese). Available at <http://english.peopledaily.com.cn/90001/90782/92900/6354887. html> (accessed 7 July 2008).

Perrow, C. (1986) *Complex Organizations: A Critical Essay*, 3rd edn. New York: McGraw-Hill.

Philp, J. and Mercer, D. (1999) Commodification of Buddhism in contemporary Burma, *Annals of Tourism Research*, 26: 21–54.

Picard, M. (1996) *Bali: Cultural Tourism and Touristic Culture*. Singapore: Archipelago Press.

Picard, M. (1997) Cultural tourism, nation-building, and regional culture: the making of a Balinese identity. In: M. Picard and R. E. Wood (eds), *Tourism, Ethnicity, and the State in Asian and Pacific Societies* (pp. 181–214). Honolulu: University of Hawaii Press.

Picard, M. (2003) Touristification and Balinization in a time of reformasi, *Indonesia and the Malay World*, 31: 108–118.

Pile, S. (1997) Introduction: opposition, political identity and spaces of resistance. In: S. Pile and M. Keith (eds), *Geographies of Resistance* (pp. 1–32). London and New York: Routledge.

Pitchford, S. R. (1995) Ethnic tourism and nationalism in Wales, *Annals of Tourism Research*, 22: 35–52.

Pretes, M. (2003) Tourism and nationalism, *Annals of Tourism Research*, 30: 125–142.

Rapoport, A. (1982) *The Meaning of the Built Environment: A Nonverbal Communication Approach*. Beverly Hills, Calif.: Sage.

Rawski, T. G. (1999) Reforming China's economy: what have we learned, *The China Journal*, 41: 139–156.

Rees, H. (2000) *Echoes of History: Naxi Music in Modern China*. New York: Oxford University Press.

Relph, E. C. (1976) *Place and Placelessness*. London: Pion.

Reuters News (17 June 2008) U.S. and Chinese officials welcome first-ever Chinese Tour groups to America. Available at <http://www.reuters.com/article/pressRelease/ idUS143139+17-Jun-2008+BW20080617> (accessed 4 July 2008).

Reuters News (5 February 1996) More tremors rock quake-hit China town of Lijiang. Reuters Limited.

Richards, G. (1995) Politics of national tourism policy in Britain, *Leisure studies*, 14: 153–173.

Richards, G. (1996) Production and consumption of European cultural tourism, *Annals of Tourism Research*, 23: 261–283.

Richards, G. (2007) *Cultural Tourism: Global and Local Perspectives*. New York: Haworth Press.

Richter, L. K. (1989) *The Politics of Tourism in Asia*. Honolulu: University of Hawaii Press.

Ritzer, D. G. (2004) *The McDonaldization of Society*. London: Pine Forge Press.

Ritzer, G. and Liska, A. (1997) 'McDisneyization' and 'post-tourism': complementary perspectives on contemporary tourism. In: C. Rojek and J. Urry (eds), *Touring Cultures: Transformations of Travel and Theory* (pp. 96–112). London: Routledge.

Robins, K. (1991) Tradition and translation: national culture. In: J. Corner and S. Harvey (eds), *Enterprise and Heritage: Crosscurrents of National Culture* (pp. 21–44). London: Routledge.

Rock, J. F. (1947) *The Ancient Na-Khi Kingdom of Southwest China*. Cambridge, MA: Harvard University Press.

Rojek, C. and Urry, J. (eds) (1997) *Touring Cultures: Transformations of Travel and Theory*. London and New York: Routledge.

Rose, G. (1994) The cultural politics of place: local representation and oppositional discourse in two films, *Transactions of the Institute of British Geographers*, 19: 46–60.

Rosemary, J. (1987) *Indigenous Enterprises in Kenya's Tourism Industry*. Geneva: UNESCO.

Round, J. (2008) Everyday tactics and spaces of power: the role of informal economies in post-Soviet Ukraine, *Social & Cultural Geography*, 9: 171–185.

Routledge, P. (2001) 'Selling the rain', resisting the sale: resistant identities and the conflict over tourism in Goa, *Social & Cultural Geography*, 2: 221–240.

Said, E. W. (1978) *Orientalism*. New York: Pantheon Books.

Salmon, P. (1992) *Achieving a PhD: Ten Students' Experiences*. Staffordshire: Trentham Books.

Sayer, R. A. (2000) *Realism and Social Science*. London and Thousand Oaks, Calif.: Sage.

Schein, L. (1989) The dynamics of cultural revival among the Miao in Guizhou. In: C. Chiao and N. Tapp (eds), *Special Issue on Ethnicity and Ethnic Groups in China* (pp. 199–210). Hong Kong: New Asia College, Chinese University of Hong Kong.

Schmitter, P. C. (2002) Participation in governance arrangements: is there any reason to expect it will achieve sustainable and innovative policies in a multi-level context. In: J. R. Grote and B. Gbikpi (eds), *Participatory Governance. Political and Societal Implications* (pp. 51–69). Opladen: Leske and Budrich.

Schubert, G. (2001) Nationalism and national identity in contemporary China: assessing the debate, *Issue & Studies*, 37: 128–156.

Scott, A. J. (2000) *The Cultural Economy of Cities: Essays on the Geography of Image-Producing Industries*. London: Sage.

Scott, A. J. (2001) Capitalism, cities, and the production of symbolic forms, *Transactions of the Institute of British Geographers*, 26: 11–23.

Scott, J. C. (1985) *Weapons of the Weak: Everyday Forms of Peasant Resistance*. New Haven: Yale University Press.

Scott, J. C. (1990) *Domination and the Arts of Resistance: Hidden Transcripts*. New Haven: Yale University Press.

Selby, M. (2004) Consuming the city: conceptualizing and researching urban tourist knowledge, *Tourism Geographies*, 6: 186–207.

Seligmann, A. (1992) *The Idea of Civil Society*. New York: Free Press.

Shanghai Star (1 August 2002) Lijiang, poetic place for living. Available at <http://app1.chinadaily.com.cn/star/2002/0801/tr16-1.html> (accessed 17 July 2008).

Shao, Y., Zhang, L., and Dun, M. (2004) Conservation and social development of Ancient Towns of Lijiang (in Chinese), *Ideal Space*, 6: 52–55.

Sharp, J. P., Philo, C., and Paddison, R. (eds) (2000) *Entanglements of Power: Geographies of Domination/Resistance*. London and New York: Routledge.

Shaw, G. and Williams, A. M. (1998) Entrepreneurship, small business culture, and tourism development. In: D. Ioannides and K. G. Debbage (eds), *The Economic Geography of the Tourist Industry: A Supply-side Analysis* (pp. 235–255). London and New York: Routledge.

Shaw, G. and Williams, A. M. (2004) *Tourism and Tourism Spaces*. London: Sage.

Shenghuo Xinbao (9 June 2006) Lijiang Airport is Operated and the Naxi Kingdom is flying (in Chinese). Available at <http://news.carnoc.com/list/70/70251.html> (accessed 17 July 2007).

Shields, R. (1992) The individual, consumption cultures and the fate of community. In: R. Shields (ed.), *Lifestyle Shopping: The Subject of Consumption* (pp. 99–113). London: Routledge.

Shin, L. K. (2006) *The Making of the Chinese State: Ethnicity and Expansion on the Ming Borderlands*. New York: Cambridge University Press.

Shotter, J. (1998) Action research as history making, *Concepts and Transformation*, 2: 279–286.

Sibley, D. (1995) *Geographies of Exclusion: Society and Difference in the West*. London Routledge,.

Sidaway, J. D. (2002) *Imagined Regional Communities: Integration and Sovereignty in the Global South*. New York: Routledge.

Sidaway, J. D. (2007) Enclave space: a new metageography of development? *Area*, 39: 331–339.

Singapore Tourist Promotion Board (1996) *Tourism 21: Vision of a Tourism Capital*. Singapore: Pagesetters Services.

Skeggs, B. (2002) Techniques for telling the reflexive self. In: T. May (ed.), *Qualitative Research in Action* (pp. 349–374). London: Sage.

Smith, C. J. (2002) From 'leading the masses' to 'serving the consumer'? newspaper reporting in contemporary urban China, *Environment and Planning A*, 34: 1635–1660.

Smith, M. K. and Robinson, M. (eds) (2006) *Cultural Tourism in a Changing World: Politics, Participation and (Re)presentation*. Buffalo, NY: Channel View Publications.

Smith, N. (2002) New globalism, new urbanism: gentrification as global urban strategy, *Antipode*, 34: 427–450.

Smith, V. L. (ed.) (1977) *Hosts and Guests: The Anthropology of Tourism*. Philadelphia: University of Pennsylvania Press.

Sofield, T. H. B. and Li, F. M. S. (1998) Tourism development and cultural policies in China, *Annals of Tourism Research*, 25: 362–392.

Soja, E. (1989) *Postmodern Geographies: The Reassertion of Space in Critical Social Theory*. London and New York: Verso.

Soja, E. (2000) Thirdspace: expanding the scope of the geographical imagination. In A. Read (ed.), *Architecturally Speaking: Practices of Art, Architecture and the Everyday* (pp. 13–30). London and New York: Routledge.

Soja, E. and Hooper, B. (1993) The spaces that difference makes: some notes on the geographical margins of the new cultural politics. In: M. Keith and S. Pile (eds), *Place and the Politics of Identity* (pp. 183–205). London and New York: Routledge.

Squire, S. J. (1994) Accounting for cultural meaning: the interface between geography and tourism studies re-examined, *Progress in Human Geography*, 18: 1–16.

Strange, I. (1996) Local politics, new agendas and strategies for change in English historic cities, *Cities*, 13: 431–437.

Strinati, D. (1995) *An Introduction to Theories of Popular Culture*. London and New York: Routledge.

Su, X. and Huang, C. (2005) The impacts of heritage tourism on public space in historic towns: a case study of Lijiang Ancient Town, *China Tourism Research*, 1: 401–442.

Su, X. and Teo, P. (2008) Tourism politics in Lijiang, China: an analysis of state and local interactions in tourism development, *Tourism Geographies*, 10: 150–168.

Swain, M. B. (1990) Commoditizing ethnicity in southwest China, *Cultural Survival*, 14: 26–32.

Swyngedouw, E. (1997a) Excluding the other: the production of scale and scaled politics. In: R. Lee and J. Wills (eds), *Geographies of economies* (pp. 167–176). London: Arnold.

Swyngedouw, E. (1997b) Neither global nor local: "glocalization" and the politics of scale. In: K. Cox (ed.), *Spaces of Globalization: Reasserting the Power of the Local* (pp. 137–166). New York: Guildford Press.

Tang, W. (2002) Political and social trends in the post-Deng urban China: crisis or stability? *The China Quarterly*, 168: 890–909.

Teo, P. (2003) The limits of imagineering: a case study of Penang, *International Journal of Urban and Regional Research*, 27: 545–563.

Teo, P. and Huang, S. (1995) Tourism and heritage conservation in Singapore, *Annals of Tourism Research*, 22: 589–615.

Teo, P. and Leong, S. (2006) A postcolonial analysis of backpacking, *Annals of Tourism Research*, 33: 109–131.

Teo, P. and Lim, H. L. (2003) Global and local international in tourism, *Annals of Tourism Research*, 30: 287–306.

Terkenli, T. S. (2002) Landscape of tourism: towards a global cultural economy of space? *Tourism Geographies*, 4: 227–254.

The Asian Wall Street Journal (23 November 2001) Setting the tourist trap. The Asian Wall Street Journal, w1.

The New York Times (17 May 2006) Next wave of camera-wielding tourists is from China. Available at <http://www.nytimes.com/2006/05/17/world/asia/17travel.html?_r=1&oref=slogin> (accessed 20 August 2008).

The State Council (1986) *The Report on Issuing out the List of the Second Round National Historic and Cultural City* (in Chinese). Available at <http://www.china-fpa.org/memories/chinagov/> (accessed 27 July 2008).

The Times (7 October 2006) The lost horizon in Yunnan. Available at <http://travel.timesonline.co.uk/tol/life_and_style/travel/destinations/china/article662907.ece> (accessed 23 March 2008).

The Toronto Star (22 October 2004) Tourist hordes storm world's world's gate, p. A01.

Thompson, C., O'Hare, G. and Evans, K. (1995) Tourism in the Gambia: problems and proposals, *Tourism Management*, 16: 571–581.

Thompson, J. B. (1990) *Ideology and Modern Culture: Critical Social Theory in the Era of Mass Communication*. Oxford: Polity Press.

Thrift, N. (2000) Entanglements of power: shadows? In: J. P. Sharp, P. Routledge, C. Philo and R. Paddison (eds), *Entanglements of Power: Geographies of Domination/Resistance* (pp. 269–278). London and New York: Routledge.

Thrift, N. (2006) Re-inventing invention: new tendencies in capitalist commodification, *Economy and Society*, 35: 279–306.

Thrift, N. and Glennie, P. (1993) Historical geographies of urban life and modern consumption. In: G. Kearns and C. Philo (eds), *Selling Places: The City as Cultural Capital, Past and Present* (pp. 33–48). Oxford: Pergamon Press.

Tian, Q. (2004) China develops its west: motivation, strategy and prospect, *Journal of Contemporary China*, 13: 611–636.

Tong, E. (2002) Magicians, magic, and shamanism in ancient China, *Journal of Early Modern History*, 4: 27–73.

Tonkiss, F. (2005) *Space, the City and Social Theory*. Cambridge: Polity.

Tuan, Y. F. (1977) *Space and Place: The Perspective of Experience*. Minneapolis: University of Minnesota Press.

Tucker, H. (2003) *Living with Tourism: Negotiating Identities in a Turkish Village*. London and New York: Routledge.

Tucker, H. and Hall, C. M. (2004) *Tourism and Postcolonialism: Contested Discourses, Identities and Representations*. London and New York: Routledge.

Tunbridge, J. E. and Ashworth, G. J. (1996) *Dissonant Heritage: The Management of the Past as a Resource in Conflict.* Chichester: Wiley.

Turner, C. (2005) Yunnan, China: minority peoples observed, *Asian Affairs*, XXXVI: 12–34.

UNESCO (1999) *Brief Descriptions of Sites Inscribed on the World Heritage List.* Paris: UNESCO.

UNESCO (2005) China – Ancient Naxi Dongba Literature Manuscripts. Available at http://portal.unesco.org/ci/en/ev.php-URL_ID=7260&URL_DO=DO_TOPIC&URL_SECTION=201.html(accessed 23 March 2007).

Urry, J. (1994) Cultural change and contemporary tourism, *Leisure Studies*, 13: 233–238.

Urry, J. (2000) *Sociology beyond Societies: Motilities for the Twenty First Century.* New York: Routledge.

Urry, J. (2002) *The Tourist Gaze*, 2nd edn. London: Sage.

Veblen, T. (1934 [1899]) *The Theory of the Leisure Class: An Economic Study of Institutions.* New York: The Modern Library.

Waitt, G. (1997) Selling paradise and adventure: representations of landscape in the tourist advertising of Australia, *Australian Geographical Studies*, 35: 47–60.

Waitt, G. and McGuirk, P. M. (1996) Marking time: tourism and heritage representation at Millers Point, Sydney, *Australian Geographer*, 27: 11–19.

Walker, R. and Buck, D. (2007) The Chinese road: cities in the transition to capitalism, *New Left Review*, 46: 39–66.

Walks, R. A. (2008) Urban form, everyday life, and ideology: support for privatization in three Toronto neighbourhoods, *Environment and Planning A*, 40: 258–282.

Wall, G. and Xie, P. F. (2005) Authenticating ethnic tourism: Li dancers' perspectives, *Asia Pacific Journal of Tourism Research*, 10: 1–21.

Wang, M. and Liu, W. (2005) A study on the protection of heritage resources and governmental behavior in the course of tourism development (in Chinese), *Tourism Tribune*, 20: 21–24.

Wang, N. (1999a) Rethinking authenticity in tourism experience, *Annals of Tourism Research*, 26: 349–370.

Wang, N. (1999b) *Tourism and Modernity: A Sociological Analysis.* New York: Pergamon.

Wang, S. and Hu, A. (1999) *The Political Economy of Uneven Development: The Case of China.* Armonk, NY: M. E. Sharpe.

Wang, Y. (2007) Customized authenticity begins at home, *Annals of Tourism Research*, 34: 789–804.

Warde, A. (2005) Consumption and theories of practice, *Journal of Consumer Culture*, 5: 131–153.

Waterman, R. W. and Meier, K. J. (1998) Principal–agent models: an expansion? *Journal of Public Administration Research and Theory*, 8: 173–202.

Wells, M.J. (1996) *Strawberry Fields: Politics, Class, and Work in California Agriculture.* Ithaca, NY: Cornell University Press.

Wen, J. J. and Tisdell, C. A. (2001) *Tourism and China's Development: Policies, Regional Economic Growth and Ecotourism.* Singapore: World Scientific.

White, G. (1992) *Riding the Tiger: The Politics of Economic Reform in Post-Mao China.* Stanford: Stanford University Press.

White, S. D. (1997) Fame and sacrifice: the gendered construction of Naxi identities, *Modern China*, 23: 298–327.

Whitson, R. (2007) Hidden struggles: spaces of power and resistance in informal work in urban Argentina, *Environment and Planning A*, 39: 2916–2934.

Wilkinson, P. F. (1997) *Tourism Policy and Planning: Case Studies from the Commonwealth Caribbean.* New York: Cognizant Communication Corporation.

Williams, A. M. (2004) Toward a political economy of tourism. In: A. A. Lew, C. M. Hall, and A. M. Williams (eds), *A Companion to Tourism* (pp. 61–73). Malden, Mass.: Blackwell.

Williams, P., Hubbard, P., Clark, D., and Berkeley, N. (2001) Consumption, exclusion and emotion: the social geographies of shopping, *Social & Cultural Geography*, 2: 203–220.

Williams, R. (1958) Culture is ordinary. In: N. Mackenzie (ed.), *Conviction* (pp. 74–92). London: MacGibbon and Kee.

Williams, R. (1977) *Marxism and Literature*. Oxford: Oxford University Press.

Williams, R. (1980) *Problems in Materialism and Culture: Selected Essays*. London: New Left Books.

Winchester, H., Kong, L. and Dunn, K. (2003) *Landscape: Ways of Imagining the World*. Harlow: Person.

Winter, T. (2005) Landscape, memory and heritage: New Year celebrations at Angkor, Cambodia. In: D. Harrison and M. Hitchcock (eds), *The Politics of World Heritage: Negotiating Tourism and Conservation* (pp. 50–65). Clevedon: Channel View Publications.

Winter, T. (2007) Rethinking tourism in Asia, *Annals of Tourism Research*, 34: 27–44.

Winter, T., Teo, P., and Chang, T. C. (eds) (2008) *Asia on Tour: Exploring the Rise of Asian Tourism*. London: Routledge.

Wood, R. E. (1997) Tourism and the state: ethnic options and constructions of otherness. In: M. Picard and R. E. Wood (eds), *Tourism, Ethnicity, and the State in Asian and Pacific Societies* (pp. 1–34). Honolulu: University of Hawaii Press.

Wu, F. (2002) China's changing urban governance in the transition towards a more market-oriented economy, *Urban Studies*, 39: 1071–1093.

Wu, F. (2003) Commentary, *Environment and Planning A*, 35: 1331–1338.

Wu, F. (2008) China's great transformation: neoliberalization as establishing a market society, *Geoforum*, 39: 1093–1096.

Wu, F. and Ma, L. J. C. (2005) The Chinese city in transition: towards theorizing China's urban restructuring. In: L. J. C. Ma and F. Wu (eds), *Restructuring the Chinese City: Diverse Processes and Reconstituted Spaces* (pp. 260–290). London and New York: Routledge.

Xie, P. F. (2003) The bamboo-beating dance in Hainan, China: authenticity and commodification, *Journal of Sustainable Tourism*, 11: 5–16.

Xinhua News Agency (7 September 2004) The implication of Lijiang's success (in Chinese). Available at <http://www.yn.xinhuanet.com/reporter/2006-03/30/content_6610952.htm> (accessed 21 May 2006).

Xinhua News Agency (29 September 2005) The gradual formation of Great Shangri-la Tourism Zone (in Chinese). Available at <http://www.xz.xinhuanet.com/2005-09/29/content_5250785.htm> (accessed 11 February 2006).

Xinhua News Agency (4 April 2006) Tourism helps more rural people get rich (in Chinese). Available at <http://www.chinadaily.com.cn/chinagate/doc/2006-04/11/content_565113.htm> (accessed July 24).

Xinhua News Agency (29 April 2006) Yunnan's tourism development is an example for China (in Chinese). Online. Available at <http://www.yn.xinhuanet.com/newscenter/2006-04/29/content_6879908.htm> (accessed 4 September 2008).

Xinhua News Agency (20 August 2006) The project of Yunnan Dali-Lijiang railway (in Chinese). Available at <http://www.yn.xinhuanet.com/newscenter/2006-08/20/content_7824455.htm> (accessed 30 Octorber 2006).

Xinhua News Agency (31 August 2006) The Bureau of Environmental Protection stopped a 80-million project of reconstructing tradition-simulated building in Changsha (in Chinese). Available at <http://news.xinhuanet.com/society/2006-08/31/ content_5029537.htm> (accessed 25 March 2008).

Xu, G. (1999) *Tourism and Local Economic Development in China: Case Studies of Guilin, Suzhou and Beidaihe*. Richmond, Surrey: Curzon Press.

Xu, J. and Yeh, A. G. O. (2005) City repositioning and competitiveness building in regional development: new development strategies in Guangzhou, China, *International Journal of Urban and Regional Research*, 29: 283–308.

Yale, P. (1991) *From Tourist Attractions to Heritage Tourism*. Huntingdon: Elm.

Yamamura, T. (2004) Authenticity, ethnicity and social transformation at world heritage sites: tourism, retailing and cultural change in Lijiang, China. In: D. Hall (ed.), *Tourism and Transition: Governance, Transformation and Development* (pp. 185–200). Wallingford: CABI.

Yan, A. and Li, H. (2002) On the physical environment in the Lijiang Old City (in Chinese), *Industrial Construction*, 32: 1–4.

Yang, H. (2002) A thought on the relation between tourism development and the fortune of Lijiang Ancient City (in Chinese), *Journal of Central University for Nationalities (Philosophy and Social Sciences Edition)*, 1: 69–72.

Yao, S. (2007) *Can China Really Become the Next Superpower?* Nottingham: China Policy Institute, The University of Nottingham (Briefing Series – Issue 21).

Yao, S. and Souchou, Y. (2002) *Confucian Capitalism: Discourse, Practice and the Myth of Chinese Enterprise*. London: Routledge.

Yeoh, B. S. A. (2001) Postcolonial cities, *Progress in Human Geography*, 25: 456–468.

Yeoh, B. S. A. (2005) The global cultural city? Spatial imagineering and politics in the (multi)cultural marketplaces of South-east Asia, *Urban Studies*, 42: 945–958.

Yeoh, B.S.A. and Chang, T.C. (2001) Globalising Singapore: debating transnational flows in the city, *Urban Studies*, 38(7): 1025–1044.

Yeoh, B. S. A. and Kong, L. (1994) Reading landscape meanings: state constructions and lived experiences in Singapore's Chinatown, *Habitat International*, 18: 17–35.

Yeoh, B. S. A. and Kong, L. (1999) The notion of place: in the construction of history, nostalgia and heritage. In: K. Kwok (ed.), *Our Place in Time: Exploring Heritage and Memory in Singapore* (pp. 132–151). Singapore: Singapore Heritage Society.

Yeoman, I., Brass, D., and McMahon-Beattie, U. (2007) Current issue in tourism: the authentic tourist, *Tourism Management*, 28: 1128–1138.

Yeung, H. W. C. (1998) Capital, state and space: contesting the borderless world, *Transactions of the Institute of British Geographers*, 23: 291–309.

Yunnan Committee for Five Series of Books on Ethnic Issues (ed.) (1983) *Socio-historical Investigation on Naxi Ethnicity* (in Chinese). Kunming: Yunnan minzhu chubanshe.

Yunnan Daily (29 October 2000) Yunnan steps into a strong tourism province (in Chinese). Available at <http://search.yndaily.com/cgi-bin/detail.exe?430714+yndaily> (accessed 10 December 2006).

Yunnan Daily (15 June 2004) My perspectives on building an ethnic cultural province (in Chinese). Available at <http://www.yn.xinhuanet.com/leader/2004-06/15/content_2318513.htm (accessed 10 December 2006).

Yunnan Daily (7 February 2006) The steady development of yunnan's tourism economy (in Chinese). Available at < http://www.yndaily.com> (accessed 25 July 2008).

Yunnan Daily (29 April 2006) Yunnan tourism conference (in Chinese). Available at <http://data.yunnan.cn/Articles/ly1/2006-7/25/20060725142675.htm> (accessed 10 December 2006).

Yunnan Daily (9 June 2006) If the town is not the homeland of Naxi people any more . . . (in Chinese). Available at <http://paper.yunnan.cn/html/20060609/news_89_243693.html> (accessed 25 July 2008).

Yunnan Institute of Designing (1987) *The Conservation Planning of Lijiang Historic Town* (unpublished). Kunming: Yunnan Institute of Designing.

Yunnan Tourism Bureau (2004) *A Plan to Double Yunnan's Tourism Development* (in Chinese). Kunming: Yunnan Tourism Bureau.

Zeppel, H. and Hall, C. M. (1992) Arts and heritage tourism. In: B. Weiler and C. M. Hall (eds), *Special Interest Tourism* (pp. 47–68). London: Belhaven.

Zhang, G. (2003) China's tourism since 1978: policies, experiences and lessons learned. In: A. A. Lew, L. Yu and J. Ap (eds), *Tourism in China* (pp. 13–34). New York: Haworth.

Zhang, H. Q., Chong, K., and Ap, J. (1999) An analysis of tourism policy development in modern China, *Tourism Management*, 20: 471–485.

Zhang, L. (1999) Debating 'Chinese postmodernism', *Postcolonial Studies*, 2: 185–198.

Zhang, L. (2006) Contesting spatial modernity in late-socialist China, *Current Anthropology*, 47: 461–484.

Zhang, W. (2003) Understanding tourism development in Yangsuo: a review of socio-cultural impacts of tourism (in Chinese), *Tourism Tribune*, 18: 15–20.

Zhao, D. (2002) An angle on nationalism in China today: attitudes among Beijing students after Belgrade 1999, *The China Quarterly*, 172: 885–905.

Zhao, R. (1998) *The History of Chinese Geography: Qing Dynasty* (in Chinese). Beijing: The Commercial Press.

Zhao, S. (2000) Chinese nationalism and its international orientations, *Political Science Quarterly*, 115: 1–33.

Zhao, S. (2004) *A Nation-State by Construction: Dynamics of Modern Chinese Nationalism*. Stanford: Stanford University Press.

Zhao, S. (2006) China's pragmatic nationalism: is it manageable? *The Washington Quarterly*, 29: 131–144.

Zheng, Y. (1999) *Discovering Chinese Nationalism in China: Modernization, Identity, and International Relations*. Cambridge: Cambridge University Press.

Zong, X. (2005) A study on the form and impact of the destination's spatial commoditization: with Lijiang Ancient Town as a case study (in Chinese), *Tourism Tribune*, 4: 30–36.

Zukin, S. (1991) *Landscapes of Power: From Detroit to Disney World*. Berkeley: University of California Press.

Zukin, S. (1995) *The Cultures of Cities*. Cambridge, MA: Blackwell.

Zukin, S. (1998) Urban lifestyles: diversity and standardisation in spaces of consumption, *Urban Studies*, 35: 825–839.

Zukin, S. and Maguire, J. S. (2004) Consumers and consumption, *Annual Review of Sociology*, 30: 173–197.

Index